Understanding Belize

Understanding Belize
A Historical Guide

Alan Twigg

HARBOUR PUBLISHING

Copyright © 2006 Alan Twigg

1 2 3 4 5 10 09 08 07 06

All rights reserved. No part of this publication may be reproduced, stored in a retrieval system or transmitted, in any form or by any means, without prior permission of the publisher or, in the case of photocopying or other reprographic copying, a licence from Access Copyright, the Canadian Copyright Licensing Agency, 1 Yonge Street, Suite 1900, Toronto, Ontario M5E 1E5, www.accesscopyright.ca, 1-800-893-5777, info@accesscopyright.ca.

Harbour Publishing Co. Ltd.
P.O. Box 219
Madeira Park, BC
V0N 2H0
www.harbourpublishing.com

Page design by Peter Read
Cover Photograph by Alan Twigg, design by Anna Comfort
Printed and bound in Canada

Harbour Publishing acknowledges financial support from the Government of Canada through the Book Publishing Industry Development Program and the Canada Council for the Arts, and from the Province of British Columbia through the British Columbia Arts Council and the Book Publisher's Tax Credit through the Ministry of Provincial Revenue.

Library and Archives Canada Cataloguing in Publication

Twigg, Alan, 1952-
    Understanding Belize : a historical guide / Alan Twigg.

 Includes bibliographical references and index.
 ISBN 1-55017-325-1

    1. Belize—History. I. Title.

F1443.T95 2006   972.8205   C2006-900285-1

Contents

Islands and Districts	6
Towns	7
Chapter 1: Welcome to Belize	9
Chapter 2: The Maya	23
Chapter 3: Spanish Eyes	31
Chapter 4: Pirates, Puritans and Politics	39
Chapter 5: The Sucking Colony	51
Chapter 6: Despard's Plight	59
Chapter 7: Mahogany and Other Industries	67
Chapter 8: Humans for Sale	79
Chapter 9: Abolition and Patriotism	93
Chapter 10: Garifuna Exodus	101
Chapter 11: British Honduras	113
Chapter 12: Garveyism to Unionism	121
Chapter 13: Liberator of Belize	135
Chapter 14: Growing Pains	155
Chapter 15: Free at Last	167
Chapter 16: The New Millennium	175
Chapter 17: Tourism	195
Timeline	223
Further Reading	232
Acknowledgements	233

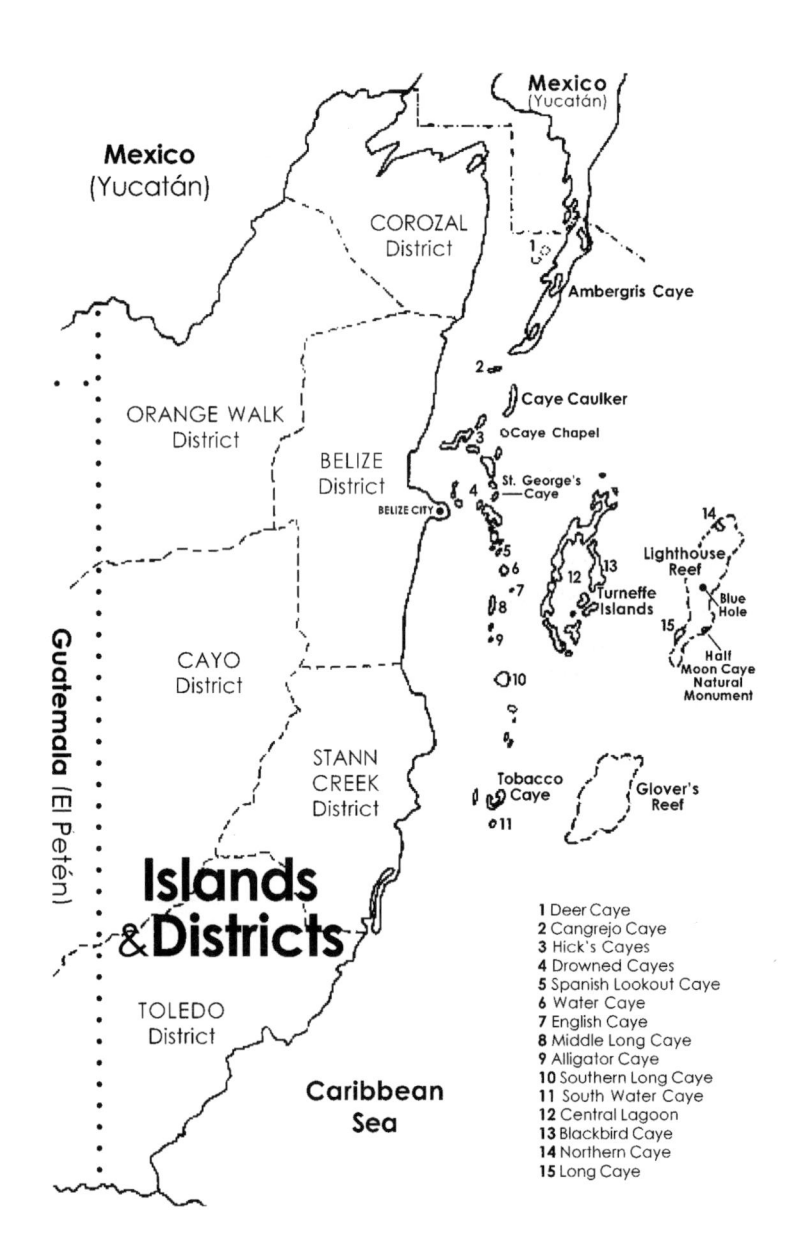

Understanding Belize

6

Islands & Districts

Mexico (Yucatán)

Mexico (Yucatán)

COROZAL District

Ambergris Caye

ORANGE WALK District

BELIZE District

BELIZE CITY

Caye Caulker
Caye Chapel
St. George's Caye

Lighthouse Reef
Turneffe Islands
Blue Hole
Half Moon Caye Natural Monument

Guatemala (El Petén)

CAYO District

STANN CREEK District

Tobacco Caye
Glover's Reef

TOLEDO District

Caribbean Sea

1 Deer Caye
2 Cangrejo Caye
3 Hick's Cayes
4 Drowned Cayes
5 Spanish Lookout Caye
6 Water Caye
7 English Caye
8 Middle Long Caye
9 Alligator Caye
10 Southern Long Caye
11 South Water Caye
12 Central Lagoon
13 Blackbird Caye
14 Northern Caye
15 Long Caye

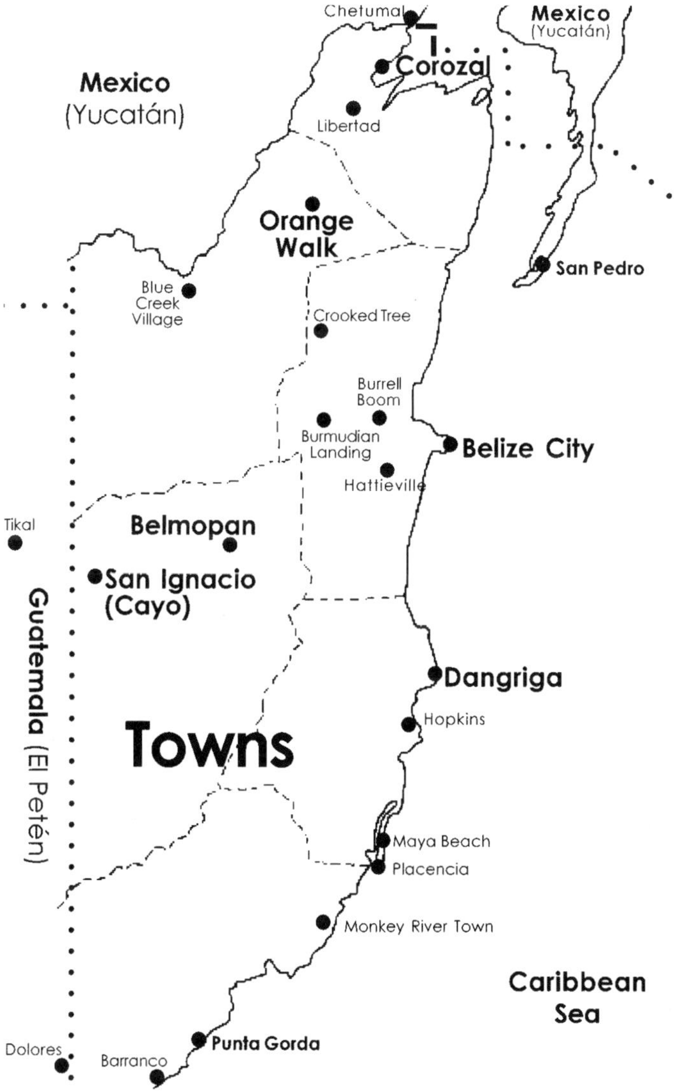

Chetumal
Mexico
(Yucatán)
Corozal
Mexico
(Yucatán)
Libertad
Orange
Walk
San Pedro
Blue
Creek
Village
Crooked Tree
Burrell
Boom
Burmudian
Landing
Belize City
Hattieville
Tikal
Belmopan
San Ignacio
(Cayo)
Guatemala (El Petén)
Dangriga
Hopkins
Towns
Maya Beach
Placencia
Monkey River Town
Caribbean
Sea
Punta Gorda
Dolores
Barranco

The epi-centre of Belizean life has long been this hand-operated Swing Bridge in Belize City, built in Liverpool and installed in 1923. As shown, it takes at least six men to crank it open to accommodate marine traffic along Haulover Creek. *Thor Janson photograph.*

Chapter 1: Welcome to Belize

How Belize Got Its Name

Most people on the planet still don't know how to pronounce Belize (Bay-leeze), let alone find it on a map. Belizeans themselves like to say their little country is located "south of paradise and north of frustration." Formerly known as British Honduras, it was renamed Belize in 1973, eight years prior to independence in 1981.

The credit for discovering Belize from a European perspective is often accorded to Captain Peter Wallace, a Scottish buccaneer who briefly controlled the pirates' lair of Tortuga off the coast of present-day Haiti. The claim that Belize is named after Wallace emanates mainly from the *Honduras Almanack*, a propaganda vehicle for the British in Caribbean colonies. There is no written proof that Wallace reached Belize.

Some have guessed the origins of the word "Belize" could be French, from *balise*, meaning beacon or lighthouse. Or it could be Spanish, from the equivalent of beacon, *balisa*. But neither the French nor the Spanish are known to have made encampments at the Belize River. At the third annual Studies on Belize Conference in 1989, David Hernández suggested the word might have African origins. Belizean historian Leo Bradley has suggested Belize might be derivative of the Mayan term *Belikin*, meaning "land that looks toward the east (or seas)." These are all theories without proof.

The earliest recorded reference to Belize dates from 1677. In that year a Dominican priest named Fray José Delgado was making his way north, through Belize, only to be apprehended and stripped by buccaneers. Reputedly he advised his companions not to kill their captors after they had all fallen into a drunken sleep. Fray Delgado was rescued by the much-feared pirate Bartholomew Sharp, an accomplice of Captain Morgan, after Sharp sent word to have the Spanish priest brought to his headquarters on St. George's Caye. Although Bartholomew Sharp would become famous as one of the most successful English pirates on the west coast of the Americas, he was a religious man whose ship was called *Most Blessed Trinity*. Sharp allowed Delgado to reach safety at the Spanish fort of Bacalar in return for the acquisition of the priest's translator.

This translator—possibly Mayan—had provided Delgado with the names of the major rivers in Belize as they travelled. In this way, Delgado had recorded the earliest geographical reference to *Balis* in his journal (now housed at the Spanish archives in Seville). Delgado identified three major riverways: Rio Soyte, Rio Xibum and Rio Balis.

The Sittee River, Sibun River and Belize River of today correspond to Delgado's 1677 notes. Soyte is clearly Sittee; Xibum is clearly Sibun – so Balis is Belize. Sometimes spelled *belix*, the Mayan word *beliz* means muddy-watered. That's an adjective apropos of the Belize River.

So the truth is clear as mud. Even if Captain Peter Wallace had lived at the mouth of the Belize River for a few months around 1640, it's not feasible for the Maya to have adopted a Scottish surname for their river after such minimal contact. Belize simply means muddy, from Muddy River. So the word Belize has Mayan, not British, origins.

Discovering Belize

The most riveting moment in Belizean history occurred in Australia when American sprinter Marion Jones held aloft the flag of Belize, along with the Stars and Stripes, during a tearful victory lap for the 100-metre event at the Sydney 2000 Olympics. As Jones wrapped herself in the blue flag of her mother's homeland, all 250,000 citizens of tiny Belize felt a strange adrenaline rush of pride. Only 19 years old, the fledgling Central American nation had never been associated with superiority before. "I consider myself half-Belizean," declared the Los Angeles superstar. Waving and crying, she flashed her cover-girl smile (*Vogue, Time, Newsweek* and *Ebony*) and alerted billions to the existence of a rectangular democracy about the size of Massachusetts or Wales, only 68 miles wide and 174 miles long. "This was a heart-swelling moment of sheer exhilaration," cooed Belizean Prime Minister Musa.

As grateful as an asphalt-challenged country could be, Belize invited Marion Jones to visit. The soccer stadium was renamed the Marion Jones Sports Complex, and she accepted keys to Belize City and the Order of Belize, as well as a diplomatic passport as Ambassador at Large of Sport. Nike was positioning Jones to be the female equivalent of Tiger Woods. She could do no wrong.

Marion Jones was the biggest thing to hit Belize since Hurricane Hattie. She autographed this program of events held in her honour in 2001. *Author's collection.*

In 2002, competing on a sport celebrity version of *Who Wants* to *Be a Millionaire*, the "half-Belizean" won the first fast-finger round of the game. "Doesn't surprise me," host Regis Philbin said. "You are always the fastest." The World's Fastest Woman donated her prize money to victims of Hurricane Iris. "Bravo, Marion, bravo," cheered *The Belize Times*. "Ambassador Jones not only gave Belize $64,000 [BZ] in hard cash, but also at least a cool million in free publicity."

The only problem was her Beauty-and-the-Beast marriage to training partner C.J. Hunter, the former world champion shot putter who had tested positive four times for a performance-enhancing steroid called nandrolone. When this doping scandal emerged, O.J. Simpson's lawyer Johnnie Cochran rushed to Jones's side, having defended her honour back in 1993 when she was suspended for missing a drug test. In '94, Jones had turned down an offer to be an alternate on the 4 x 100 US Olympic relay team. At Sydney in 2000, Marion Jones vowed to stand by her man. Six months later her marriage was over. Hunter said Jones's performances were drug-enhanced. In 2003 Jones was implicated in a doping scandal along with superstar slugger Barry Bonds. Under suspicion, Marion Jones performed poorly at the 2004 Olympics at Athens. All that's gold doesn't always glitter.

Ecotopia

From a distance, Belize looks perfect, too. There are 250 varieties of orchids. The water is safe to drink. It's one of the warmest and least populated English-speaking countries on earth. Buses and planes run on time. In the 20th century, there wasn't a single McDonald's restaurant. What's not to like?

If the United Nations were to hand out a gold medal for nature management, Belize might win. Belize has claimed that 42 percent of its territory is protected for conservation, the highest percentage in the world. The Las Cuevas Research Station in the Chiquibul Forest Reserve has studied the relationship between the rainforest and the environment since 1994. There are 70 varieties of forest, more than 700 species of trees. The government created a 6,000-acre Medicinal Plant Reserve (Terra Nova) in 1993 and an even larger rainforest reserve for "bush medicine" was designated in 2001, honouring Don Elijio Panti, a famous Mayan healer.

There's a butterfly farm and there are jaguars. After the American zoologist Alan Rabinowitz proposed the world's first preserve for jaguar habitat, the 155-square-mile Cockscomb Basin Wildlife Sanctuary was created southwest of Dangriga Town. (A national survey, completed in 2005, reported the killing of 64 jaguars and 10 mountain lions by ranchers in recent years in order to protect their herds from predation.) Belize also boasts sanctuaries for howler monkeys, baboons, the red-footed booby and the jabiru stork, the largest flying bird in the Americas.

Belize is a magnet for twitchers (birders) who can view 500 species that include macaws, king vultures, parrots, herons, egrets, American kestrels, roadside hawks, oscillated turkeys and citreoline trogons. The Belize Audubon Society manages the jaguar preserve, the Guanacaste National Park, Blue Hole National Park (different from the Blue Hole dive site), the Crooked Tree Wildlife Sanctuary and it protects the keel-billed toucan, the national bird of Belize.

The national flower is the black orchid. There are 4,000 species of flowering plants, 400 species of fish and 139 species of reptiles and amphibians. Walrus-like manatee can be seen surfacing at the Gales Point Manatee Preserve. The national animal, the Baird's tapir or "mountain cow," can weigh up to 650 pounds.

The 185-mile-long Belize Barrier Reef is second only to Australia's Great Barrier Reef in length. UNESCO declared the postcard-perfect barrier reef a World Heritage Site in 1996. There are four atolls in the Caribbean and Belize has three of them: Lighthouse Reef, Glover's Reef and the Turneffe Islands. The circular

Blue Hole dive site is a cobalt blue lagoon that attracts the world's most skilled divers. The 412-foot-deep cavern was first made famous by a Jacques Cousteau documentary. It is protected as a natural monument within a 1,023-acre marine park. There are more than 200 islands called *cayes* (as in Florida Keys). Water temperatures are usually in the low 80s.

On the western side of the Maya Mountains, spelunkers and trogophiles (explorers of caves) can exercise their deepest and darkest speleological urges in the Chiquibul zone. Hard-to-reach Thousand Foot Falls cascades 1,600 feet into Hidden Valley, with swimming holes at the bottom, making it the highest waterfall in Central America and the ninth-highest in the world.

When you clamber over a Mayan temple, hover over a banana plantation in a propeller-driven plane or snorkel amid candy-striped fish, you know you're not in Kansas anymore. Belize is the final frontier for Mayan archaeology. You can explore a 2,000-year-old Mayan burial site, by canoe, inside the Barton Creek Cave. Ruins at Caracol are possibly more extensive than the more famous Mayan site of Tikal in Guatemala.

Belize is a politically stable democracy. Most people speak English. A Belizean dollar is always worth 50 cents US. There are only six main highways. And, best of all, as soon as you squeeze onto a Novelo's bus, jostling over potholes and overhearing indecipherable Creole, those two powerful words, *black* and *white*, can be recognized as racial misnomers, even hateful ones.

Shades of Brown

The most remarkable natural resource of Belize is its diverse population. As nation founder George Price repeatedly declared, "All ah we da won." There are eight main racial groups. They speak at least seven languages. The range of skin tones defies classification, but there are some basic social divisions.

- Mestizos (almost half of the population) are mainly mixed-blood descendants of Mexicans and the Maya who fled into northern Belize in the 1800s, escaping the Caste War in Mexico. They are Spanish-speaking and tend to be poorly educated agrarians, near the bottom of the economic ladder, although "Mestizo" is a term that can be loosely applied to any Latin in Belize. Seasonal labourers and illegal immigrants from Guatemala, El Salvador and Honduras have swelled their numbers in recent decades. At the turn of this century it was estimated Mestizos could comprise 66 percent of the populace by 2010 if growth rates didn't change. In accordance with their numbers, Columbus Day was replaced by Pan American Day.

- Creoles (about one-quarter of the population) were dominant politically and numerically until the 1990s. Now many are seeking immigration to the USA. They are Afro-Belizeans with some white ancestry, or else direct descendents of Free Coloureds. Traditionally prominent within government and the civil service, Creoles, mostly based in Belize City, speak English and a Jamaica-related patois—regarded by some linguists as a separate language—full of droll aphorisms and aggressive humour. The Creoles had the slowest rate of growth in the 1990s (0.5 percent).

- The Maya (roughly 10 percent) live mainly in the south, in the Toledo district, or along the Guatemala border. There are two distinct groups: the Q'eqchí (or Ketchi) and the Mopan. Although they're both within the Yucatec stream of the Maya, they speak different languages. It can be persuasively argued that the indigenous peoples of northern Belize were never conquered and neither were the Manche Chol Maya in the south, although most were once forced to evacuate to Guatemala by the British. The oldest evidence of Mayan settlement in Belize is at Cuello, dating from 2500 BC.

- The Garinagu (about six percent) are proudly different Afro-Amerindian Belizeans with renegade slave origins. Runaway slaves, primarily on the island of St. Vincent, forged an original "Garifuna" culture and language. Their exodus to Belize is a remakable story of persecution and endurance. They now live mostly in Dangriga and southern coastal villages. Elders retain the Garifuna language and a Garifuna dictionary has been published, as well as a Bible translation. The Garinagu and Creoles look alike, but their customs and viewpoints don't coincide.

- Mennonites (about three percent) emigrated from Manitoba, Canada, and Chihuahua, Mexico, in the late 1950s to settle as farmers in northern Belize. They have preserved their orthodox Protestant solidarity with their own schools, financial institutions and military exemptions. They speak an archaic Low German dialect in rural communes at Shipyard, Little Belize, Progresso, Blue Creek, Spanish Lookout and Barton Creek. Mennonites are widely respected in Belize; their poultry and eggs have become dietary staples for the country.

- East Indian and Chinese Belizeans operate many shops and restaurants. The British brought Chinese and East Indian servants after slavery was abolished in 1838. A merchant class of Lebanese Belizeans is also evident, along with some Rastafarians from Jamaica. Taiwanese entrepreneurs began arriving in significant numbers in the 1990s, making Chinese Belizeans the fastest-growing ethnic group. According to the 2000 census, their numbers were up 13 percent from the 1991 census, making the selling of passports into a lightning rod for dissatisfaction among many disgruntled Belizeans.

- Americans and Canadians in particular have sought an antidote for First Worlditis in Belize as retirees and investors. American citizens and companies have long since become the primary landowners, essentially replacing the British as real estate kings during the 20th century. Caucasians are ubiquitous as owners and managers within the ever-expanding tourism industry.

Crime

But for all that, Belize isn't paradise unless your vision is restricted to scuba goggles. There are lots of reasons why it took Belize more than four centuries to reach the one-quarter-million mark in population.

The streets of Belize City are definitely not safe at night. The murder rate in Belize has been approximately three times higher than that of the US in recent decades. From the summer of 1998 to the summer of 1999, there were at least 56 murders for a population of less than 250,000. "Perhaps no existing issue requires a more rapid and comprehensive solution than that of crime," said Prime Minister Musa in 2002. While tourists are seldom targets for rape, murder and machete attacks, such crimes are not uncommon on the mainland.

Some of the violence is imported. As in Los Angeles, gangs in Belize City emerged as Crips and Bloods. Belizeans can partly blame their crime wave on President Ronald Reagan (1981–89) and his White House efforts to stifle a once-thriving marijuana industry. At the behest of Nancy Reagan's "Just Say No" campaign, the United States said "Yes" to the hiring of small planes to spray paraquat on the crops after the US identified Belize as its fourth-largest supplier of marijuana.

By the end of the 1980s, the US Drug Enforcement Administration could boast it had reduced exports of "Belize Breeze" from 200 tons to 50 tons, but the indiscriminate spraying ruined legal crops and put marijuana growers out of work. That's when Belize graduated to the harder stuff. The same mangrove-ridden shorelines and islets that had once sheltered pirates and privateers became a haven for narco-traffickers. By 2001, Belize was identified by the World Drug Report as the fastest-growing transshipment point for South American drug dealers.

Drug users, beware. When Britain's Minister of Defence Peter Kilfoyle toured Belize's notoriously violent Hattieville

Correctional Institute in 2000, he declared it the worst prison he had ever seen. Two years later, the government downloaded its responsibility for the prison to the Kolbe Foundation, resulting in controversial cutbacks. The "Hattieville Ramada" remains so crowded that Belize took steps to reinstitute the death penalty.

In September 2005, anti-drug police seized 5,000 pounds of suspected cocaine near Tobacco Caye, in the Stann Creek Area, and claimed its estimated street value was US$83 million.

Hurricanes and Road Kills

Like the crime waves, everybody talks about the weather in Belize and nobody can do much about it.

Hurricane season lasts from June to November. Hurricane Keith (2000) killed eight people and the 140-mph winds of Hurricane Iris (2001) wrecked the southern towns of Independence, Seine Bight, Placencia and Monkey River, killing 20 and ruining 10,000 homes. Hurricane Wilma narrowly bypassed Belize in October of 2005. Most famously, Hurricane Hattie (1961) was a Category Four hurricane and tidal wave that levelled one-quarter of the housing in Belize City, prompting the government to build the inland capital of Belmopan. A monument to remember the 264 people killed by Hurricane Hattie in 1961 was unveiled 44 years later in 2005 at the Lord Ridge Cemetery in Belize City where victims had been buried in a communal grave.

The Saffir-Simpson Hurricane Scale determines the severity of hurricanes according to wind speed, ascending from one to five in severity. When Hurricane Janet hit Corozal in 1955, it was Category Five. Hurricanes Abby (1960), Anna (1961), Francelia (1970), Carmen (1974), Fifi (1974) and Greta (1978) were followed by a Category Five calamity, Hurricane Mitch (1988). It killed 100,000 Hondurans and Nicaraguans, sending refugees streaming into Belize. Shortly after Category Four Hurricane Emily bypassed Belize in July 2005, the Caribbean Community Climate Change Centre opened in Belmopan to coordinate Caribbean responses to climate change.

But it's the driving climate that most merits concern. In 2002 the *Belize Times* stated that "Traffic accidents have claimed more lives than gang warfare, jackings and AIDS combined." In tiny Belize, with few roads and cars, there were 55 road fatalities in 2000, followed by 70 fatalities in 2001. The highway speed limit is 45 mph for trucks and buses, 55 mph for other vehicles, but few signs are posted. "Drive 55 and stay alive" isn't catching on. Most accidents occur in the Belize City District.

Bring a Thick Book

Other drawbacks include tropical diseases such as malaria and Dengue fever, scorpions, Yucatecan "American" crocodiles (called *alligators*), police corruption, high unemployment, alcohol abuse and domestic violence. Nurse sharks and barracudas are rarely hostile; the green moray eels have been known to bite.

Few tourist guides mention tarantulas. Other disagreeable Belizean ambassadors are mozzies (mosquitoes), troublesome sand fleas, bottlas (flies, pronounced *bottle-ass*), ticks, scorpions, Africanized killer bees and nine types of poisonous snakes among the 54 species. The deadliest is the yellow-jawed Tommy Goff, or *fer-de-lance*, with its heat-seeking fangs.

Belize is home to more than 500 species of birds, including pelicans. *Vivien Lougheed photograph.*

It's no shame to prefer Hawaii.

If you're within VISA and MasterCard territory, much of the

time the backwardness of Belize can seem charming. Until the 1990s there were just two traffic lights. One was at the one-lane Hawksworth Bridge that spans the Macal River, a suspension bridge modelled on the Brooklyn Bridge. The other light controlled the flow on the venerable Swing Bridge, built in Liverpool, at the heart of Belize City. Installed in 1923, this bridge was reputedly the only hand-operated swing bridge for vehicular traffic still operational in the Americas by century's end; at 5:30 a.m. and 5:30 p.m. daily, eight men cranked it open for marine traffic along Haulover Creek. Haulover Creek was one of the many open sewers in Belize City until Canadian Prime Minister Pierre Elliott Trudeau befriended nation founder George Price and personally ensured funding would be made for sanitary sewerage and also improved water systems.

The fourth major bridge to span the Belize River, the 374-foot Agripino Cawich Memorial Bridge, opened near Roaring Creek, in 2005.

Camera, Action

With the likes of Madonna and Ringo Starr discovering Belize, Hollywood has set up shop. Based on an Ernest Hemingway short story about a man searching for pirate treasure, the first entirely-filmed-in-Belize movie was Trimark's *After the Storm* (2001). The TV series *Temptation Island* has filmed in Belize, as did *Dogs of War* (1981) and a low-budget adventure flick, *Caribe* (1987).

Francis Ford Coppola now offers writing workshops at his five-star Blancaneaux Lodge, named after turn-of-the-century naturalist François Blancaneaux. Coppola first came to Belize in the 1980s, trying to convince the government to establish a satellite address for a telecommunications hub. The jungles reminded him of the Philippines, where he made *Apocalypse Now*, so he bought a run-down tourist lodge and installed a river-powered hydroelectric plant. "It's like being a movie on location," he says.

"You just bring everything with you or you build it yourself."

Belize is now in danger of becoming trendy. It's home to Coppola's *Zoetrope* magazine, where "the river powers your laptop and the birds are your alarm clock," and the *X-Files* cast and crew from Vancouver bought a former banana and coconut plantation south of Hopkins, subdivided 65 beachfront lots, and laid plans for two new hotels and a golf course—the second in Belize. "I bet we get more jaguars on our land than the Cockscomb Basin Wildlife Sanctuary," boasted one of the buyers.

When director Nicholas Roeg sought a backdrop to adapt Joseph Conrad's *Heart of Darkness* (1993), Belize City didn't require much modification. Earlier Belize had served as the mosquito-infested backwater for Hollywood's adaptation of Paul Theroux's novel, *Mosquito Coast* (1986). That movie starred Harrison Ford, who became a benefactor to the Belize Zoo and supported the international efforts to scuttle the controversial Chalillo Dam project in the Cayo District. The star of *Indiana Jones* and *Star Wars* stayed at the prim Victoria House resort on Ambergris Caye, commuting to the set by helicopter.

Few tourists will ever see a jaguar unless they visit the Belize Zoo, completed in 1991 with the help of actor Harrison Ford and songwriter Jimmy Buffet. *Vivien Lougheed photograph.*

Pride vs. Pursestrings

Tucked against Guatemala, facing Jamaica, attracting only one-tenth as many tourists as Costa Rica, Belize was discovered by the cruise ship industry as of 2002. The government must now balance its crucial need to boost tourism with its recognized aim to protect the integrity of a post-colonial society. Having endured piracy, anarchy, slavery, British chauvinism, flimsy housing units from Cuba, strings-attached American meddling and four centuries of foreign ownership, Belizeans are not keen to serve as the latest Eliza Doolittle of the Caribbean. This pride is the legacy of a remarkable politician named George Price, the most central figure in Belizean history, who led the colony of British Honduras to independence and beyond.

Chapter 2: The Maya

Belize only turned 24 in 2005. To present Mayan history as a subsidiary of Belizean history is necessarily to scratch the surface. The Maya were in Belize first. To classify the Maya strictly as an ancient people of stargazers, yanking out hearts of sacrificial victims atop pyramids, just makes the struggle of yet another indigenous people more difficult.

People of Corn

Forerunners of the Maya developed agriculture in Central America more than 5,000 years ago. Food was stored, people became sedentary and populations increased. A class system emerged with corn growers and a priestly aristocracy. Tool and basket makers were added. Trade began and chiefdoms arose. Ideas were circulated, ritual exchanges of rare items occurred—cultures spread. Mesoamerica's first major

"The Mayans gave the world the concept of zero," says Maya leader Gregorio Ch'oc, "and in return for it, what they got was zero." *Twigg photo.*

culture arose with the Olmecs, from 1500 BC to about 500 BC, on both coasts.

The Olmecs traded pottery, jade, shells, obsidian and magnetite. They also built ball courts for a traditional and often deadly game in which players from two opposing teams were not permitted to use their hands while trying to manoeuvre a ball through ringed hoops embedded in the walls of the ball court. Olmecs also developed rudimentary calendar and writing systems to keep track of their inventories and to schedule their *mercados*, or markets, for trading.

In Mexico the Olmecs were followed by the Zapotecs, based in the Oaxaca Valley, then by the Mixtecs, giving rise to the name Mexico. Roughly speaking, the Maya emerged as the dominant culture after the Mixtecs.

Long before the Spanish brought diseases and enslavement, Belize was the centre of a vast trading system. A settlement on Ambergris Caye, called Bacalar, served as a major trading centre connecting inland states with the Yucatán. Its ceremonial centre of Chac Balam has since divulged evidence of 300 burial sites containing necklaces of conch pearl and jaguar teeth, pots and jade earrings. This meant that Mayan islanders, linked to Altun Ha on the mainland, must have swapped their salt for jade.

Ambergris Caye, facing the bays of Corozal and Chetumal near the mouths of the Hondo and New Rivers, served as a conduit for ideas and the exchange of other products such as wax, salt, furs, feathers and cotton. Anthropologists have presumed that a mile-long canal only several feet wide was dredged to separate Ambergris Caye from the Yucatán peninsula, thereby reducing travel time for the traders.

As accomplished long-distance traders and mariners, the Maya were eventually recognized as the Phoenicians of the New World. "These people, even in the later days of the 16th century," according to William Gates, translator of *Yucatán Before and After the Conquest*, "were higher in polity, science and all that really makes civilization, than the invaders who only had gunpowder, horses, lusts... [and] the Cross." Their society lacked only the wheel and the archway to surpass most other cultures.

Aboriginal Rights

For decades, Mopan and Q'eqchí *naturales* in the Toledo District of southern Belize have been resisting an apartheid system of reservations, created by the British, with increasing militancy. They have sought international help to establish a 500,000-acre Maya Homeland since 1996.

Under the leadership of Julian Cho (1962–98), the Maya Mapping Project in Toledo was conceived to assert ancestral and custodial rights. More than 40 communities pooled their resources to publish a village-by-village *Maya Atlas*. Concurrently the Toledo Maya Cultural Council protested incursions by Malaysia-owned logging companies.

Belizean Maya, affiliated with spokesperson Gregorio Ch'oc of the Maya Leaders' Alliance, filed a lawsuit via the Indian Law Resource Center in the USA to assert indigenous, collective land rights, much to the irritation of some Belizean government officials such as nation founder George Price. The Maya don't want government permission to live on reserves; they want ownership rights to communal land.

The Maya and other indigenous Amerindians have been resisting European invaders ever since 13 shipwrecked Spaniards were captured on the Yucatán coast in 1508. Two survived. Most were eaten. "The Maya are, for all their apparent docility," wrote Michael D. Coe in *The Maya*, "the toughest Indians in Mesoamerica."

The case for aboriginal rights in Belize is a strong one, bolstered by the work of Mayanists such as Rutgers anthropologist Norman Hammond, who uncovered Mayan settlements at Cuello dating from 2400 BC. In 1973, Hammond spotted traces of a possible ceremonial site on an aerial photograph and registered the area with Joseph Palacio, Archaeological Commissioner of Belize.

Using carbon-14 dating, Hammond verified the discovery of some of the oldest pottery in Central America. Cuello's central plaza also revealed the earliest known Mayan sweat house, dating from 900 BC. Placement of the sweat house indicated to Hammond its importance to Mayan community life and reflected the sophistication of the society. Hammond told the *New York Times* the sweat houses were for "the simple cleansing of the body, the purging of nasty things and opening of communications with the supernatural." The Maya in Belize still use sweat houses for bathing, especially women seeking to purify their bodies after childbirth.

Belize is the only country in which Mayan sites are found throughout its territory.

Bush Medicine

Having worshipped a primordial god as early as 3300 BC, the Maya continue to accumulate valuable medical knowledge and maintain their distinct culture with distinct customs. One of the best-known contemporary practitioners of Mayan "bush medicine" has been Ovencio Canto of San Antonio village in southwest Belize, but such men are by no means rare.

The most renowned San Antonio healer, Don Elijio Panti, MBE, died at age 103 in 1996. The 13,006-acre holistic Noj Kaax Meen Elijio Panti National Park at San Antonio, Cayo District, was opened on June 2, 2001, in his honour. Don Elijio Panti learned the ancient skills of Mayan healing—including massage, prayers, acupuncture, crystal balls and herbal baths—from a Maya, Jeronimo Requena, when they worked as *chicoleros* (chicle collectors) in El Petén, Guatemala. Neither man could read or write. Panti began practising Mayan medicine at San Antonio in 1931.

The venerable healer conducted fieldwork for a collaborative project between Rosita Arvigo's Ix Chel Tropical Research Foundation and the New York Botanical Garden before he died. He collected a trove of plant samples for AIDS and cancer research in association with the US National Cancer Institute. For his lifelong work as a spiritualist, healer and community leader, Don Elijio Panti received the Distinguished Citizen Award from University College in Belize, a Distinguished Contribution to Science Award from the New York Botanical Garden and was made a Member of the British Empire by Her Majesty, Queen Elizabeth.

Panti also shared much of his knowledge with Chicago-born Rosita Arvigo, a "naprapath-herbalist-activist." Arvigo's company, Rainforest Remedies, is an offshoot of her tutelage with Panti. Some of the profits are meant to help save the rainforests in Belize. Shaman Pharmaceuticals, traded on NASDAQ, has contracted with Arvigo to help provide research for health remedies.

The issue of respecting Mayan medical know-how on a monetary basis has been spurred by a growing awareness that Mesoamerican women and Mayan bush medicine led researchers to develop the modern birth control pill.

With direction from Rosita Arvigo, traditional Maya healers in Belize have co-founded the Traditional Healers Foundation to ensure healers will receive compensation for intellectual property rights. She was also a driving force behind the allocation of 6,000 acres of rainforest for Belize's first "bio-medical" reserve, Terra Nova.

Panti's Mayan niece, Marcia Garcia, chairperson for the Itzamna Society and the "inheritor" of his work, endured years of meetings and complex negotiations to create the much larger Noj Kaax Meen Elijio Panti National Park. *Noj Kaax* means "canopied rainforest"; *Meen* refers to Mayan spiritual healers.

There are 90,000 acres of canopied rainforest in the Panti reserve. At the park's official opening, 175 spiritualists from Belize and Guatemala gathered for an all-day inauguration ceremony. The forested "pharmacopia," developed by the Maya-run Itzamna

Society, has the potential to make Don Elijio Panti the most famous Belizean.

Mundo Maya

Spain could not conquer the Maya of Belize. According to the *Encyclopedia Britannica*, Spanish attempts to conquer the various Mayan enclaves in the Central American isthmus between 1527 and 1547 cost "the lives of more Spaniards than had been expended in wresting from the Incas and Montezuma [the Aztecs], the wealthiest empires of the New World." To escape Christianization, the Maya sought refuge in the Maya Mountain Range of Belize. The Mopan Maya call these people *Che'il*; the Q'eqchí Maya call them *Chol*. The Q'eqchí resented Christianity more than the Mopan. British loggers and colonialists also pushed the Maya into the mountains, but not all the Maya left Belize. According to Mayanist Dr. Grant Jones, "The principal inhabitants of the Toledo District during the 16th through 18th centuries were Mayas who spoke Yucatecan languages, Chol and Mopan."

The Maya migrated back into Belize in the late 19th and 20th centuries to escape warfare in Mexico and taxation in Guatemala. In the north they intermarried with Latinos. In the south, Mopan and Q'eqchí Maya settled in the Toledo District as "the forgotten ones" of Belize. Government statistics in the 1990s indicated their average annual family income in Toledo was US$600—a high estimate.

As more Maya learned modern communication skills, their political savvy increased. By 2002, Belizean Foreign Minister Assad Shoman and Gregorio Ch'oc had forged a Framework Agreement to implement ten steps to be taken "for the protection of the Maya people's rights with respect to land and resources in Southern Belize."

Shoman decried the treatment of modern Maya in his lucid and emotional *13 Chapters of a History of Belize*. "What does it mean when we want to make big tourist bucks off the 'Mundo Maya' project," he asked, "but never thought to invite the Maya to have a say in it? That we take visiting dignitaries to visit Maya 'ruins,' but don't give a thought to how we continue to ruin the lives of the Maya? The architecture of the dead Maya was used to fashion the National Assembly, but the living Maya have not been allowed to be architects in the fashioning of the nation."

Shoman and Ch'oc reached an accord partly because the government of Belize was increasingly sensitive about the Maya village network along the controversial Guatemala-Belize border. For trade and diplomacy purposes, Belize was eager to upgrade and expand highway connections to Guatemala. This placed the Maya in a precarious but potentially influential position if they could organize themselves politically—a task that fell onto the shoulders of Ch'oc, who was introduced to the world's indigenous people's movement while attending university in Saskatchewan, Canada.

"Toledo must be one of the most studied places in the world," he says, echoing Shoman's view. "The anthropologists, the scientists, they are always coming here to study the people and what we know. But they go away and nothing changes for us."

Traces of Mayan ancestry can be seen in the faces of many Belizeans, from nation founder George Price to Armin Bochub, daughter of a curandero (herbalist) who lives near Punta Gorda. *Twigg photo.*

Columbus's navigator Vicente Yáñez Pinzón saw Belize in 1508. *Belize Archives.*

Chapter 3: Spanish Eyes

Columbus's Navigator

Known in the history books as the first European to reach Brazil, and as the discoverer of the Amazon, Vicente Yáñez Pinzón, one of Columbus's navigators on his first voyage in 1492, co-"discovered" Belize in 1508. That year Pinzón (1461–1513) and his sailing partner Juan Díaz de Solís reached the coastline of Belize by sailing north from Bonacca along the Toledo Coast.

Raised in the shadow of his brother Martin Alonzo, 20 years his senior, Vicente Yáñez Pinzón had accompanied his brother on his commercial trips along the Atlantic and Mediterranean coasts, not without a few incidents of piracy. Accused of mutinous behaviour at sea, the elder Pinzón had returned to Spain and established a shipbuilding firm in their native seaport of Palos. That's how the Pinzón brothers got hooked up with Columbus.

After sailing with Columbus to the New World in 1492, commanding the *Niña* and bringing Columbus back to Spain when the *Santa Maria* foundered and was abandoned, Vicente Yáñez Pinzón embarked with four caravels from Palos in 1499. Dragged off course, he accidentally reached the coast of Brazil and became the first Spaniard to sail beneath the equator. During his four months along the Brazilian coast, he discovered the mouths of the Orinoco and Amazon Rivers and assumed the Amazon must be the Ganges. He sailed north to the coast of Venezuela, past the Leeward and Windward Islands, Puerto Rico and Hispaniola, and lost two ships near the Bahamas, before returning to Palos in September.

For his extraordinary voyage, Pinzón was decorated by King Ferdinand II and later named Governor of Puerto Rico in 1505, though he never took up the posting. In 1508 King Ferdinand convened a council with Pinzón, veteran navigator Juan Díaz de Solís and Amerigo Vespucci to discuss how best to reach the Indies. The New World reports of Amerigo Vespucci (1451–1512) from Florence had circulated widely in Europe prior to the publication of Columbus's journals. Vespucci claimed he had visited the New World in 1497 when it was really 1499. As a result, Martin Waldseemüller had published a speculative map in 1507 that designated the New World as America, in honour of the pretender Amerigo Vespucci.

On July 29, 1508, Vicente Yáñez Pinzón sailed one last time, with de Solís, to explore the east coast of the Yucatán. On that voyage he glimpsed the Cockscomb Mountains of Belize but never went ashore. It has been suggested that de Solís and Pinzón named *Cabo de Honduras*, Cape of the Deep Waters, not Columbus.

Juan Díaz de Solís, the co-discoverer of Belize, was born about 1470 in either Spain or Portugal. In the early 1500s he had returned home from the sea to find he had been cuckolded. He murdered his wife and fled from criminal justice, only to run afoul of the law for debts and for his work with French privateers. In 1508–09 de Solís sailed alongside Vicente Yáñez Pinzón within sight of the Belize shore. In 1512 de Solís gained the highly paid position of pilot-major, succeeding Vespucci. In 1516, after passing the present sites of Montevideo and Buenos Aires, de Solís was killed in the River Plata area while exploring onshore, 35 degrees south of the equator.

The Father of Mestizos

The first European to have sustained contact with the Maya of Belize was the remarkable Gonzalo Guerrero, a soldier who was born Spanish but died Mayan. His story is rarely told in English.

In 1511, an ill-fated expedition led by Pedro Valdivia set sail from Panama for Santo Domingo, carrying 20,000 ducats of gold, only to run aground on shoals south of Jamaica called *Las Viboras* (the vipers). There were approximately 18 Spaniards set adrift (accounts vary), including two women and Guerrero. They had a small boat but no sails, candles, oars or food. For 13 days, they drifted. Seven died at sea. The current brought them to the shoreline of eastern Yucatán, above Belize.

Possible landing sites include Cozumel, Tulum (then called Zama) or Cancún, but the consensus is, when considering currents and the time of year, they must have arrived somewhere between Tulum and Playa del Carmen. The Indians captured the Spanish and promptly ate Valdivia and four others. The Maya of the early 1500s were not widely known for cannibalism, so it's possible the flesh eaters were Caribs from the south, originally from the Orinoco River.

The rest of the Valdivia survivors were placed in cages to be fattened. Among them was Gonzalo Guerrero. He and Jeronimo de Aguilar managed to escape, or were traded. They became the property of a Maya chief, Aquincuz of Xamanzana, who accepted them as slaves. Aguilar lived among the Yucatec Maya for eight years, first with Aquincuz, then under his successor Taxmar. Having studied as a priest, the celibate Aguilar was not tempted by women, to the amazement of his keepers. He carefully kept track of his Christian holy days with a Book of Hours, a medieval religious schedule still popular in the 16th century.

In 1519, while repairing their ships at Cozumel, Hernán Cortés and his men heard tales of two bearded men on the mainland. He sent letters requesting the release of both men, accompanied by green glass beads that resembled jade. Aguilar successfully pleaded with his *cacique*, Taxmar, for his release. Upon the priest's arrival at Cozumel, Cortés mistook the ragged sunburnt man carrying a paddle for an Indian. "Where is the Spaniard?" he asked. Aguilar would prove invaluable to Cortés as a translator when he undertook his conquest of the Aztecs.

Guerrero, meanwhile, had "gone native." Around 1512 or 1513, Gonzalo Guerrero was given or traded to the chieftain at Chetumal, a trading centre south of the present-day Mexican city of that name. Guerrero was therefore the first European to set foot in Belize. He became "Mayanized" as the son-in-law to Nachancan, lord of Chetumal, who placed him in charge of military operations. Guerrero helped the Maya successfully attack his countryman Francisco Hernández de Córdoba and his expedition in February of 1517 after they had landed atop the Yucatán peninsula, looking for slaves and gold.

Guerrero taught the Maya how to construct forts and bastions, tattooed his body, grew his hair and wore earrings. According to 16th-century reports of an acting governor of Honduras–Higueras, found in the Guatemalan section of Spanish archives, Guerrero was responsible for the ousting of the first known Spanish settlement in Belize in the late 1520s.

As a mobile commander of Mayan forces for 20 years, based in Chetumal, Guerrero would have become familiar with the Belizean coast. In 1531, to entrap 50 Spanish soldiers led by Alonso Dávila, the Maya built a crude fort with one door. With the approach of the Spanish, the Maya retreated, leaving the soldiers to "capture" the fort without a fight, and renaming it Villa Real. The Maya were then able to lay siege to the fort for more than a year, as the Spanish died or were killed. Eventually the few remaining

Spaniards were permitted to escape by canoe, alerting Spaniards not to approach the Maya along the Hondo River.

When Jeronimo de Aguilar travelled south to find Guerrero and announce the splendid news that Cortés was waiting for them, Guerrero pointed to his three sons and said, "Look how handsome these boys of mine are." He refused to be "saved" by the Spanish. He had "married" a noblewoman, recorded as dona Elvira Toznenitzin. She reproached Aguilar for his impudence as a slave, telling him to leave. Aguilar gave Guerrero some green beads as a gift for Nachancan.

The acting governor of Honduras–Higueras, Andrés de Cerezeda, once described Guerrero leading an attack south of Belize to avenge killings of Maya chiefs by the Spaniards. During this encounter Guerrero was shot and killed. Mention of his death was found in a document dated August 14, 1536. "He is the one who lived among the Indians of the province of Yucatán for twenty years or more," wrote the Spanish administrator, "and in addition is the one whom they say brought ruin [to] *Adelantado* [Francisco] de Montejo. He came with a fleet of fifty canoes to aid the natives of this province, to destroy those who were here then. This was about five or six months before the arrival of the *Adelantado* [Pedro de Alvarado], at the time when I executed certain *caciques* [chiefs]. This Spaniard who was killed was naked, his body decorated, and he wore Indian dress."

Just as the Argentinian-born doctor Che Guevara fought imperialism for Cuba, Guerrero was a transplanted rebel in adopted territory. He was not, however, the New World's first great resistance fighter. That distinction belongs to the Taino leader named Hatuey, originally from Hispaniola, who was burned at the stake in Cuba on February 2, 1512.

In Mexico, novelist Eugenio Aguirre has published *Gonzalo Guerrero* and Salvador Campos Jara has produced an historical novel. In the Mexican state bordering Belize to the north,

Quintana Roo, Gonzalo Guerrero is acknowledged as the "Father of Mestizos" in the state anthem. There is also a monument in Chetumal and a bronze statue of Guerrero, by sculptor Raul Ayala, on Mérida's immense Montejo Boulevard. A plaque commemorates Guerrero's arrival at Playa del Carmen. But in English, Guerrero is rarely mentioned even though he began the long tradition of fighting off the Spanish.

Hernán Cortés Penetrates Belize

In 1524, having conquered Mexico, Hernán Cortés learned Cristóbal de Olid had proclaimed the independence of Spanish Honduras. To remove this upstart official, Cortés began a gruelling, fantastical overland trek toward Spanish Honduras that ranks with Hannibal's journey over the Alps. Departing from Vera Cruz on the Mexican coast, he marched in a straight line toward Trujillo on the east coast of Central America, torturing and hanging the Mexican chieftain Cuauhtémotzin along the way. This *entrada* of about 140 soldiers and several thousand natives had to traverse high mountains and dense jungles. While slashing his way through uncharted territory, Cortés would have passed through the southwest corner of Belize; thus he and his men became the first Europeans to set eyes on Belize from the east. Order was easily restored in Honduras in 1525. Cortés once said it was more difficult contending with his own countrymen than fighting against the Aztecs.

Several attempts by Cortés to return to Mexico by sea ended in shipwrecks. Becoming despondent, Cortés began dressing in the black robes of a Dominican monk, issuing morose premonitions of his own death. He returned by sea to Mexico, via Cuba, thereby encircling Belize. A flurry of lesser-known explorers and would-be conquerors of Belize arrived on the Atlantic coast of Central America after Columbus and Cortés, including Francisco Hernández de Córdoba, Anton de Alaminos, Juan de Grijalva, Francisco Montejo the Elder, Alonso Dávila, Francisco de Montejo the Younger, Alonso Pacheco, Martín Rodriguez and Juan de Garzon.

The Leftover Pawn

The failure of Spain to permanently affix Belize is downright bizarre. By the time Cortés died, Spain had already claimed territory from Oregon, Colorado and the Carolinas—approximately 40 degrees north—to the middle of Chile and Argentina—approximately 40 degrees south. After Spain had established a Viceroyalty to govern Mexico in 1535, it created a subdivision called the *Audiencia* of Guatemala in 1544 to oversee Guatemala, El Salvador, Honduras, Nicaragua and Costa Rica. In Central America, only Belize never had direct, ongoing Spanish administration.

Wallios Valix,

Wallis, Valis,

Walix Valx.

Walis, Balix

Waliz, Balis

These variations of pirate Peter Wallace's surname have helped perpetuate a myth that he "founded" Belize. *Belize Archives.*

Chapter 4: Pirates, Puritans and Politics

"The Queen of England understands not why her or any prince's subjects should be debarred from the Trade of the Indies."
— QUEEN ELIZABETH, DECLARATION OF POLICY, 1587

The quip about Belize City being built on a foundation of rum bottles is not, in itself, without foundation. As much as Australia is a country born of convicts, Belize arose from pirates, buccaneers and privateers such as Sir Francis Drake and Captain Henry Morgan.

The more Spain and Portugal sought to enforce trade monopolies assigned by the Pope in 1493, the more England, France and Holland enlisted privateers to get their share of New World cargoes. English privateers mostly embarked from London in the spring, hoping to return prior to hurricane season in the fall. Mere pirates, on the other hand, didn't have that luxury of returning to English waters.

It was open season on Spanish shipping, year-round, but it was frequently necessary to hole up for repairs and replenishments. Therefore the "class" of English mariners who gravitated to Belize could not have been the highest. With its exceptionally long reef and its offshore Turneffe Islands, Belize likely provided lairs aplenty for the likes of Blackbeard (Edward Teach), Calico Jack (John Rackham), John Coxon, Bartholomew Sharp, Nicholas van Horn, William Bannister, Edward Low, Bartholomew Roberts, Captain Yankey, Abraham Blauvelt (a.k.a. Abraham Bluefield) and "Admiral" John Benbow—allegedly the inspiration for Long John Silver in *Treasure Island*.

Every English villain who chortled hardy-har-har-har in the 16th and 17th centuries didn't necessarily hide out in the islands of Belize, but enough did to make the non-aligned Belizean coastline off-limits for any merchant Spanish ships. It is often cited that Benbow became a semi-respectable logwood cutter in Belize prior to his death on November 4, 1702.

Tales of cruelty abound. The routine business of extracting information about where treasures were hidden could entail "woolding." A band was tied around the captive's forehead, and was slowly tightened by means of turning an attached stick. This torture was continued until the victim's eyes popped out.

Tortuga, the Pirates' Lair

The piratical tradition in the northern Caribbean that gave rise to settlement of Belize in the late 17th century was centred, at first, on a small, 20-mile-long island that Columbus called Tortuga—Spanish for "turtle"—off the northern coast of present-day Haiti. Frenchmen from Tortuga lived off wild herds and notoriously harassed the Spanish. These drifters wore tanned skins and acquired the name *boucaniers*—a term drawn from the French word *boucan*, meaning the place where strips of meat were dried in the Indian style, or from the Mayan word *buccan*, referring to dried manatee meat. Either way, *les boucaniers* from tiny Tortuga could range at great distances with a secure storage of food. As more English, Scottish, Dutch, French, Irish, Portuguese, Danish and Swedish adventurers spread to more Caribbean islands, the term was Anglicized to buccaneers.

The privateer attacked only if a "letter of reprisal" or a "letter or *marque*" was obtained from his king, lord admiral or governor. Such paperwork sanctioned plundering at sea on a retaliatory basis, specifically targeting ships from one country, mainly Spain. It was akin to bounty hunting at sea, but on a national scale. During times of war—and England was usually at war to some degree—private citizens could be "permitted" to "annoy" the enemy. Such licences clearly instructed these privateers not to harm their captives. Again, if murders or rapes occurred, the king or admiral who had issued the licence could claim innocence of any wrongdoing.

Captain Morgan

The most renowned of the Jamaica-based privateers who passed through Belizean waters was Captain Henry Morgan. Born of Welsh ancestry near Tredegar, Glamorganshire, in 1635, he arrived in Barbados in 1655 as a junior officer in an expedition commanded by General Venables. It's assumed Morgan participated in the English takeover of Jamaica in 1655, under the direction of Venables. That same year, Morgan attacked the town of Campeachy on the Gulf of Mexico, with Captains Morris and Jackman and 107 men, then sailed past Belize and sacked the Honduran port of Trujillo.

While sacking Trujillo, Captain Morgan was abetted by the Mosquito Indians who would become essential allies of the English settlers in Belize. But Captain Morgan of rum bottle renown was not the first Englishman to befriend the Mosquito Indians. The Puritans had preceded him.

Puritans, Ahoy

It's probable the first Englishmen to set foot in Belize were Puritans. In 1633, English Puritans settled on the island of Roatan, within easy sailing distance of Belize, when Captain William Claiborne received a grant for settlement in exchange for one quarter of Roatan's profits. Roatan was briefly named Rich Island before the Puritans were driven off the island by the Spanish in 1643.

The Puritans on Roatan were adjuncts of a larger settlement established in 1630 called Providence, 110 miles off the coast of present-day Nicaragua. It was discovered for the English in 1625 by Captain Sussex Camock aboard a ship called *Warwicke & Somer Islands*. Captain Camock was subsequently instructed to commence trade with the black-skinned Indians at Cape Gracias á Dios—where Columbus gave thanks to God in 1502—south of Belize at the present border between Honduras and Nicaragua, on behalf of the Earl of Warwick and the Puritan Providence Island Company.

Camock gained the English lasting favour with the Mosquito Indians as a trader around Cape Gracias á Dios from 1633 to 1635. This relationship would prove integral to Belize. The Mosquito Indians crowned their kings in British Honduras and repeatedly came to the rescue with military backup. At least one historian has suggested Captain Camock was likely the first Englishman to reach Belize but this conjecture is rarely mentioned by other historians, perhaps because Camock was sailing toward Belize long before the English established colonial records in Jamaica in 1655.

Around the late 1630s Tortuga was briefly governed by Captain Peter Wallace—whose surname is often cited as the root of the word "Belize." The supposition that Peter Wallace reached Belize first has been greatly inflated to the detriment of other theories. English historian Stephen L. Caiger makes an assertion that Camock's privateering colleague Captain Daniel Elfrith was cultivating silk grass, pumpkins and potatoes and selling them from two stands, or "stanns," in the Stann Creek area of Belize. Philip Bell has been credited with operating a large plantation at Placentia Point—possibly present-day Placencia in Belize. It has also been suggested that Captain Samuel Axe oversaw tobacco cultivation on Tobacco Caye.

Other candidates for First-Englishman-in-Belize honours include privateer William Jackson, who served the Providence Island Company from 1639 to 1641. Captain Anthony Hilton of Tortuga once originated a plan to use slave labour for the harvesting of logwood and one of the best sources for logwood in the northern Caribbean was Belize.

Ultimately the colony of Providence Island came to a disastrous end: nine Spanish ships and 2,000 Spanish soldiers took 350 English colonists and 381 slaves as prisoners in May of 1641.

The Wallace Myth

The credit for founding Belize is most commonly accorded to Captain Peter Wallace, sometimes cited as a short-lived governor of Tortuga. The designation that Wallace arrived first, and the claim that Belize is named after him, emanates primarily from the *Honduras Almanack*, a propaganda vehicle for the British in the colonies.

The *Honduras Almanack* of 1839 claims the founder of Belize was born at Falkland, Scotland, and that he settled in Belize in 1640. It is known that a Captain Wallace lived with a small party of French rogues on Tortuga, near Hispaniola, in the late 1630s, because he marooned about 40 Frenchmen on Hispaniola. The aggrieved French reached St. Kitts and complained to Governor de Poincy, who commissioned a contingent of about 50 men, under the French Protestant Le Vasseur, to seek retribution at the pirate stronghold of Tortuga in 1640.

According to some historians, Wallace wasn't there. We know Spain had attacked Tortuga in 1638. Either Wallace was killed or he took flight from Tortuga, most likely to Providence. But according to Stephen L. Caiger, the avenging Le Vasseur, or Levasseur, captured Wallace in August 1640 but was soon overcome by a larger English force. Wallace besieged Le Vasseur for 10 days but the "doughty Huguenot" would not budge. Wallace and his followers, who included former Providence settlers, sailed away, possibly headed to Providence.

By 1640 Providence had degenerated into a refuge for privateers. Spain had unsuccessfully attacked it in 1635. Fearing another attack, English authorities were granting privateer licences to legalize attacks on Spanish ships. Providence was located west of Cartagena, the largest city on the Spanish Main, on the coast of Colombia. "From the beginning," historian Peter Earle claims, "the [English] colony's main function was to annoy the King of Spain in the Indies."

Spain unsuccessfully attacked Providence again in 1640. This jives with the vague hypothesis that Wallace could have arrived at the mouth of the Belize River around 1640, either directly from Tortuga or if he fled there from Providence.

Mexican historian Justo Sierra contributes this hypothesis: "In association with the most resolute of his comrades, [Wallace] determined to search for a site where he could establish his lair. So he made a thorough survey of those reefs and shoals, and then found a river entirely protected by cays [small islands] and shallows. At the mouth of this river he landed with some 80 buccaneers, and started to build some houses, surrounding them with a palisade of breastwork—in short, a rude fortress. The place was called Wallace (Belize) after him."

By 1640, silt had not built up sufficiently to cover the mangrove swamps for a stockade. Had Wallace made a "thorough survey" of reefs and shoals, he would not—as an experienced explorer who had overseen the settlement at Tortuga—have sought refuge at the inhospitable river mouth. An Englishman named John Fingas reported to the Council of Trade in London in 1705 that the Yucatán shore "is a great part drowned." A survey of the Belize River mouth in 1787 demarcates the perimeter as "All Swamp & large Mangrove."

Mad dogs and Englishmen might go out in the midday sun, but they don't take the trouble to erect stockades in godforsaken and remote swamps where the Spanish have never bothered to go.

Bloodwood

The raison d'être for settlement along the coast of Belize in the late 1600s, and for centuries thereafter, was the exportation of timber: logwood and mahogany. The logging began with the cutting of logwood, a dyewood that was sought by the woolen industry. The alternate English term "bloodwood" arose because handling it resulted in an almost permanent red stain on the skin.

Logwood (*Haematoxylon campechianum*) grows abundantly in two main areas—along the coasts of the Yucatán and at Campeche—and along the riverbanks of Belize. It has scented yellow flowers and rough, ash-coloured bark. Mature trees grow to about 25 feet tall, rising to as much as 50 feet, with a crooked trunk about 18 inches in diameter. The branches are flecked with whitish spots, sometimes with sharp spines underneath. The outer purplish-black wood conceals a cherry-red wood that was once primarily sought for its dye.

Less appreciated by the Europeans were logwood's medicinal qualities. As a tonic and non-irritating astringent, logwood extracts are said to treat hemorrhages from the uterus, lungs and bowels, and treat diarrhea and dysentery. It is also reputedly beneficial for constitutions broken down by various diseases, mercury or dissipation, and may be used as a treatment for weak bowels following cholera. These healing attributes probably account for one of logwood's alternate names, heartwood.

The transition from piracy to landlubbing began after England captured Jamaica in 1655. In 1659 English sailors attacked Campeche and temporarily took control. Logwood cutters from Jamaica took hold of the Spanish logging centre of Cape Catoche in 1662.

In 1667 Spain signed an important treaty with England in which Spain granted greater English access to trade if England promised to restrict, but not necessarily criminalize, its privateers and buccaneers. The accord encouraged more buccaneers to consider logging as an adjunct to their maritime exploits. Unused logwood territories were seemingly up for grabs.

As recorded by English adventurer William Dampier in the 1670s, the English and Scottish ruffians who undertook the logging first subsisted on a diet of "pork and pease, or beef and doughboys." British loggers of the Caribbean were known as Pork and Doughboys ever afterward.

World traveller William Dampier described widespread drunkenness among the "Logwood-Cutters" in the 17th century.
Portrait by Thomas Murray, circa 1697, National Gallery

Ungovernable Wretches

"I had but little comfort living among these Crew of ungovernable Wretches."
—NATHANIEL URING

Shipwrecked in Belize in 1726, the English sea captain Nathaniel Uring wrote, "The Wood-Cutters are generally a rude drunken Crew, some of which have been Pirates, and most of them Sailors; their chief Delight is in Drinking; and when they broach a Quarter Cask or a Hogshead of Wine, they seldom stir from it while there is a drop left. There was little else to be heard but Blasphemy, Cursing and Swearing."

Drinking sprees, he reported, lasted up to a week. If the woodcutters were chronically half-cut themselves, it's unlikely they cared a great deal about the tenuousness of their position within the diplomatic circles of Europe.

Godolphin's Folly

In 1670, Spain and England signed the Treaty of Godolphin in which England outlawed privateering. In return, Spain conceded English sovereignty of Caribbean territories that England occupied, including Jamaica with its sugar cane. But this treaty, named for the English ambassador to Spain who negotiated it, did *not* specify tiny Belize. Either Godolphin simply overlooked Belize, or else England didn't wish to risk a squabble over a few logwood camps.

The earliest written proof, in English, of English habitation in Belize came from Governor Modyford of Jamaica, also in 1670, when he reported that a dozen vessels—formerly privateering ships—were harvesting logwood at 25 to 50 pounds per ton. Barbados and Jamaica were paying duties on their exports in return for England's governance and military protection. Hence Governor Modyford suggested similar taxed revenues from Belize might be "very considerable to his Majesty, paying 5 pounds per ton custom" if the squatters were granted some official encouragement.

The hyperbolic Modyford reported to King Charles II, in 1671, that the logwood taxes from woodcutting could enhance the National Commerce "more than any of His Majesty's Colonies." But Modyford was ignored. England was wary of offending Spain so soon after the Godolphin Treaty was signed. There were barely 700 settlers in Belize, hence the Settlement, as it was mostly called, was left as a haven for drifters and thieves. In this way the Settlement became an unprotected pawn in a deadly game of geopolitical chess for more than 100 years.

The logwood harvested from Belize was initially taken to

Spanish and Italian ports, and to New England. In 1671, of 2,000 tons of logwood harvested, 600 tons were transported to Boston. "For God's sake," pleaded the next governor of Jamaica, Sir Thomas Lynch, to his superiors in London, "give your commands about the logwood."

Resenting such English incursions into the logwood trade, the Spanish attacked an English settlement of logwood cutters on the Gulf of Mexico in 1675; some 260 loggers "ended their days in the mines." Three years later the English took over the logwood centre of Campeche, but their control was only temporary. In 1680 the Spanish dislodged English logwood cutters from the island of Triste.

Ultimately the Spanish controlled most of the Yucatán and Campeche logwood groves, leaving the Belizean groves undefended for those who preferred the Jolly Roger to the Union Jack.

Still wary of France forming an alliance with Spain, the English became so reticent to offend the Spanish that Sir Thomas Lynch recruited the privateer John Coxon to remove English settlers from Belize in 1682. Coxon's men mutinied, displeased with their wages. "He was in danger of losing his ship and life," Lynch reported. "His men plotted to take the ship and go privateering." Some of Coxon's men were punished upon their return to Jamaica but Coxon remained in Belize as a logwood cutter until 1689.

The Dye Is Cast

The unofficial dividing line between the Baymen and the Spanish continued to be the Hondo River, but there were few laws. From all accounts, an English logwood camp was a tropical Wild West outpost replete with scorpions, tarantulas, mosquitoes and lethal fevers, relieved only by hunting, drinking and rape.

The annals of world traveller William Dampier and the ship's doctor, John Atkins, almost 50 years apart, confirm this impression. Atkins recalled ex-pirates along the coast in 1722 "often made sallies in small parties among the nearest Indian towns, where they plundered and brought away the Indian women to serve them at their huts, and sent their husbands to be sold in Jamaica." More than a century later, the *Honduras Almanack* would put it more delicately. "The sacred institution of marriage was not only neglected, but despised; drunkenness and c---- were among the besetting sins of the land; and virtue and decency were but little known, and less thought of."

Much earlier, Dampier recalled logging with the English woodcutters at Campeche in 1676. These men "would still spend 30 or 40 pounds at a sitting aboard the ships that came thither from Jamaica, carousing and firing off guns three or four days together. And though afterwards many sober Men came into the Bay to cut Wood, yet by degrees the old Standers so debauched them that they could never settle themselves under any Civil Government, but continued in their Wickedness."

Dampier, a mapmaker, provided the most in-depth account of the English logging methods, including their use of explosives, in his 1697 memoir, *A Voyage Around the World*:

> During the wet season, the Land where the Logwood grows is so overflowed, that they step from their Beds into the Water perhaps two feet deep, and continue standing in the wet all day, till they go to bed again; but nevertheless account it the best Season in the Year for doing a good Day's labour in...
>
> The Logwood-Cutters are generally sturdy strong Fellows and will carry Burthens of three or four hundred Weight; but every man is left to his choice to carry what he pleaseth, and commonly they agree very well about it: For they are contented to labour very hard.
>
> But when Ships come from Jamaica with Rum and

Sugar, they are too apt to mis-spend both their Time and Money. If the Commanders of these Ships are Free, and treat all that come the first Day with Punch, they will be much respected, and every Man will pay honestly for what he drinks afterwards; but if he is niggardly, they will pay their worst wood, and commonly they have a stock of such laid for that purpose; nay they will cheat them with hollow Wood filled with dirt in the middle and both ends plugg'd with a piece of the same drove in hard, and then sawed off so neatly, that it's hard to find out the Deceit; but if any Man come to purchase with Bills payable at Jamaica, they will be sure to give him the best wood.

In Belize, logwood trees were floated down the New and Belize Rivers to the coast. Near the mouth of the Belize River, ships could anchor safely around a nearby mangrove island. The Spanish called it *Cayo Cocina*—Kitchen Island—but it would later be named St. George's Caye. Spain and the Baymen would jostle for control of this island for more than a century.

Chapter 5: The Sucking Colony

Despite their allegiance to rum, not royalty, the original, free-trading Baymen of Belize supplanted the monopoly-minded Spanish in the logwood trade in the 1700s. Little direction was provided from London.

The politics of the Caribbean shifted appreciably in 1713. Britain "forced a trade" upon Spain in the aftermath of Queen Anne's War whereby British ships were granted unimpeded access to the Caribbean slave trade. Having called the shots in the Caribbean for more than two centuries, Spain resented the meddling of its main seafaring rival. In response, Spain repeatedly harassed the "sucking colony" of Belize.

If there was a turning point in the struggle to defray Spanish aggression, it came on April 5, 1754, when a force of 250 machete-wielding loggers somehow turned back 1,500 Spaniards invading from El Petén in Guatemala—stopping them at Labouring Creek. Although the "Battle of Labouring Creek" doesn't quite merit a national anthem, it rallied the spirits of the Settlement enough to mount a successful counter-offensive with reinforcements of 500 men.

In 1755, the Spanish responded by routing the Baymen,

forcing them to seek refuge en masse on the Mosquito Shore (now known as the Mosquito Coast). Burning the Settlement to the ground, the Spanish assumed the location was not worth occupying. "The Spaniards have done no great damage to the Bay," cheerily reported Superintendent William Pitt, "neither have they built any Battery or left any People there: for they say it is only fit for Englishmen who can always have a supply of Provisions which they can not."

Mahogany and Cook's tour

The Baymen hired a military engineer named Jones to construct a fort a few miles up Haulover Creek. Soldiers from the Mosquito Shore stood guard during its erection. The humiliating retreat of 1755 had also been costly; self-defence appeared to be a cheaper option than running away.

From 1756 to 1763, England fought successfully against Spain and France in the Seven Years War. At its conclusion, Spain conceded in the Treaty of Paris to allow Baymen to cut and export logwood if, in return, the British demolished their fortifications—most notably the stockade at Haulover Creek with its enclave of

Rivers

1. Hondo River (Mexican border)
2. New River
3. Blue Creek (Mexican border)
4. Northern River
5. Rio Bravo
6. Yalbec Creek
7. Belize River
8. Sibun River
9. Mullins River
10. North Stann Creek
11. Sittee River
12. Silver/Jenkins Creeks
13. Monkey River
14. Warrie Creek
15. Rio Grande
16. Moho River
17. Temash River
18. Sarstoon River (Guatemalan border)

soldiers with cannon. The fort was removed. The Baymen were once again vulnerable to any major Spanish aggression. They had paid for their stockade; there was no compensation for its removal.

The Treaty of Paris, written by the Marquis de Grimaldi, generated an increasingly uncomfortable truce because it only specified the right of the Baymen to harvest logwood, not mahogany or any other wood. By this time, mahogany furniture was fast becoming a status symbol in England. The Baymen were aware mahogany (*Swietenia mahagoni*) found in Belize was as good as any in the world. It was being used for beams and stanchions in shipbuilding.

To find mahogany, the Baymen needed to search beyond the riverbanks. Permission to seek logwood was vaguely worded to incorporate the "Bay of Honduras and other parts of the World." Governor Estenoz of Yucatán ordered all loggers removed from the Hondo River because they had commenced logwood cutting "without waiting to settle limits with the necessary solemnity." Estenoz wanted logging restricted between the Belize and New Rivers, no farther than 20 leagues from the coast.

It was a long way to London or Madrid to file a grievance. Defenceless without their stockade, the loggers felt unfairly treated and appealed to Governor Lyttleton of Jamaica. Six months of diplomatic exchanges between Spain and Great Britain ensued. To investigate the situation in Belize and to ensure the safety of the woodcutters, Governor Lyttleton sent Admiral Sir William Burnaby to visit the Bay Settlement, accompanied by a competent and eager subordinate named James Cook.

When Burnaby arrived on HMS *Active*, with three other ships, to investigate the expulsion of loggers from the Hondo River, he summoned his young lieutenant, Cook, to consult with the new governor of Yucatán in Mérida. Cook dutifully returned with explanations.

It turned out the Spanish had been harassing the Baymen

because the fort commander at Bacalar and the Yucatán governor had been in cahoots—selling goods at inflated prices. The Baymen, seizing an opportunity, had been bribing Spanish soldiers with liquor and other goods in order to cut wood on the Spanish side of the Hondo River. The Spanish governor had resented commercial competition. This situation resolved itself when the corrupt governor of Yucatán had died and the Bacalar fort commander had been replaced.

Burnaby's Code

In the beginning, there had been honour among thieves. If you crossed the Tropic of Cancer in a pirate ship, it was believed you had drowned your former self. The rules of Europe were no longer applicable—you were free to remake yourself, adopt a different name. You subscribed to the Ship's Articles, agreed upon prior to sailing. No prey, no pay. An honour-among-thieves ethic evolved. Mock pirate gatherings held around the world—not unlike Star Trek conventions—have playfully revered such rules of Olde:

- Anyone caught stealing from his fellow sailor will have his nose or ears sliced off. For a second offence, the culprit will be marooned with only water and a musket.
- Loss of an eye or a finger will gain compensation of 100 pieces of eight or one slave; loss of the right arm will gain 600 pieces of eight...
- Every man has a Vote in Affairs of Moment; has equal title to the fresh Provisions, or Strong Liquors, at any Time seized, and use of them at Pleasure, unless a Scarcity make it necessary, for the good of all, to Vote a Retrenchment.
- The Captain and Quarter-Master to receive two Shares of a Prize; the Master, Boatswain and Gunner, one Share and a half, and other Officers, one and a Quarter.
- That Man that shall strike another while these Articles

are in force shall receive Moses's Law (that is 40 Stripes lacking one) on the bare Back.

- That Man that shall snap his Arms, or smoke Tobacco in the Hold, without a cap to his Pipe, or carry a Candle lighted without a Lanthorn, shall suffer the same Punishment as in the former Article.
- If at any time you meet with a prudent Woman, that Man that offers to meddle with her, without her Consent, shall suffer present Death.

When pirates and privateers became loggers in Belize, they adapted their at-sea codes in a similar spirit of egalitarianism. The "Articles" of the first Baymen had led to regularized town meetings in Belize and were refined into a constitution in 1765 when the upper-crust Admiral Burnaby arrived with Cook and suggested Cayo Cocina should henceforth be named St. George's Caye in honour of England's patron saint.

During Burnaby's layover, Joseph Maud and his fellow magistrates approached Burnaby to draft the common rules of the Settlement. Twelve articles of Burnaby's Code were signed by 85 people, including two women, Mary Wil and Mary Allen, on April 9, 1765. The constitutional document made some very odd allowances—such as leniency for the kidnapping of a steersman, because such men were so valuable—so it's apparent Burnaby served mostly as the draughtsman, not the creator, of the statutes.

If any person refused to comply with the verdicts, justices had full power to seize property. Fines could be paid in Jamaican currency "or the same value Merchantable unchipt Logwood" delivered to St. George's Caye. For enforcement, 13 good and lawful subjects could be selected to assist the seven justices: John Douglas, James Farrell, David Fitzgibbon, Basil Jones, John Lawrie, Joseph Maud and Christopher Sinnott.

Most significantly, in article eight, the Settlement ceded

its authority to the commander of any of His Majesty's Ships of War during any war. The Baymen, by choosing subservience to any British naval vessel, were courting some assured British protection against the Spanish. The Baymen mostly wanted a rough-hewn constitution to impress Spain. Admiral Burnaby's name appeared on the code because the Baymen hoped the Spanish would take notice of their formalized attachment to him and think twice about further incursions.

Burnaby attached little significance to the code. In Jamaica, he reported the Baymen only subscribed to them when it suited them. Returning to Belize at the end of 1765, Burnaby found the Baymen "in a state of Anarchy and Confusion" and recommended a superintendent should be provided.

Horatio Nelson at the Bridge

Increasingly the outside world was bumping into Belize. In 1777, a year after the Boston Tea Party, an American privateer arrived at St. George's Caye in his sloop *General Washington* and successfully demanded to be replenished with supplies, chiefly rum. He promptly sailed south from Belize and captured three British ships.

In 1778, France decided to set its forces upon England, increasing conflicts within the West Indies. In 1779, Spain and Holland decided they might as well declare war on Britain, too. The Baymen soon discovered waving a piece of paper with Admiral Burnaby's name on it wasn't much of a deterrent. There was yet another Spanish attack.

In 1779, taking advantage of Spain's declaration of war, the new Yucatán governor sent a flotilla of 15 *perriaguas* and one schooner to easily capture St. George's Caye. The Spanish absconded with some 140 captives, destroying camps and burning homes up the New River as they proceeded north. Prisoners, including women and children, were forced to march all the way to Mérida. From there they were shipped to dungeons in Havana—a proverbial fate worse than death—until they were released in 1782.

The famed "wooden walls of England" arrived in the form of a sloop called the HMS *Brig Badger*, commanded by a 20-year-old named Horatio Nelson. He was in the area patrolling for the new bane of Britain's existence—American privateers. Nelson had participated in the unsuccessful attack on the Spanish port of San Juan in Nicaragua in 1779, having been promoted to serve as captain aboard the frigate *Hinchingbrook*. Nelson's arrival at Belize facilitated the safe journey of retreating small vessels to Roatan and the Mosquito Shore.

To seek some revenge, in 1780 some of the vanquished Baymen sailed with the newly appointed governor of "Rattan," a former shipmate and friend of Nelson named Colonel Edward Despard, and successfully destroyed the Spanish port of Black River. This was followed by their participation in a larger naval offensive on the Spanish Honduran port of Omoa. Under the direction of Despard, the Baymen returned to St. George's Caye and Belize City, erecting another stockade up Haulover Creek.

Between a Rock and a Swamp Place

The resilience of the Baymen was little appreciated in London. Instead Britain concentrated its diplomatic efforts on securing its tenancy in Gibraltar. When the Treaty of Versailles finally resolved hostilities with Spain in 1783, the rock of resistance that was swampy Belize remained designated as a Spanish territory. Spain granted permission for logwood cutting only. Mahogany had by this time eclipsed logwood as the economic basis for the Settlement but permission to extract mahogany was not mentioned in any treaty.

Territorial rights of the Baymen were actually limited by the British victory. They were forbidden to occupy any islands and were obliged to dismantle all fortifications. Reduced to narrower confines, Baymen resented overcrowding and unemployment. To make matters worse, Britain tried offloading some of its convicts. Then a 12-hour hurricane struck in November 1785.

Spain was willing to review the Treaty of Versailles of 1783—a treaty that Baymen detested—only because they were eager to somehow retrieve Gibraltar. In the Convention of London, Spain agreed the boundaries for logwood cutting could be extended as far south as the Sibun River with the proviso that Baymen couldn't attempt any form of government. The Baymen could once again occupy St. George's Caye and fishing would be permitted. As well, they could also use islands for careening of ships. (Careening entailed moving a vessel ashore and hauling it onto its side by pulling ropes attached to the masthead.) Most importantly, the Baymen would be allowed to cut mahogany. A legal economy could finally arise from the mouth of the Rio Balis after a century of piracy, privation and debauchery. All London had to do was decide who might best oversee the lucrative logging trade and supervise the Baymen who had been described by Admiral Parry as "a most notorious, lawless set of Miscreants."

Chapter 6: Despard's Plight

Colonel Edward Marcus Despard, an Irishman, was sent to administer the settlement sometimes known as "Haulover" in 1780. Despard's official title was "Superintendent of His Majesty's Affairs within the district which, by the late Treaty of Peace, has been allotted to the Log-Cutters upon the Bay of Honduras." Having led forces that retook parts of the Mosquito Shore from the Spanish, Despard was not an unpopular choice. But his job would be the death of him.

Before he was hanged as an English traitor in 1803, Marcus Despard tried his best to bring responsible government to the fledgling settlement of Haulover. *Belize Archives.*

Born in 1751, at Coolrain, near Mountrath, in Queen's County, Ireland, Despard was the youngest of six brothers. Most of them fought for the British in the American War of independence; Despard went instead to Jamaica where he worked as an engineer.

Having proven himself as an administrator along the coast of Nicaragua and Honduras, he was a logical choice to ensure the newly minted London Convention was respected and observed.

While going about his military affairs, Despard had married a black woman, Catherine, from the Mosquito Shore. It was not uncommon for European men to cohabit on an ongoing basis with slaves, or ex-slaves, or Free Coloureds, but Despard's marriage was not the norm. Catherine would remain his faithful companion, his secretary and his long-suffering advocate until his grisly death.

In Belize, Despard immediately found himself in an untenable position. The London Convention specifically forbade "the formation of any system of government either military or civil." Despard was therefore duty-bound to dismantle Burnaby's Code. This was not the way to win friends and influence people. His job, in essence, was to ensure that Baymen had no government, while at the same time he was obliged to *be* the government.

Admiral Parry of the Royal Navy had described the Baymen as "artful and cunning, having practiced every ill. [They] fly from different parts thither to avoid Justice, where they pursue their licentious conduct with impunity." They were also quick to become adversarial. It didn't help that Despard was an Irishman or that he was high-minded—and they were not. Equally problematic, Despard was instructed to evacuate all British subjects from the Mosquito Shore and the Bay Islands, including Roatan, in keeping with the terms of the London Convention.

The Influx of Shoremen

Even on paper, this didn't make sense. If the agenda was to consolidate British settlers, the Baymen should have been sent to the Mosquito Coast where Shoremen and their slaves were far more numerous. But Britain did not wish to make a fresh enemy out of Spain, so Despard was required to bring the Shoremen and their slaves to the Settlement.

Anticipating the influx, the Baymen set aside a separate area to be called Convention Town, named after the London Convention. Absentee control of timber holdings was hastily made invalid by the Baymen, enabling them to grab as much land as they could prior to the mass immigration. For good measure, Baymen also decreed no man could have access to logwood or mahogany rights unless he owned four slaves. Evicting Shoremen from staunchly loyal British enclaves in the western Caribbean—an area Despard had just liberated—was going to be hard enough without having to cope with the Baymen's wrangling for advantages prior to the move.

In 1787, some 2,214 British subjects were relocated to Belize—by far the most radical of the many immigration scenarios that would gradually give rise to the nation of Belize. With the arrival of the Shoremen, the population of the tiny Settlement increased fivefold.

Neither the Shoremen nor the Baymen could appreciate that the London Convention was mostly about who controlled Gibraltar. Britain had agreed to evacuate the Mosquito Shore and Bay Islands, knowing full well the Mosquito Indians would remain as British allies, whereupon Spain stipulated new logging concessions for Belize to the Sibun River. Affecting magnanimity, Spain then asked for the return of Gibraltar. Britain said no, it had already matched Spain's bid by agreeing to evacuate the Mosquito Shore.

To further complicate Despard's situation, London specifically directed him to "give preference to the Mosquito Shore arrivals." Without any cohesive police force to back him up, Despard couldn't force the minority Baymen to easily integrate the new majority from the Mosquito Shore. To enforce the terms of the Convention, Despard had to sometimes call upon the neighbouring Spanish militia. It didn't help that, in the process of fulfilling his duties, he became friends with the leading Spaniard from

Bacalar, Don Juan Gual, who was instructed to inspect the Settlement every six months.

Not surprisingly, Despard became the most hated man in Belize.

Despard's Disgrace

The late 18th century was a period of radical transformation and uncertainty for the Settlement. A few British captives liberated from the dungeons of Havana were also relocated to Belize at this time. Under Despard, a ruling was made in 1787 that forbade possession of more than two mahogany works on any river, no matter how many slaves the harvester might claim. Some Baymen were forced to relinquish their holdings.

The Baymen reported to Jamaica and London that Despard's despotic rule was "too degrading for an Englishman to suffer." Threats of armed resistance arose. The more the Baymen who controlled the timber industry objected to Despard, the more prudent it became for London to sacrifice him, after he had done most of the dirty work for them. As Spain and England returned to less than cordial relations in Europe, it became less necessary to maintain the cordial relations Despard had developed in Belize.

Despard's replacement, Colonel Peter Hunter, arrived on His Majesty's Sloop of War *Cygnet* in April 1790. Only two days after disembarkment, the second superintendent of Belize issued a proclamation to restore Burnaby's Code. Hunter reappointed magistrates who had been in charge prior to Despard's arrival. When a new election of magistrates was held, Colonel Despard was elected to serve as one of the nine, but departed the "Bay of Honduras Settlement" soon thereafter. So did Hunter, who was recalled to Jamaica in 1791. Magistrates once again controlled their own timber trade.

Embittered, Despard returned to London to defend his record. He spent much of his time in London seeking compensation for debts and writing lengthy justifications for his actions.

For two years his protestations fell on deaf ears. Ultimately he was told there was no charge against him worthy of an investigation. He could not be reinstated simply because the job of superintendent in Belize had been abolished.

Despard turned his support to radical causes, becoming the United Irishmen's principal organizer in London. When the United Irishmen attempted a brief uprising in 1798, Despard was imprisoned in Coldbath Fields, under the Habeas Corpus Act, until 1801. Upon his release, he went to Ireland where his relatives dismissed his wife as a "black housekeeper." Their son James— a "flashy Creole"—failed to pass muster.

On his return to London, Despard became the focal point for a small party of malcontents who met in public houses. He was arrested as their ringleader on November 16, 1802, in the Oakley Arms, along with 40 working men and soldiers, mostly Irish. According to a police informant, Despard and his followers had sworn an oath to assassinate King George III.

Despard was tried first. Lord Nelson provided a character reference to no avail. The jury found Despard guilty of treason along with six other conspirators. Lord Ellenborough pronounced the sentence: "You are to be drawn on hurdles to the place of execution, where you are to be hanged by the neck, but not until you are dead; for while you are still living your bodies are to be taken down, your bowels torn out and before your faces, your heads then cut off, and your bodies divided each into four quarters, and your heads and quarters to be then at the King's disposal; and may the Almighty God have mercy on your souls."

Then there came a reprieve of sorts: their bowels would not be removed and burned and their bodies would not be quartered. A scaffold and gallows were erected atop the jail. Extra police were placed on duty. Seven coffins were brought, plus the block for beheading and two large bags of sawdust. At 4:00 a.m. the drums signalled the cavalry to assemble. A bell rang at half-past six and the cells were opened. At 7:00 a.m. on February 21, 1803, Despard and the others were removed from irons. The first superintendent of Belize met his solicitor and shook his hand, thanking him for his efforts. Upon seeing the 100 spectators, scaffolding, executioner's block and coffins, Despard declared, "Ha! What nonsensical mummery is this!" Then he was hanged and beheaded.

Battle of St. George's Caye

British military forces were depleted following the American War of Independence. The British Treasury was low and remote Belize was near the end of the pecking order in terms of defensive allotments.

The French were making successful attacks in the eastern Caribbean. More hostilities with Spain were on the horizon—and the Baymen were wary of history repeating itself. In lieu of troops, Britain sent Major Thomas Barrow to fortify the Settlement in December 1796.

As the third-ever superintendent, the newly appointed commander-in-chief discovered nearly half his constituents preferred to vamoose rather than fight. This attitude riled Thomas Paslow, a former Irish artillery colonel who was eager to wear a uniform he owned that had once belonged to King George II. Another patriot was Magistrate Marshall Bennett who had too much invested in the Settlement to lose. A more realistic group, led by Colonel James Pitt Lawrie, a former Superintendent of the Mosquito Shore, was advocating evacuation.

Even if British soldiers could be found in the 1790s, they wouldn't necessarily prove effective. European troops in the West Indies were frequently victims of two unforeseen adversaries: tropical diseases and the "New" Rum. Soldiers and sailors commonly fell victim to typhoid during the passage from Britain. Once in the Caribbean, yellow fever, known as "Yellow Jack," took a heavy toll. As well, the early sugar producing equipment dispersed a high lead content into the soldier's rum ration. The situation was exacerbated by the common belief that drinking rum in large quantities was a protective measure against yellow fever. In fact, over-consumption led to undiagnosed afflictions such as encephalitis, liver cirrhosis, liver necrosis, nephritis, anemia and gout.

"What shall we do with the drunken sailor?" is more than an amusing song. Proximity to two of the world's rum-producing capitals, Jamaica and Barbados, made liquor part of the staple diet for soldiers. Entire military garrisons in the West Indies became incapacitated from drinking.

By the time Commander-in-Chief Barrow arrived in Belize, Spain had already declared war and captured three of the Baymen's ships. A crucial public meeting was held on June 1, 1797, to determine whether settlers would defend Belize or not. The vote was 65 to 51 in favour of defending Belize, with 11 abstentions.

In preparation for battle, St. George's Caye was evacuated in August. It was judged indefensible; its buildings were burned to the ground. When Spanish forces arrived in September, their large ships ran aground in mud behind Caye Chapel. For three days they failed to secure St. George's Caye as a base for mounting their offensive on the Settlement.

Maritime passageways were narrow, so the flotilla of Spanish warships could not attack simultaneously. Captain Ralph Moss and 50 men aboard HMS *Merlin*, the lone warship, were supplemented by five local sloops, *Towser*, *Tickler*, *Mermaid*, *Swinger* and *Teaser*. Each had volunteer crews of approximately 25 men each. Tinier vessels ran reconnaissance, tracking every move made by the Spanish.

By a combination of luck, pluck and Spanish incompetence, the invaders' superior fleet of 31 ships carrying 2,000 troops and 500 seamen was held in check. The defenders had manoeuverability on their side, plus local knowledge of the shoals. The Spaniards were beset by dysentery, malaria and yellow fever and they buried their dead on a daily basis on Caye Chapel.

The British slaves fought bravely alongside their white masters—seemingly as equals—leading overseers to report, "Negroes in an undaunted manner rowed their boats, and used every exertion to board the enemy." The slave owners would use the behaviour of their slaves in the battle to claim that slavery in Belize was not as exploitive as slavery in other West Indian colonies.

When 14 of the Spanish ships attempted to land soldiers on St. George's Caye, the *Merlin* and smaller craft attacked as Spanish vessels were temporarily stationary targets. After considerable losses, the Spanish retreated on September 6 and waited three days. On September 10 they turned tail. Not a defender was lost.

The battle has served as grist for an anthem officially called the "Ballad of the Battle of St. George's Caye Composed in Belize Under the Name of the Tenth Day of September." Not the catchiest of titles, but the tune has stuck.

> *It was the tenth day of September*
> *In ninety-eight Anno Domini,*
> *When our forefathers won the glorious fight—*
> *The Battle of St. George's Caye.*
> *Then cheer them, hail them!*
> *Let our grateful loyal hearts not fail them,*
> *As we march and shout and sing with merry glee:*
> *The Battle of St. George's Caye!*

Chapter 7: Mahogany and Other Industries

Exportation of mahogany was the economic focus of Belize for almost three centuries. Mahogany does not grow in groves and it's more awkward to harvest than a logwood tree; consequently timber merchants needed many more slaves when the demand for mahogany eclipsed that of logwood. Because mahogany was scattered over broader areas than logwood, Baymen and their gangs infiltrated the interior of Belize, granting themselves larger timber reserves as they went. According to a series of "locations laws" that were drafted prior to Spain's approval of mahogany works,

The harvesting of "bloodwood" (logwood) by ex-pirates was eventually replaced by a mahogany industry dependent on slave labour. These mahogany loggers are from the early 20th century. *Belize Archives.*

mahogany works comprised up to three miles of river frontage, receding for up to eight miles. These 24-square-mile holdings were treated as freehold properties, bought and sold, in contradiction to the formal allowances made by the Spanish.

At the outset of the mahogany industry, the Baymen viewed the traditional slash-and-burn agricultural methods of the Maya as threatening to their income. The Maya responded violently as early as 1788; troops were sent to punish them for "committing depredations upon the mahogany works." Arms and ammunitions were sent to repel the Maya at a place called Hogstye Bank, near present-day Belmopan, in 1807. The Maya attacked a mahogany camp up the New River as late as 1817, but they were not able to organize their villages to fight en masse. The Maya increasingly disappeared into the mountains, shunted outside the mainstream of Belizean society.

During the dry months, between January and September, huntsmen searched for mahogany trees. To rise above the broad base of the tree, the axemen stood on platforms notched into the trunk. Other slaves used oxen to haul the fallen tree to the nearest river. According to verbal accounts only, slaves were used as beasts

Mahogany logs were floated down the rivers and prepared for transport as "mahogany squares." *Belize Archives.*

of burden if oxen were not available. At a place called a *barquadier*, untrimmed logs were formed into rafts. Logs were sent downriver in the rainy season to make booms, and at the river's mouth, they were squared in preparation for loading.

The growth of the mahogany trade gave rise to institutionalized control and systemic expansion. Ignoring accords with Spain, cutters went beyond the Sibun River. The Settlement could expand with relative impunity after Napoleon invaded Spain in 1808, installing his brother as King. British loggers reached the Moho River by 1814. Unchallenged, they advanced as far south as the Sarstoon River.

In 1814, the newly arrived Superintendent George Arthur identified the "monopoly of the part of the monied cutters" and petitioned the secretary of state to withdraw land control rights from settlers for unused land. Three years later, when a militia was founded, he issued a proclamation to hinder the monopoly: in essence, anyone who claimed to own land had to explain how they got it and nobody could occupy unused land without his permission. Unfortunately Arthur appointed a commission to investigate the legitimacy of private land holdings that was chiefly comprised of the self-interested aristocracy who controlled the trade—and they found little was amiss. Superintendent Arthur's initiative was nonetheless significant because it formalized the principle that all unclaimed land was Crown land.

Arthur's unusually long tenure (1814–22) proved significant. The first wooden bridge connecting the two halves of Belize City was built in 1818. The Criminal Court was created by an Act of Parliament in 1819. The Supreme Court held its inaugural session in 1820. By 1821, Spanish territories were disassembling, veering toward republicanism. Much too distracted by interior concerns, Guatemala and New Spain (Mexico) were unable to stifle the territorial expansion that emanated from Belize City.

In the 19th century, mahogany production reached its zenith

in the 1830s and early 1840s during Europe's railway boom, when mahogany was in vogue for railway coaches.

As Colonel Arthur had correctly surmised in 1814, those who controlled the land controlled the mahogany trade; and those who controlled the mahogany trade controlled Belize. In the late 1850s, the mahogany elite sought to undo some of Arthur's diligent inquiry into land use. A lawyer in England, employed by a company that would become part of the British Honduras Company (BHC), drafted the Honduras Land Titles Acts to essentially permit land ownership to be sold or transferred even if legal title could not be clearly proven. This prompted a flurry of real estate speculation. The venerable James Hyde & Co. was bought by the newly formed British Honduras Company in 1859. The BHC consortium developed primarily from the businesses of the two settler families of James Hyde and James Bartlett, and a London merchant named John Hodge. It wasn't long before BHC owned more than one million acres in Belize, about one-fifth of the country.

The BHC made a brief foray into sugar production in the 1870s, but the company was almost exclusively concerned with timber—cutting it and hoarding it. The BHC couldn't use all of its massive land holdings, but its lock on Belizean real estate stymied competition. It cut and shipped trees, never replanting. The BHC changed its named to the Belize Estate and Produce Company (BEC) in 1875.

After the mahogany business faltered badly in the mid-19th century—due to falling prices, shortages of labour, political instability and dwindling natural resources—many established families in Belize became indebted to London merchants. Young, Toledo and Company went bankrupt in 1880 and with that demise, the BEC became as powerful in Belize as the United Fruit Company was in any banana republic.

By 1965, lumber accounted for only 14 percent of domestic exports (compared to 25 percent for citrus and 33 percent for sugar).

The BEC's stranglehold on the Belizean mahogany business prevailed until the 1970s when it was finally sold to an America company. By then the supply of mahogany trees in Belize was nearly exhausted. In February of 2003, Belize police seized 186 pieces of rough-sawn mahogany measuring 4,745.7 feet from a truck on the Western Highway near Hattieville. The load was worth about $5,000. Charges were laid against four men for unlawful possession of mahogany according to Section 19 of the Forest Act.

Sir Walter Raleigh went looking for gold in El Dorado in 1595, only to discover mahogany. Four centuries later, it was a rare commodity, approaching the status of a precious metal.

The Rise and Fall and Rise of Sugar

Cane production in Belize can be traced to 1847 when the Yucatán Maya revolted against white settlers of Spanish origin. The *Guerra de las Castas* almost halved the population of the Yucatán, sending thousands of Maya and Mestizo refugees spilling into Belize, bringing their sugar cane growing expertise with them. As early as 1852, Mestizos were cultivating sugar in Belize, many at the behest of a far-sighted magistrate, James Blake, in Corozal.

The fledgling industry was also dominated by the BHC. The first shipment of sugar to Europe was made on the ship *Byzantium* in 1857. Production quadrupled between 1862 and 1868, from 397,176 pounds to 1,706,880 pounds. Plantations with steam-operated machinery soon proved more efficient than small plots managed by Mestizo *rancheros*. The Maya and Mestizos devolved into a rural peasantry, increasingly dependent on larger companies that aquired more of the land.

During the sugar boom of the 1860s, the bigger estates were desperate to import more labour, en masse. Overtures were made to acquire 1,500 blacks from Havana and workers from India. In 1863, John Hodge of the BHC went to Washington, DC, and London in an effort to import recently emancipated slaves but the American agent in Belize, Dr. Charles Lea, noted that blacks would be "subjected to a species of slavery and demoralized far worse than ever existed in our country."

The BHC imported 474 Chinese labourers in 1865. About 100 soon died and another 100 fled to live with Santa Cruz Maya. The 133 Chinese listed on the 1871 census became the nucleus for the Chinese population in Belize.

The government invited Confederate soldiers at the end of the Civil War to find a haven in Belize as sugar planters. To sweeten the deal, Lieutenant Governor John Gardiner Austin wanted to sell 500,000 acres of Crown land to the impoverished white immigrants at only 20 cents per acre; the official price for others was $5 per acre. Non-whites on rented land were transforming wilderness into valuable real estate, but they would have to pay 25 times more to gain title to Crown land than the Confederates.

Austin's plan was not simply racist. He was hoping "the great landed proprietors of the Colony" and the BHC would be more willing to divest some lands to Anglo-Saxons. As well, Britain might take a greater interest in Belize if there were more white citizens. In his enthusiasm, Austin suggested white planters could "change this Colony from an unknown wilderness into a garden teeming with all the wealth and beauties of the tropics."

Ex-Confederates immigrated from 1864 to 1870, north of Punta Gorda at Cattle Landing, where 12 sugar mills were started—and failed. The Southerners went home to whistle Dixie after sugar prices fell and Belize failed to provide land prices as favourable as those promised. The main problem was that sugar could be imported to England duty-free, from anywhere, after 1874, and so subsidized beet sugar from Europe had skewered the sugar market. By century's end, the sugar industry collapsed and Belize was once more chiefly dependent on mahogany, plus one new export product: chicle.

The modern sugar industry arose from two Tate & Lyle factories operated by the British in the early 1960s. By the 1970s, sugar accounted for more than half of Belize's exports. In the 1980s, the US reduced its sugar quota and prices fell. Tate & Lyle closed its Libertad factory in 1985. Its Tower Hill factory became employee-operated. Belize Sugar Industries persevered, recording its highest bulk shipment of 17,300 tons to Canada in 1990. By 2000 Belize resembled Cuba in that it was clearly dependent on sugar and tourism, sugar accounting for almost half of export revenues.

The EU sugar market has paid preferential prices for almost 50% of the Belizean sugar output, but proposed price cuts, legislated by the EU Sugar Import Regime, will severely limit revenues during a four-year period commencing in 2006.

By Gum

Chicle is the gum of the sapodilla tree used to manufacture all chewing gum in the 19th century. The *chiclero* secured a rope around his waist and around the tree, and climbed the sapodilla tree with a machete. He then cut the bark in criss-crossing lines, bleeding the sap into the indented rivulets of the bark. Much like the process of gathering maple syrup, the sap was leaked into containers, which were carried back to the chiclero's camp. The sap was cooked and then moulded into blocks weighing about 25 pounds. Using mules or oxen, the chiclero brought his gum out of the forest for sale to a chicle buyer. With mahogany prices unpredictable, the production of chicle was encouraged by British authorities to provide some ballast for a fragile economy. "From the exhaustion of Mahogany the hitherto staple commodity," wrote Superintendent Macdonald in 1839, "the permanent welfare of this place must mainly depend upon the rearing of colonial produce."

Even though the chicle industry waned when artificial substitutes were devised, the government issued a licence to the American Chicle Company to bleed sapodilla gum in the Toledo District as late as 1919. The Forestry Department of Belize has continued to issue chicle permits to independent collectors. Production methods haven't varied much over more than a century. Chicle is still being extracted mainly from July to February when rains induce a good flow of gum from the trees. The 1989 price on a contract of 22,000 pounds, depending on quality, varied from BZ$316 to $320 per 100 pounds. Some chicle from Belize in the 1980s and '90s was still being exported to Japanese and American firms for brand names such as Wrigley's Spearmint and Double Mint.

A chiclero taps a sapodilla tree to extract chicle for the production of chewing gum. *Belize Archives.*

Yes, We Have No Bananas

Around 1800, a few fledgling banana plantations precipitated a trade route to New Orleans, but these ventures failed. In 1899, two companies called the Boston Fruit Company and the Tropical Trading and Transport Company merged to form the United Fruit Company (UFCO). *La Frutera*, as it became known, began to aggressively establish a virtual monopoly on production and distribution of bananas in Latin America, giving rise to the derogatory term "banana republic." The banana industry got off to another false start in 1911 when UFCO purchased the Middlesex Estate in the Stann Creek District, only to have the crop succumb to Panama disease. An attempt to revive the industry in the 1930s was blighted by Sigatoka leaf spot disease. This demise reduced Monkey River Town, once thriving at the mouth of the Monkey River, to a tiny village. [The headline "Yes, We Have No Bananas" has been used many times. It's derived from a 1923 chart-topper recorded by Billy Jones and his orchestra and co-written by Leon Trotsky's nephew.]

Bananas are one of the world's oldest crops. About 10,000 years ago the first edible variety mutated from the wild banana, a mass of hard seeds. All bananas are basically clones of the first plant, meaning they're sterile, unable to evolve to combat new diseases. Consequently they are continually under threat by nature. In 2003, scientists predicted the possible extinction of the banana within 10 years due to the rampaging spread of black Sigatoka, a fungal disease that reduces the productive lives of banana plants from 30 to only two or three years. "As soon as you bring in a new fungicide, it develops resistance," said Emile Frison, director of the International Network for the Improvement of Banana and Plantain. Most banana groves in Brazil were already destroyed by 2003. The likelihood that Belize could adequately protect itself from black Sigatoka was slim.

In Belize, when diseases haven't impeded cultivation, banana plantations have been severely damaged by hurricanes. In the latter half of the 20th century, most bananas were bought by Fyffes, once a subsidiary of United Brands, formerly UFCO. Fyffes claimed to be the world's second-largest produce company.

As one of the original Caribbean signatories to the Lomé Convention in 1975, Belize had a promising banana industry until the late 20th century. The Convention was an important agreement between the European Economic Community and 42 former European colonies whereby colonies and former colonies gained preferential access for agricultural products. In essence, Europe was lending a helping hand to little guys like Grenada, Guyana, Uganda (which became the world's second-largest producer) and Belize. Only about 7 percent of the EU imports were the sweet, smaller fruit of the smaller Caribbean producers but this was productive for Belize.

Unfortunately this subsidy system was deemed threatening by Cincinnati's Carl Lindner, boss of Chiquita Brands. On April 11, 1996, at Lindner's request, US trade representative Mickey Kantor officially complained to the World Trade Organization, which obligingly decreed the European Union could no longer provide favourable trade terms for bananas. Caribbean bananas started to rot. Coincidentally Lindner had been responsible for a $15,000 donation to the Clinton Democrats. The day after Kantor lodged the WTO complaint, Lindner upped his Democratic allegiance with a reported $500,000 contribution to state party funding. He then stayed overnight in the Lincoln Bedroom at the White House.

In 2002, Belizean banana exports fell another 18.7 percent. The Americans' proposed $10-trillion Free Trade Area of the Americas deal spooked more than a few Central American and Caribbean leaders, including members of the People's United Party (PUP). Consequently Belize has played a formative role in forging trade alliances within its geographic zone. The fate of the Caribbean banana industry hangs in the balance.

Citrus

Treaties with Spain long prohibited commercial agriculture. Only the Maya, poor Mestizos and Garinagu developed continuous knowledge of subsistence farming. Harvesting mahogany was "man's work"; conversely gardening was not. For these reasons Belize failed for centuries to take full advantage of its agricultural potential, a potential only recently exploited by the Mennonites.

One exception is citrus. In 1913, William Jex Bowman imported 300 budded grapefruit trees. He opened the first citrus-packing plant, at Sarawee, in the Stann Creek District, in 1925. The citrus industry in Belize has shown intermittent promise but harsh weather conditions, uncertain labour conditions, foreign ownership and management problems have prevented citrus farming from reaching its full potential. In 2002, Minister of Works, Transport, Citrus and Bananas, Dr. Henry Canton, resigned to take a job offered by the Belize Citrus Growers Association. The industry has never maintained consistency despite some excellent growing conditions in the Stann Creek District. In 2002, revenues from citrus juices fell by a third, representing a drop of 25.6 percent in citrus deliveries.

The Measure of Intelligence

The United States is far and away the foremost trading partner with Belize, but Taiwan has forged surprisingly strong ties with Belize, providing loans and foreign aid. Some frictions and resentments are bound to arise when a robust little country with 22.4 million people, 1,800 people per square mile and a GDP of $297 billion in 2001 decides to suddenly befriend a struggling country with 28 people per square mile. Under Said Musa's administration, the government continuously issued press releases about various donations made to Belize by Taiwan, but not all Belizeans have been impressed.

"This is the measure of intelligence in Belize in the third millennium—money," commented newspaper publisher and writer Evan X Hyde. "It wasn't like that when I was growing up in Belize. Money didn't mean anything where respect in the community was concerned. You couldn't buy respect in Belize 40 years ago. Now you can. That's the truth of it, and there's no turning back the hands of time."

Olaudah Equiano from Gambia was one of the precious few African slaves who survived and wrote his memoirs.
Frontispiece for The Interesting Narrative *(commissioned by Equiano, painted by William Denton, engraved by Daniel Orme)*

Chapter 8: Humans for Sale

"When I looked round the ship and saw a large furnace or copper boiling and a multitude of black people of every description chained together, every one of their countenances expressing dejection and sorrow, I no longer doubted fate; and quite overpowered with horror and anguish, I fell motionless on the deck and fainted. I asked if we were not to be eaten by those white men with horrible looks, red faces and loose hair."

— OLAUDAH EQUIANO, SLAVE

In Belize, the ancient Maya constructed temples; Spaniards made sovereignty claims; pirates plundered Spanish galleons; Anglicans prevailed in historical records—and for several formative centuries, black-skinned people did most of the work.

The story of how slaves arrived in the New World can't be told enough. "Approximately one-fourth of the slaves who landed in the New World between the sixteenth and the nineteenth centuries traveled under the British flag," writes Colin A. Palmer in *Human Cargoes: The British Slave Trade to Spanish America, 1700–1739*. "This proportion was more than any other nation could boast."

The first African slaves were reported in the Caribbean in 1502. The first shipment of slaves en masse, from Guinea, arrived for sale in 1517. The Englishman John Hawkins made the first of his three voyages carrying slaves as merchandise in 1568. Brazil received more African slaves than any Spanish or British possession, but English seafarers dominated the business of slave trafficking by 1700.

Neophyte timber merchants in the Settlement would have had difficulty competing with the Spanish buyers in the 1600s. The governor of Jamaica complained in 1717 that all the "able, stout and young negroes" were being sold to the Spanish, leaving English planters only "the old, sickly and decrepit, or what are called Refuse. If a choice Negro is sold to a planter, he must give as much or more than the Spaniard and that in ready money."

The presence of African slaves in Belize was first recorded in a missionary's journal in 1724. Of 151 slaves delivered to the British logwood centre of Campeche between 1730 and 1733, five were purchased; the rest were bartered, so it's likely the first slaves in Belize were purchased only a few at a time. The slave trade didn't take off until the economy of the Settlement was based on mahogany extraction.

Slaves in Belize were purchased mostly via the markets of Jamaica and Bermuda—chiefly Jamaica. Their African origins are roughly traceable due to collective terms such as Congoes, Ashantees and Eboes. The Ibo or Ebo, from the Bight of Biafra region, west of the Benin River, were sought after because they were considered tractable. A poor section of Belize City, located between South and Berkley Streets running from Regent Street to the canal, was called Eboe Town. It was destroyed by fire on November 9, 1819.

Slavery and Creoles

The Caribbean slave trade was chiefly in support of English-run sugar plantations and Spanish-run mines. Belize was an exception: there, approximately 80 percent of male slaves were used for mahogany gangs. The different labour situation in Belize has led to claims that slave masters were more tolerant than elsewhere in the Caribbean. In cutting and hauling mahogany, slaves worked with minimal supervision, or alongside their masters, hence it has been imagined that a bond of trust and co-operation necessarily evolved.

In fact, the system of slavery in Belize was unusually "backward" in terms of evolving basic rights for non-whites and the penalties for disobedience, or even suspected disobedience, could

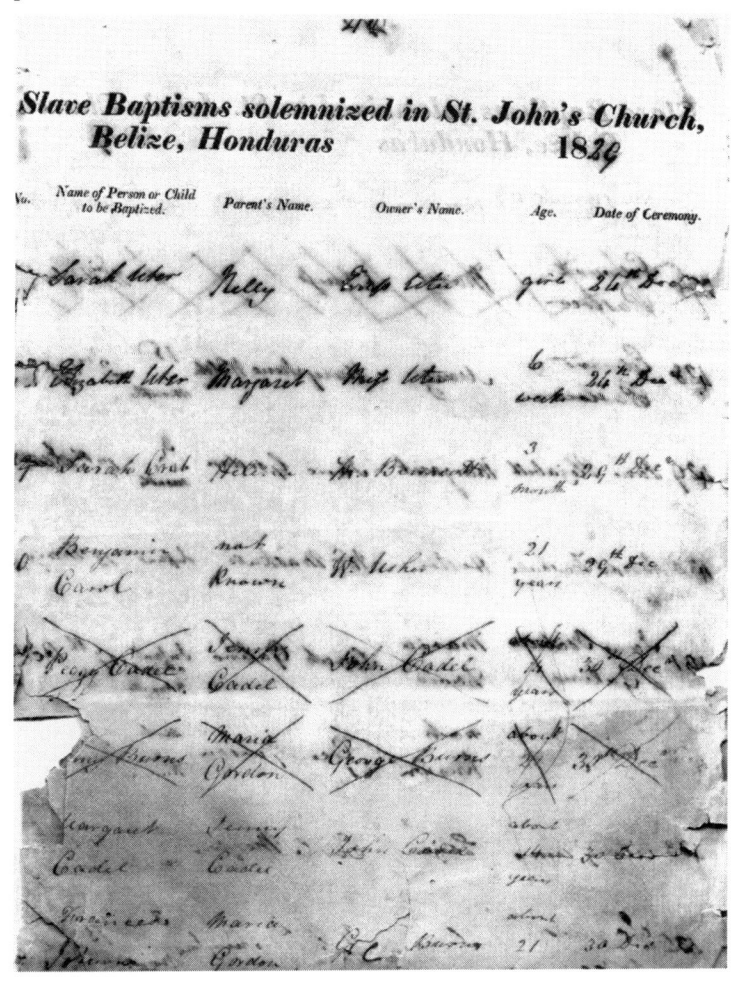

Blacks were the backbone of Belize. A few of their Anglicized names have been preserved in church records of baptisms. *Belize Archives*

be brutal and swift. Magistrates of Belize were slave owners untrained in law, concerned far more with business than justice. It was within their self-interest to sanction cruelty, to excuse fellow slave owners who went too far, because their own slaves had to be intimidated to prevent them from running away.

Runaways and Rebels

Runaways were a constant problem. Even before surrounding Spanish jurisdictions had outlawed slavery, it was widely known that the Spanish would accept runaway slaves as freemen. A slave owner in the early 1790s complained, "unless some means is speedily devised to render their conditions more safe, and to prevent the Desertion of the Negroes in future, the Settlement of Honduras must be inevitably ruin'd."

Penalties against disobedient slaves were stringent and harsh. On February 6, 1795, jurors unanimously convicted James, a slave belonging to James Usher, for the crime of "intending to desert to the Spaniards." He was sentenced to receive 40 lashes with a cat-o'-nine-tails at three different public places. Immediately afterward he was to be "put in irons and transported from the Settlement never to return under pain of death." Convicted "on suspicion of inveigling slaves to run to the Spaniards," a Free Black named Charles Freeman was to "receive this day, on his bare back, well laid-on, thirteen lashes at each of the three public places at this River Mouth, the like number of lashes on Friday and Monday next." After receiving his flagellation on Monday, Charles Freeman was "to have his right ear severed from his head."

There *were* limits. Having flogged to death one of his slaves named Murphy, a slave owner named Thomas Clark argued in court that he didn't know it was against the law to flog his slave with the intention of making him do his duty. The defendant was fined 100 Jamaican pounds. It was nonetheless acceptable practice to assert some firm, physical control in order to protect one's property and prohibit escapes. "No Man however well disposed he may consider his Negroes," reported another slave owner, "can think his property safe for a single Night. It is but a Week ago since a whole Gang about Twelve in number Deserted in a Body to the Spaniards." These 12 runaways "got safe to the Lookout & were as usual joyfully received, this last Desertion has caused a general dread & apprehension amongst the Inhabitants of the Settlement, who perceive nothing less than the total ruin of their Property, should a speedy Stop not be put to a practice so disgraceful to Society & so repugnant to Justice."

Contrary to the wishful thinking of some historians, master and slave were not always enjoined by a spirit of brotherly labour. On May 28, 1794, magistrates concurred that a slave named Dick must be hung on gallows to be constructed on the Yarborough Plantation on May 30 for having attacked his proprietor, Owen Ellis, with a machete. The owner received "Sixty Pounds in Jamaica currency out of Public Funds" for compensation, out of which prosecution expenses were to be deducted.

The first recorded slave revolt in Belize occurred in 1765 when a slave owner named Thomas Cooke and his carpenter were slain on the banks of the New River. The rebels killed three more men on the New River who arrived on a schooner to load logwood. "And they still continue in Rebellion," wrote one settler to the superintendent, "and have entirely stopped the communication of the New River."

Another 23 armed slaves escaped from the New River area in 1768. Commerce was halted. The only militia that might be summoned comprised mainly black pensioners and it was not certain they would vanquish their black brethren.

In 1773, six white Belizeans were murdered and five encampments were overrun in May along the Belize River. Three search parties of 150 men in total couldn't capture the rebels. A Captain Davey encountered 50 rebels armed with 16 muskets and cutlasses "but the Rebels after discharging their Pieces retired into the woods and it being late in the afternoon we could not pursue them." Fourteen rebels surrendered but the rest remained defiant, limiting all trade in the area. The HMS *Garland* arrived in August with troops to augment the Settlement's forces. Captain Judd's men chased 19 rebels as they fled their way through 100 miles of bush. Five months after the uprising, 11 of them reached the Hondo River and found freedom with the Spanish.

In 1791, news of an unprecedented slave uprising in present-day Haiti (Santo Domingo) spread throughout the Caribbean. Although François Dominique Toussaint L'Ouverture would die in prison in 1803, his black revolutionary forces defeated English, Spanish and French forces to create the independent black republic of Haiti in 1805. So when, in 1791, a French ship carrying 200 of the black rebels from Santo Domingo arrived, panic-struck settlers refused to allow mooring to "such an infectious cargo." The public meeting decried the "horrors of St. Domingo."

By 1816, runaway slaves had established an independent encampment "near Sibun River, very difficult to discover and guarded by poisonous snakes." In 1820 Superintendent Arthur confirmed "two slave towns" existed north of the Sibun River. After two slaves known only as Will and Sharper led an armed uprising that spread along both the Belize and Sibun Rivers, martial law was declared for a month. Authorities later discovered Will and Sharper "had been treated with very unnecessary harshness by their Owners, and had certainly good grounds for complaint." Pardons were offered to any runaways who would "deliver themselves" but a reward was offered for the apprehension of Will and Sharper. They were never caught. In 1823, another 39 slaves escaped to the El Petén region of Guatemala over the course of one month.

Manumission

Between 1807, when slave trading was criminalized, and 1834, when slavery itself became illegal, more than 500 slaves were manumitted—granted free coloured status. Many were the mistresses or offspring of their owner. It was particularly difficult to achieve manumission in Belize because the cost of buying one's freedom was higher than in other English slave colonies. Although most of the slaves in Belize were male, more than three-quarters of the manumitted slaves were women and children.

In 1832, according to a census, there were 31 Free Coloureds who owned slaves in Belize and only 26 white slave owners. The rise of Free Coloureds created a middle class who became useful to the ruling elite as a supervisory buffer class between ex-slaves and their masters. The Free Coloureds in Belize were among the last of their kind in the British West Indies to acquire equal rights with whites. For many years they were not permitted to serve as jury members. They were required to own more property than whites, and to attain longer residency requirements than whites, in order to vote.

The effect of the criminalization of slave trading in 1807 and the manumission of more than 500 slaves after 1800, prior to outright abolition in 1834, is evident in census figures for slaves.

DATE	TOTAL	% OF POPULATION
1745	120	71
1779	3000	86
1790	2177	75
1803	2959	75
1806	2527	72
1809	3000	73
1816	2742	72
1823	2468	60
1826	2410	46
1829	2027	52
1832	1783	42

During this transition period, prior to Abolition, the British authorities took measures in 1838 to restrict grants of Crown land in Belize. No Crown land was sold between 1838 and 1855; precious little of it was sold by 1868. These deliberately racist policies not only kept the bulk of land ownership within British hands, it forced the emancipated blacks to continue serving as the labouring class.

Paslow the Patriot

Much is known about Thomas Paslow. He was a quarrelsome Irishman who maintained a Free Coloured woman named Clarissa Carter. He had logging camps near the present-day sites of Paslow Falls and Clarissa Falls on the Mopan River. In 1791, Thomas Paslow was convicted of mutilating two of his slaves, which probably meant he castrated them. He was unanimously found guilty and fined 10 pounds of Jamaican currency. Details are sketchy. Apologists have explained it was common practice to castrate rapists.

When news arrived that the Spanish were planning to attack the Settlement in 1797, Paslow adamantly maintained everyone should stay to fight. "A man who will not defend his country is not entitled to reap the benefit thereof," he wrote. He outfitted a scow and took part in the Battle of St. George's Caye, during which slaves won the admiration of their masters for providing such valiant support. Fifteen years after this battle, according to the Settlement superintendent, 15 slaves escaped from Paslow "because of ill treatment and starvation." He died penniless in the 1820s.

The Justice Building in Belize City was long called the Paslow Building. When it was severely damaged by fire in 2002, attempts were made to reopen it until the structure was deemed unsalvageable.

Upon his arrival in 1814, Superintendent George Arthur

observed, "The People of Colour have already privileges far beyond what are granted in any other part of the West Indies and our security certainly requires that they should be curtailed rather than extended."

Paslow was not singular in his treatment of slaves. In 1816, a slave owner named Michael Carty was taken to court for torturing his female slave. She was "stripped naked, and her hands being tied to her feet with tight Cords, a stick was passed under her knees, and above the elbow-bend of her arms a large cattle chain was fastened round her kneck with a padlock and, in this agonizing posture, was this wretched female tortured from morning until night flogged in the most barbarous manner her wounds festered to such a degree that her life was considered in the greatest danger." Carty had to pay a fine to the Settlement—which was unusual.

In 1820, a slave owner named Duncanette Campell went on trial for punishing his Free Coloured concubine named Kitty. He had chained her in the loft of her house and repeatedly whipped her until, according to an attending physician, "her whole countenance was so disfigured that it was some time before I could recognize her." Kitty's case concerned whether or not the legal limit of 39 lashes had been exceeded. An all-white jury of landowners took only a few minutes to acquit the accused: Campbell could have whipped her more than he did.

Peggy's Case

In 1821, a slave named Peggy complained about treatment she received from Dr. Mansfield William Bowen. Without much evidence, he'd accused her of stealing some handkerchiefs. He tied her up, flogged her, and placed her, handcuffed and shackled, into a rat-infested storehouse. Peggy languished for five days until her common-law husband promised to pay Dr. Bowen an exorbitant amount of compensation for the allegedly purloined hankies. She was released on a Sunday and, remarkably, went to the civic authorities. Just as promptly, Dr. Bowen recaptured Peggy and ordered her to be punished for insubordination.

"On looking through a hole," an eyewitness later told the court, "I saw a woman named Peggy fastened to four stakes placed in the ground, and laying on her belly, her legs and arms being distended, and tied to the stakes by cords, so that she had no power to alter her position. Her clothes, when I first saw her, were fastened round her hips, and after she was flogged some time by a woman, with a cat, her clothes were dragged down until they were below the small part of the thigh, when the whole of her posteriors were exposed. The woman again flogged her on the posteriors, at which I was so disgusted that I turned away. Doctor Bowen was present during the whole of the punishment." Peggy was kept chained and handcuffed in the storehouse for two weeks, sometimes taken outside and chained to a tree so she would wash clothes. She received two mackerel and 20 plantains per week for food.

The prosecution called eight witnesses to verify Peggy's story. But Dr. Mansfield William Bowen was himself a magistrate, and his three fellow magistrates who heard the case, James Hyde, Charles Evans and John W. Wright, were all slave owners. The jury consisted of twelve white slave owners.

Dr. Bowen was found not guilty of maltreatment.

Creole Society

The conceit that slavery was more humane and civilized in Belize has been cultivated by whites and non-whites alike.

During slavery and its aftermath, the shortage of white women led to sexual relationships between black women and white men as a community norm. Children born of concubines, mistresses, common-law wives or rape victims had varying degrees of acceptability, but when the mothers were freed by their masters, their offspring were categorized as free people of colour, or Free

Coloureds. Usually lighter-skinned than full-blooded Africans, many of these mixed blood Belizeans evolved into an interim managerial class within a striated system of prejudice. Often the Free Coloureds had slaves of their own, if they could afford them.

The emerging Creoles—Afro-European blacks—in Belize mingled with Europeans at social events and had some flexibility to be upwardly mobile. They tended to look down upon the black labouring class, thereby cementing the power of the dominant whites. As the whites failed to reproduce or increase their numbers by immigration, the relatively well-educated Creoles graduated into controlling positions within society.

Creoles have cited linguistic connections with the Twi language of the Ashanti people of Ghana, but many contemporary Creoles can also trace their origins and family names to some of the oldest Baymen families. Roughly speaking, Creoles became numerically dominant in Belize in the 19th century, dominant as merchants in the first half of the 20th century and politically dominant in the second half.

The term "Creole" isn't explained often—because it's confusing. In Portuguese, *criar* means "to raise a child or a servant born into one's household." A derivation *crioulo* was used by the Portuguese to describe slaves in the New World, chiefly in Brazil. In Mexico, however, a *criollo* refers to a Mexican of pure Spanish blood. And both of these antithetical meanings don't coincide with the French (*créole*), Dutch (*creol*) and English (creole) adaptations. In Belize a Creole is someone born in the Americas with mixed European and African ancestry. Belizeans at an Orthology Workshop in 1994 decided to promote the spelling *kriol* in reference to Creole speech. Leaders of the Creole cultural community maintain their playful, indecipherable Kriol is not "bad English" or a bastard dialect; it is proudly viewed as unique unto itself.

Creoles developed towns along the waterways and coastline in conjunction with logging. The main Creole towns outside

Belize City are Ladyville, Biscayne, Bermudian Landing and Hattieville in Belize District; Roaring Creek, Camalote and Santa Elena in Cayo District; Mango Creek/Independence and Placencia in Stann Creek District; and Forest Home, Cattle Landing and Monkey River in Toledo District. Creole society evolved organically, not according to any sectarian basis. Many Mestizos, Garinagu and Asians have intermarried to join the dominant Creole culture. While sharing religious and cultural practices of Africa, Creoles have freely integrated random influences such as dory

Brukdown dancing (above) and punta rock music are just two of many original facets of Belizean culture. *Belize Archives.*

building from the Mosquito Indians, cooking from the Mestizos, cricket from the British, basketball from the USA, and so on. Forestry work culminated each year with several weeks of festivities at Christmas that featured partying (heavy drinking), *brukdown* music, dancing, singing and boat racing. Large pitpans with as many as 40 paddlers competed from different mahogany camps during the traditional *bram* celebrations.

Traditional Creole culture has included Anancy tales, distinctive Creole proverbs, games such as *bruk maka chista* and *moon shine baby*, and fire dances such as the *sambai* fertility dance during the full moon. In keeping with African origins, coconut milk is used extensively in Creole cuisine. The traditional boil up can include cassava, sweet potatoes, plantains, cocoa, boiled fish and pigtail. Some West African dishes such as *bambam*, *bami*, *dukunu* and *wangla* augment rice, beans, fish and crab dishes.

Creole folk remedies are numerous. Eye infections should be treated with breast milk. For boils, apply a poultice of bread and breast milk. Wild yam tea can improve the blood. Boiled orange peel tea is a treatment for gas. Earaches can be treated with groundhog, mint leaf, garlic and sweet oil stew, applied with a cotton swab. For diarrhea, boil a green plantain with the peel still on it, drink the water, then mash the plantain and eat it. For fevers, catch a toad or a young chicken, split it in half, and bandage each half onto the bottoms of the feverish person's feet.

Superstitions linked with pregnancy and infancy are numerous. A snake will not bite a pregnant woman. A baby will get the gripe if it is stared at. Passing a child over a coffin can prevent the dead from returning to take the life of the child.

The United Black Association for Development (UBAD) was formed during the rise of the Belize independence movement to unite Creoles as a political and cultural force. The National Kriol Council was formed in 1995 to lobby for establishment of a National Kriol Day, a proposed holiday similar to Garifuna Settlement Day for the Garinagu, the distinct black minority group based in Dangriga. In 1996, UBAD created an Educational Foundation to promote the education of increasingly crime-ridden black youth. Prior to the 1970s, the dominant Jesuit orthodoxy within the educational system of Belize was reticent to teach black history, but the government of Said Musa encouraged the teaching of more black history within the schools. Creoles are increasingly disenchanted by their loss of clear dominance within an increasingly multicultural and complex social structure.

The national emblem of Belize now depicts one black and one white woodcutter. This duo from a government publication in 1953 "tells it like it was" in British Honduras.

Chapter 9: Abolition and Patriotism

The Sacred Tie

Generations of administrative whites in Belize embedded an essentially self-congratulatory view of employer-labour and master-slave relations. The promulgation of a live-and-let-live cultural patina has been akin to wilful forgetting. "All classes," reported Governor James Longden in 1870, "whether Chinese, Creole, Charib, Negro or Indian, are in as good if not in a better position than the labouring class in the West Indies." In 1896, the *Times of Central America* stated, "In the political as well as social life caste did not depend altogether upon the colour of the skin." The *Colonial Guardian* in 1898 found "hostility of race and class peculiarly absent from British Honduras."

"Strangers are aghast by the confusion," wrote Emory King in the late 20th century, "but we Belizeans are the most tolerant people in the world." The folksy columnist has reiterated the myth of superior tolerance in his books about Belize. "Slavery in Belize was far different than elsewhere in the West Indies or the American colonies or later States," he wrote, advertising one of his books. "It was a family affair."

The most obvious example of obscuring the nature of Belizean slavery is the national flag with its motto "Flourish in the Shade." The flag depicts an idealized image of master-slave relations: master and slave are shown shoulder to shoulder, as equals. A heraldic shield between them features an axe, saws and a ship to signify the formative importance of the mahogany trade.

A coat of arms inside a white circle and surrounded by a greenish garland shows a mahogany tree (the national tree) with two bare-chested woodcutters, one on each side. The man on the left has light skin and holds an axe over his right shoulder. The man on the right has very dark skin and holds a paddle over his left shoulder. Both have white leggings. Beneath the shield is a flowing scroll with the Latin motto about flourishing in the shade of mahogany trees.

This image of racial equality can be traced to the Battle of St. George's Caye of 1798. One of the victorious Baymen provided a retrospective account of the Baymen's victory in 1821: "Our slaves marshalling themselves under their respective owners, cheerfully and manfully fought for and defended their Master's lives and their Master's property. There appeared a sacred tie between the Slave and the Master, which bound the one to the other clearly evincing the marked preference of these faithful Slaves to their state of bondage than to the freedom offered by the Spaniards."

In 1890, Dr. Frederick Gahne, a "coloured" man, was editor of the *Colonial Guardian*. When Britain rejected appeals for an elected legislature—because there were too few Europeans in the colony to vote—he noted, "even in the days of slavery the men of European descent, those of mixed European blood and those of purely African descent, stood shoulder to shoulder to resist the Spaniard."

In August, 1888, hoping to celebrate the anniversary of Abolition in Belize, some Creoles advanced the notion of a new library and an emancipation institute. It was not supported. Queen

Victoria's Silver Jubilee in 1897 presented another occasion for recognizing heritage and progress so Belizeans petitioned London for a new stamp commemorating the Battle of St. George's Caye. It was not supported. These two initiatives and Gahne's phraseology encouraged two Creole shopkeepers, Wilfred Haylock and Percy Hyde, to reprise the request for a stamp in 1898—the battle's centennial—by submitting their design for one. It depicted a white soldier and a black soldier holding hands. Beneath them was a banner saying "Shoulder to Shoulder."

It was within the best interests of the Creole middle class to propagate the ideal of co-operation between races. Responding to the working-class riots of 1898, the white Creole editor of the *Clarion*, P.S. Woods, lectured, "What a lesson in loyalty and confidence it would constantly be to those very people if their minds were turned back vividly to that September day at St. George's Caye when the sturdy Baymen masters and slaves willingly stood shoulder to shoulder." H.H. Cain of the *Belize Independent* later agreed this model for equality should be propagated in the schools. A British loyalist named M.S. Metzgen produced a tract called *Shoulder to Shoulder* in 1928.

Historian Assad Shoman has best traced and understood the psychological and political implications of the shoulder-to-shoulder myth. "When the time came for Belizeans to assert their independence from the Empire, this myth was clearly a major obstacle to struggle—indeed it glorified the negation of struggle—and had to be debunked."

The Union Jack traditionally flew in Belize until 1907. From 1907 until 1919 the Union Jack appeared in the upper left quarter of the British Honduran flag, leaving room for a rudimentary coat of arms on the right side. In February 1950, two woodcutters, a Latin motto and a circular garland were added. A rare copy of a government promotional pamphlet produced in 1953, printed in Ipswich, shows two black men as the woodcutters. A revised version of that pairing, with the requisite white man substituted for the black man on the left, became the accepted one around the time George Price became leader of the People's United Party (PUP). The Union Jack still appeared within the official flag into the 1970s.

The modern flag of Belize is closely connected to the original PUP flag with its royal blue background. Because the emblematic woodcutters flag with its slogan has been so difficult to reproduce, George Price urged his PUP followers to simply place a white circle against a blue background for demonstrations. Hence the flag of PUP and the flag of independence and equality became advertisements for one another in the 1950s. Red is the colour of the United Democratic Party. To keep everyone happy, two red stripes were added as horizontal borders when a committee was convened to redesign the flag for independence in 1981.

Abolition

As production methods in the British Colonies became more mechanized, the extraction of resources such as sugar cane in Jamaica and Barbados required less manpower. But Belize was still reliant on its labourers to cut mahogany.

The greatest inducement for the Belizean gentry to accept Abolition was that their slaves kept running away. Each time one more slave left his "family" in Belize, the master lost his investment. "[British] Honduras is now in the centre of countries which have declared Slavery illegal," wrote James Stephen of the British Colonial Office in 1830, "and if we persist in maintaining it we must look for a rapid depopulation of the settlement by slaves passing the border line, and returning no more."

The British Colonial Office threatened to have the Baymen's public meeting process revoked unless progress was made on abolition. Partially in deference to this threat, civil rights were granted to Coloured Subjects of Free Condition on July 5, 1831. After Abolition in 1834, the *Honduras Almanack* confidently asserted few former slaves "are to be found entirely exempt from those low propensities which are exhibited in a state of barbarism."

The emancipation process was designed not to adversely inconvenience businessmen. All registered slaves over six years old were to become unpaid apprentices. Depending on the type of work they did, they could only gain their complete freedom after four to six years of "apprenticeship." A man could have been cutting mahogany for 30 years but he would still be termed an apprentice.

Slave owners were granted compensation by Britain on a per-slave basis. Slaves did not receive any reciprocal payment. The rates of compensation were to be based on the industrial value of slaves. The more backward colonies would receive much higher rates because the costs of transporting slaves from Jamaica and Barbados were significant. In the case of Belize, especially strong and healthy slaves were required to harvest mahogany, so Belizean slave owners were granted the highest rate of compensation per slave in the Caribbean. The colony rates of compensation per slave in English pounds were: British Honduras 53.6; British Guiana 51.1; Trinidad 50.1; Barbados 20.1; Jamaica 19.5; Bermuda 12.1. The other two colonies that received more than double the rates of Barbados, Jamaica and Bermuda—Trinidad and British Guiana—were significantly more agreeable to the terms of free apprenticeship than Belize.

For the Caribbean, the conversion system from slavery to apprenticeship was drafted mainly in Trinidad; some statutes proved impractical in Belize. It wasn't feasible to have a magistrate visit every plantation once a fortnight. Superintendent Cockburn therefore announced he would appoint local men to serve as the inspectors on the Crown's behalf. Cockburn was worried that workers on mahogany gangs would be prone to "idleness, profligacy and insubordination" if they knew limited freedom was at hand. Hence the inspection system in Belize was interpreted as a policing mechanism for the owners.

In advance of implementing the switchover, a new law was passed by a public meeting to settle any disputes that might arise between servants and masters. It was modified by the superintendent to allow some complaints against masters to be heard before three magistrates. There was a good deal of trepidation as to how it would all work. The new "apprenticeship" system throughout the British Empire required ex-slaves to continue working 45 hours per week—without pay. Employers in Belize stretched the mandatory work period to 50 hours per week, or more, without punishment.

The apprenticeship system was in place from 1834 to 1838. Whereas poorly paid special magistrates around the rest of the Caribbean were obliged to make monthly reports to authorities, the superintendent in Belize established police gangs. During the first year of the new system, 117 apprentices were punished. When the apprenticeship period ended, August 1, 1838, was declared a public holiday throughout the West Indies.

The Dark Rainbow

The liberated slaves didn't have much to celebrate. When wages became available, laws were enacted in Belize to force workers to enter into six-to-twelve-month contracts, effectively binding them to their former masters. If an employer reneged on a contract, he could be fined, but if a worker failed to meet the terms of the contract, he or she could be imprisoned and subject to public whipping.

Land grants were no longer made available after 1858. It was determined that if ex-slaves could obtain access to land, this would "discourage labour for wages." Laws had already been passed in 1803 and 1810 to forbid slaves from undertaking any independent work. "Slaves of either Sex shall not be permitted to hire themselves to themselves for any purpose whatever," magistrates had decreed. Such actions could "create Insubordination thereby diminishing respect to the proprietors."

Men who knew only one trade, mahogany cutting, by necessity had to live away from home on mahogany gangs, while women only worked as domestics. Hence the tradition of the absent father in Belize runs deep. It has been suggested the "limited pattern of work experience during slavery" also kept Afro-Belizeans tethered to their masters more than in other British colonies.

Abolition also affected the method of government. After 1821, when neighbouring Latin republics emerged, diversified trade based in Belize gradually allowed for the emergence of a middle class. The likes of Marshall Bennett, who had 271 slaves, weren't keen to share power, either economic or political. They had accordingly raised the membership requirements for the public meeting. Whereas British-born whites needed one year's residency and property worth 500 pounds (Jamaican currency) to vote, Free Coloureds born in the Settlement needed property valued at twice that much.

The relatively few families that had controlled Belize for more than 100 years didn't wish to endure the time-consuming responsibilities of governance; the elite only wanted the advantages of such. With impending abolition, the Settlement was becoming more complicated and arduous to manage. In 1830 the superintendent consequently introduced legislation, by proclamation, to terminate the public meeting process, assuming the right to appoint members of a newly formed executive council. In effect, on the eve of Abolition, Belize reverted to an anti-democratic system comparable to the one that was once imposed by Colonel Despard. The new executive council was largely composed of men who had been magistrates. The superintendent enjoyed a freer hand to do the bidding of slave-owning merchants. Any potential political clout of an emerging black working class was effectively muted well in advance, even though British Common Law replaced Burnaby's Code in 1840.

Ex-slaves were also stymied by a code of colourism: the dark rainbow of racism was understood by all. "From the black to the white by law," the *Honduras Almanack* declared, "there are seven or eight legalized ranks, through which descent must be proved to have passed before the privileges of a European are open to them." In Santo Domingo, it had once been determined by law that Negro blood decreased for six generations until it could be said to have vanished completely. The mulatto in the Caribbean wouldn't always be a mulatto: given time, his offspring could theoretically evolve into a white.

A stratified apartheid system replaced a simple white-master/black-slave system in Belize. It was possible to rise in this system by subjugating those below. Such a hierarchy allowed individuals at the top to convince themselves that they were responding generously. The educated Creoles who were willing and able to serve white interests emerged as an elite in Belize City.

Chapter 10: Garifuna Exodus

Now dominant along central and southern coasts of Belize, the Garinagu are descendents of runaway slaves and Carib Indians who fused an original, anti-European culture and a distinct, hybrid race on the island of St. Vincent from the 1500s. Theirs is an epic story worthy of Homer.

Carib Country

Around 1000 AD, agrarian-based Arawak Indians from the Orinoco River region of South America moved north, followed soon afterward by fierce Caribs. Allegedly cannibals, these Caribs gave rise to the pervasive term Caribbean. Caribs overran and dispersed the Arawaks, mating with Arawak women and establishing strongholds on Dominica and St. Vincent, two mountainous islands in the Lesser Antilles, west of nearby Barbados. The "cassava-eating people," or *Kalipuna*, arose as an aggressively independent culture on these two islands. The more significant population was on St. Vincent, just south of St. Lucia. The Garinagu knew this island as Yurumei—and, much later, Vincyland.

On Dominica the people were known as *Karaphuna*. Contemporary leaders now prefer the collective term Garinagu, a possible derivative from *Kalinagu*, or *Kalinago*, roughly translatable as "we call ourselves so." Garifuna is also used as an adjective for Garinagu culture or as a singular noun to designate a person.

While Arawaks fell prey to the Europeans, Caribs fought to protect their homelands. Walter Raleigh reached St. Vincent in 1595 and thereafter spread tales of cannibalism. Their reputation for barbarism helped the Caribs of St. Vincent avoid colonization. Conversely, vanquished or desperate Amerindians gravitated to St. Vincent as a final refuge.

The Caribs of St. Vincent became notorious as warriors who paddled long distances in large canoes to defend Amerindian brethren, going so far as to capture some slaves from English and French ships. They invaded some plantations in the 1500s. A turning point in Carib history occurred in 1636 when two Spanish ships loaded with Nigerian slaves were wrecked off St. Vincent. The freed slaves, as well as a few Spaniards, merged with the Caribs. A slave ship from Guinea was also wrecked on one of the Grenadine Islands during this era, possibly further enhancing the population of Yurumei. The shipwrecked African slaves learned Caribbean survival skills from their Amerindian protectors and melded their African belief systems to Carib customs.

Racial divisions on St. Vincent ensued along colour lines. Black Caribs proved themselves more domineering than their sponsoring Yellow Carib brethren (black slaves racially mixed with Arawak Indians). The latter were gradually outnumbered and driven to the leeward side of the island. They consequently sought assistance and protection from the French governor of Martinique, who divided the island with a line called Barre de l'Isle in 1719. The Black Caribs were delighted to have unfettered dominion over their own half of St. Vincent, dubbed Carib Country, while the French went about cultivating the friendship of the remaining Yellow Caribs.

By 1763 there were an estimated 3,000 "free negroes" on St.

Vincent, sharing the island with slightly more French settlers and their slaves. The originating Yellow Caribs were almost extinct. Seeking greater access to land, the French governor of Martinique sent 400 volunteers under a Major Paulian to attack the Black Caribs. Using the hide 'n' seek tactics of guerrilla warfare, the Black Caribs defeated and humiliated Major Paulian and his soldiers, who scurried back to Martinique. Thereafter the French continued to settle in the area allocated to the Yellow Caribs, respecting the boundary line.

Black Caribs became increasingly prosperous as avid traders and farmers. Less threatened by the seemingly docile French, they began to coincidentally appreciate some finer aspects of French culture, adopting French names and gaining a taste for wine. Under the leadership of their chief of chiefs, Joseph Chatoyer, assisted by his brother Duvalle and his advisor named Jean Baptiste, the Black Caribs added dabs of Catholicism to their mystical religious practices.

When European powers met in 1763 and peacefully divided up the Caribbean, St. Vincent was allocated to the British. Unlike the French who had settled on a permanent basis as diversified farmers, British settlers were keen to expropriate arable lands that were unused, hoping to make their fortunes by growing sugar cane on large tracts of land, using slaves for labour. Although the Black Caribs signed a lengthy peace treaty with the British in 1773, the spirit of the French Revolution was soon in the air, inspiring major slave revolts in Santo Domingo in 1791 and Martinique in 1794.

Burgeoned by the support of the French, the Black Caribs began an island-wide uprising in May, 1795, burning a prominent English estate. The British fled their plantations. Forts were disassembled and sugar works burned. An estate manager was run through the rollers of his cane mill. British farmers were slaughtered with their cattle. It would take the British almost a year to summon enough reinforcements to win the so-called Brigand's War of 1795–96.

It was the loss of the Caribs' charismatic leader that turned the tide. The story goes that British forces were mounting an attack on Dorsetshire Hill at night, on March 14, 1796, when Joseph Chatoyer challenged a British officer named Major Leith to a duel. Leith was trained in swordsmanship; Chatoyer was not. Chatoyer's five wives were widowed. That's the British version of Chatoyer's downfall; the likelihood that Chatoyer would have agreed to engage in one-on-one combat using swords seems slim.

The clannish Black Caribs, dependent upon Chatoyer for their cohesion, fled into the mountains. Fickle French support fizzled. The British sent Lieutenant General Sir Ralph Abercrombie to the eastern Caribbean to finish the job. Ultimately, Abercrombie's forces convinced more than 5,000 disorganized Black Caribs to surrender. They were transported to the tiny Grenadine Island of Balliceaux.

An 1804 historical society report by Alexander Anderson, curator at the Botanical Gardens on St. Vincent and an eyewitness to events, reports that 2,500 Black Caribs—almost half of them—succumbed to starvation and yellow fever when kept in cramped, unsanitary conditions on Balliceaux. Those who survived were transferred, en masse, to Jamaica, embarking on March 11, 1797. In April, after even more Garinagu had perished in transit, they were unloaded onto the island of Roatan off the north coast of Honduras, expected to manage with a small supply of fish hooks, tools, cuttings, seeds and food supplies. The Black Caribs begged the Spanish on the mainland to rescue them. The commandante of Trujillo, the largest city on the coast of Honduras, surmised they could be valuable as labourers and subsistence farmers, and the 1,700 Black Caribs on Roatan were rescued on May 19, 1797.

Reaching the Mainland

The Spanish on the mainland needed the Black Caribs as much as the Black Caribs needed the sanctuary provided by the Spanish. The poor Spanish diet was augmented by traditional Garifuna foods such as fish, coconut milk, cassava, garlic, basil, banana and plantain—and the Spanish were introduced to fish boiled in coconut milk, called *serre*, served with mashed plantain, called *hudut*.

In 1802, Belize imported 150 Garinagu to serve as labourers for the expanding mahogany trade. Some slave owners were concerned about their arrival, worried that Garifuna attitudes would make their slaves unruly, but Superintendent Bassett decided this was a risk worth taking—their reputation as adept farmers and fishermen preceded them. One enclave of the Garinagu had established itself briefly along the Sibun River, just south of Belize City; they were not allowed to remain in Belize City after dark for fear they might incite the slaves to revolt. Another enclave had appeared at the present site of Punta Gorda, at the southern end of Belize.

At the turn of the century, the North Stann Creek River mouth was a preferred loading area for mahogany ships; fresh water was available from the placid waters of a "standing creek"—hence the name Stann Creek Town, also known as Carib Town. It was only 36 miles south of Belize City by sea, but beyond the reaches of the forestocracy by land. The landing site was originally called *Danreugeu Grigeu*, "a river that stands." The Garifuna townsite would grow into Belize's second-largest city, renamed Dangriga Town in 1975, in honour of the Garinagu.

The Garinagu didn't migrate north in large numbers until the outbreak of a civil war in Honduras, when the pro-independence forces of Francisco Morazan took up arms in 1823 against the insurrectionist Royalists. Having been saved by a Royalist regime in 1797, the Black Caribs sided with the pro-colonial Spaniards—a choice with deadly consequences. In 1832, when the Republicans finally triumphed and reprisals were swift, the Black Caribs became prime targets for the Republican regime.

Having already visited Belize in his teens, Alejo Beni, the son of an executed Carib-Royalist general and an Indian, loaded two dories with provisions and sailed north from Christales Village with 27 other adults and 12 children. They nudged the sandy shores of Stann Creek on November 19, 1832, establishing an encampment that would attract many more boatloads of Garinagu refugees. This date would be recognized as Settlement Day, the most important date in Garifuna history within Belize.

Discrimination and Exploitation

For the most part, the British treated the Garinagu as semi-autonomous squatters, denying them land rights, but eager to use them as labourers. But unlike the Free Coloureds who strived to climb in white society and become the Creole elite, the Garinagu were not keen on subscribing to high tea. Only one year after Beni's arrival, the forestocracy in Belize City empowered a police constable to bring any Garifuna absent from his forestry work into Belize City for interrogation. Allegations of polygamy were frequent and justified. Methodist missionaries began to visit Stann Creek in 1828; they opened Thomas Jeffrey's day school for 70 children in 1835.

After Alejo Beni was killed in a tree-cutting accident in 1847, the 1,500 Garinagu in Stann Creek were hard-pressed to protest colonial instructions in 1857 requiring them to apply for Crown leases or else risk dispossession. A Crown Land Ordinance in 1872 prevented both the Garinagu and the Maya from owning plots of land and forced them to accept collective reservations.

Jesuit and Catholic priests also arrived in the early 1800s to give the Methodists a run for their souls. An influential parochial school was operated for many years by the Sisters of the Holy Family based in New Orleans. In the long run, Catholicism would be preferred in Dangriga as an alternate to obeah, supernatural religious practices brought from Africa. By gradually melding some Catholicism into their mélange of African and Indian beliefs, the Garinagu developed a very perplexing form of spirit association that was often ignorantly confused with Voudon, or "Voodoo." Their dancing rites, directed by a shaman or *buyei*, were intended to connect future, present and past generations of a family group during a *dugu* meeting. Frenetic dancing and trance-like sessions, conducted in private, in what seemed to be a secretive language, were easily misconstrued as devil worship.

Regular steamship service to New Orleans created a market for Stann Creek bananas in the 1880s. Garifuna labour was also needed after two German immigrants experimented with some grapefruit seedlings in 1888, giving rise to "King Citrus" in Belize. A resident citrus planter, William Bowman, the first so-called "elected" legislative council member from Stann Creek, built the first citrus-packing shed in 1925.

Labour conditions were harsh and exploitive. Lieutenant Governor Frederick Barlee tried to eliminate or at least discredit an "advance system" whereby workers were indentured to the employer with the need to compensate for large advances, usually paid at Christmas time. Equally problematic was the "truck system" whereby workers were forced to accept half their wages in goods, usually sold by the employer's agents at exorbitant prices.

After Stann Creek had gained the status of a township in 1895, Garifuna women were briefly required to harvest and bag nuts for export, along with citrus products and bananas, but this marketing experiment ended. A three-foot-wide railway was built to connect Stann Creek to Mile 25 of the closest main highway in 1910. When Panama Disease dealt a death blow to the banana industry this railway was dismantled in 1937. The agro-proletariat among the Garinagu had few rights but the Garinagu remained proudly separate from Belize City, preferring their reliance on the sea and their traditional subsistence farming. Their visionary leader Thomas Vincent Ramos formed the Carib Development and Sick Aid Society (CDS) in 1924, a year after his arrival in Belize, and wrote a booklet called *Carib History* in 1943.

Thomas Ramos

Thomas Vincent Ramos (formerly Thomas Villanueva Ramos) was born in Tulian, Puerto Cortez, in the Republic of Honduras, on September 18, 1887. He fathered at least 14 children, 11 with his wife Eliza Marion, who married him in 1914. They immigrated to Stann Creek around 1929. Jack of all trades, master of none, he was the Stann Creek correspondent for the *Belize Independent*, a weekly that was published in the 1940s, plus a farmer, a candy maker, song composer and boxing manager. His sons Carl and Abraham (Kid Abe) were boxers.

Ramos spent most of his life in Stann Creek, where he supported the Universal Negro Improvement Association and co-founded numerous organizations such as the Carib International Burial Fund Society, the Colonial Industrial Instruction Association and the Independence Manhood and Exodus Uplift Society in Man-O-War, Stann Creek. Most significantly, the Carib Development Society provided sick and death benefits, undertook education initiatives and obtained 800 acres at Sarawee that were later designated as a Carib Reserve.

In 1941, Ramos and two colleagues, Mateo Avaloy and C.S. Benguche, wrote to the District Commissioner to request the establishment of a public and bank holiday originally known as Carib Disembarkment Day. The holiday was granted within Stann Creek Town in 1943 after Ramos visited the colonial governor, His Excellency Sir John Adams Hunter, with two other colleagues, Domingo Ventura and Pantaleon Hernandez. Ramos died November 13, 1955. Settlement Day was extended as a holiday to people of Garifuna origin throughout Belize; then it was adopted nationally in 1977, when its name was officially changed to Garifuna Settlement Day. It has also become a day of reflection and celebration for Garifuna communities in Los Angeles, New Orleans, New York City and Texas. It includes performances by traditional dance groups and roots musicians, plus a Miss Garifuna pageant. Given the historical alienation of the Garinagu, the integration of this holiday into the framework of Belizean society has marked an important change in traditional racial relations.

A bust of Ramos was erected in the vicinity of his gravesite at Garden of Gethsemane, Dangriga's graveyard, in 1990. Ramos was honoured posthumously with the Order of Belize when Prime Minister Said Musa visited Dangriga in November 2002 to participate in groundbreaking ceremonies for the new Buyei Juan Lambey Institute devoted to the propagation of Garifuna culture.

Another significant builder of Garifuna society was Juan Pablo Lambey. He was born on June 26, 1932, in a small coastal town in Honduras. His mother brought him to Dangriga when he was four. Married in 1957, he and his wife Alice raised eight children. Moving frequently to towns such as Gallon Jug, Mango Creek and Pomona, he worked as a truck driver, farmer, citrus picker and fisherman. As a disciple of Ramos, Lambey was a grassroots politician who fought for better wages. He served as secretary of the General Workers Development Union and for two terms as the president of the National Garifuna Council. "Pappa Lam" organized and led the annual re-enactments of Beni's fabled arrival on November 19 for Settlement Day and acquired the land for a new National Garifuna Council complex which was named in his honour upon the building's completion. Lambey died on April 17, 2000.

Cultural Renaissance

Mistrusted and misunderstood in Belize for more than 200 years, the Garinagu have nonetheless retained their cultural integrity and steadily gained political sophistication in the 20th century. The origins of their folk tales, sacred drumming, punta and wanaragu dances, burial rites and language are both African and

South American.

Punta Rock is a relatively new pop music phenomenon in the Caribbean, emanating from Garifuna musicians in Punta Gorda, Seine Bight, Hopkins and Dangriga. Its name and its rhythms are derived from the punta dance of the Garinagu, incorporating African rhythms. Artists such as Benjamin Nicholas, Austin Rodriguez and Pen Cayetano have used traditional bright colouring and unusual perspectives to illustrate historical themes.

The Garinagu began performing their Wanaragu or "Jonkonnu" dance at Christmas, going door-to-door like carollers, receiving gifts of food or money, in the 1800s. Originating from Jamaica's early colonial period, the mocking dance is called the John Canoe Dance by Creoles. Some dancers wear white masks and sport crude replicas of eighteenth century naval hats on their heads, or multi-coloured hoods, to mock the British "canoe" hat wearers. The playfulness of the dance enabled subjugated minorities a rare public opportunity to express their disdain for their masters through mimicry.

Dangriga-born Adeline Lucas of Pelican Bay Resort stands in front of Benjamin Nicholas's mural depicting Garifuna Settlement Day. *Twigg photo.*

The "Garifuna reawakening" in recent decades might not be sufficient for the Garinagu to counteract the rise of luxury condominiums near Hopkins Village, the construction of 120 new resort rooms in the Riversdale area of Stann Creek and extensive entrepreneurial ventures near Seine Bight.

The concentration of Garinagu in Dangriga has at least

provided an impregnable base for operations. The percentage of Garinagu in Dangriga's overall population in 1980 was 70 percent. Eleven years later it hadn't changed. There is little room left for Dangriga to expand, but on the other hand tourism hasn't overwhelmed the area thanks partially to a 24 percent poverty rate.

Taking on the World

In the spirit of their revered forefathers—Chatoyer, Beni, Ramos and Lambey—Garifuna representatives from the United States, Guatemala, Honduras, St. Vincent and Belize met in Dangriga in April 2001 to "right the wrongs against their fellow men and women." They created the World Garifuna Organization as the legal petitioner to pursue reparations from Britain.

"For too long we have considered ourselves as Belizean-Garifuna, Honduran-Garifuna, Guatemala and Nicaraguan Garifuna," wrote Joseph R. Flores. "So much so, that it is now with great difficulty that we can work together on any given issue that is of vital interest to us as Garinagu. This double identity must cease if there are to be any Garifuna at all remaining in the future. Our Survival as a people depends on it."

Every year, on November 19, a flotilla celebrates the arrival of the first large contingent of Garifuna settlers at Dangriga in 1832. *Belize Archives.*

The irony of escaping British conquerors only to congregate in the former colony of British Honduras does not escape Augustine Flores. He was one of the students in the original Carib Language Group that helped Father John Stochl, a Jesuit Scholastic at St. John's College, produce the first dictionary of the Garifuna language back in 1952. "We are not considered equals," says Flores. "We need very strong vigorous representation. We don't want token representation."

A retired school principal and hotelkeeper, Augustine Flores emerged at the forefront of Garifuna education and self-determination initiatives for the Garinagu ever since he completed his education in the United States. While he was president of the National Garifuna Council from 1994 to 1998, Flores oversaw the founding meeting of the Central American Black Organization, now headquartered in Honduras.

The World Heritage Center in Paris has proclaimed Garifuna culture to be "a masterpiece of the oral and intangible heritage of humanity."

Augustine Flores. *Twigg photo.*

Chapter 11: British Honduras

"An unenviable undertaking."
—D.A.G. WADDELL, HISTORIAN, DESCRIBING BRITISH HONDURAS

In 1856, the Chichanha Indians confined a foreman for Young, Toledo & Company to his residence on the Belize side of the Hondo River, demanding royalties for the mahogany floating in the river. They held the foreman under armed guard and threatened to set fire to the mahogany works. As the Creoles say, "When thief thief from thief, God laugh." Knowing the Chichanha were allies of the Yucatán administration, emissaries from the Settlement including Mr. Philip Toledo himself petitioned Mexican authorities from Mexico City and the fort at Bacalar to negotiate with the

Few institutions in Belize have been more influential than St. John's Anglican Cathedral, founded in 1812. Here kings were crowned from the Mosquito Indians, allies of the British. *Twigg photo.*

insurrectionists. This marked the first major involvement of the Settlement in the increasing turbulence of the Caste War.

La Guerra de Castas

In 1846, Mexico had gone to war against the United States, trying to retrieve Texas and other purloined states. The Maya and related Yucatán tribes seized the opportunity to revolt against Mexican authorities in 1847. A new breed of Europeanized, politically savvy Mestizos who had gained power in Yucatán ruthlessly suppressed the rebellion, ultimately halving the population.

Thousands of poor Catholics fled into northern Belize. There was no border, no military force to intimidate them. The Anglican business elite in Belize pondered a bleak future. The chief resource industry, mahogany logging, was faltering badly due to a glut in the market, lowering prices, while supplies were simultaneously dwindling in Belize, raising harvesting costs. Formal amalgamation with Britain was considered as an all-purpose antidote: contain the migrants and stabilize the economy. But London wasn't keen. An outstanding land claim by Guatemala, rendering the Belize-Guatemala border under dispute, would have to be resolved first.

Superintendents appointed from Britain were mere custodians of the territory, not problem solvers, but the overtures made by Superintendent Colonel Charles St. John Fancourt, a military man, and his successor, Philip Wodehouse, a former British civil servant, were sufficient for Britain to agree it was time to replace the Settlement's outdated public meeting process with an elected legislative assembly. The technocrats in London drafted a revised system of government. A legislative assembly, with 18 elected members and three appointed members, was created by Britain in 1853, marking the onset of a flirtation with interior self-government. To respect the importance of separating the judiciary from the political process, the chief justice was excluded from the executive council. The superintendent essentially retained veto powers, but for the most part Belize had home rule for 17 years until 1870, just prior to becoming a Crown Colony.

A new legislative assembly opened in January 1854. It comprised many of the same people who had managed the public meetings, but superior power resided with an executive council. This body included the new superintendent, William Stephenson, and three of his appointees to be approved by the governor of Jamaica. As Jamaica was itself an underling of Britain, it had little time for its poor cousin: Belize remained a feeble protectorate. The Anglican bishop of Jamaica visited the Settlement only three times in 19 years.

As economic stagnation continued, merchants in Belize were increasingly inclined to sell firearms to the Maya of Yucatán. The governor of Yucatán repeatedly protested this gunrunning but little action was taken to prohibit it. Secure in Belize City, the entrepreneurial classes couldn't foresee the prolongation of the Caste War, or its relevance to them. "The so-called Caste War of Yucatán did not merely incidentally affect Belize because of the weapons trade...or because of the influx of refugees into the territory," according to Assad Shoman. "The war was critically important with regard to the definition of Belize's northwestern border and had major repercussions on Belize's constitutional as well as social and economic development."

In 1851, near the outset of the Caste War, Santa Cruz Maya had suspected a betrayal and attacked their Chichanha brethren, who had aligned themselves with the Yucatán government. (These Chichanha became known as the Icaiche Maya after they moved to the village of Icaiche in 1861.)

In June and September of 1857, Young, Toledo & Company were again confronted with Icaiche demands, this time at Blue Creek. When British and Mexican administrations failed to mediate, the mahogany merchants of Belize relented and paid the extortion fees. The resurgent indigenous peoples of Yucatán and northern Belize had to fight back because they were pressured by Yucatán capitalists to relinquish their ancestral lands for sugar cane.

Mexico, having gained its independence from Spain in 1821, had concurrently lost its primary market for exporting cattle—the still loyal Spanish colony of Cuba, also its primary source for importing sugar and rum: hence the need for a sugar industry in Yucatán and the land grab by the new aristocracy.

In the mid-1800s, life on both sides of the Hondo River was becoming increasingly underpoliced and dangerous. Thousands of mixed-blood Mestizos, as well as the Maya, were escaping the Caste War by migrating south from Yucatán, and soon Yucatecan refugees outnumbered the people of the Settlement. The main group of immigrants were the Santa Cruz Maya, so named because they were inspired by a talking cross at their village of Holy Cross (Santa Cruz), at present-day Felipe Carrillo Puerto.

Inspired by twisted Catholic idolatry, these Santa Cruz Maya, also known as the *Cruzob*, became a fierce revolutionary force. They captured and burned a town called Tekax in November, 1857. In response, the Yucatán government reinforced its garrison at Bacalar with 500 armed Icaiche in order to confront or dispel the Santa Cruz Maya.

The Icaiche proved to be fickle friends to the Spanish. The following year the Santa Cruz Maya were able to overrun Bacalar, murdering everyone in the town except six children, one of whom—José Maria Rosado—became a community leader in Belize.

Looking to London

In 1847, at the outset of the Caste War, the Settlement was home to 1,700 Garinagu at Stann Creek, and the Garinagu to the south already represented a potential threat to the all-white oligarchy.

The influx of potentially violent Maya and Mestizos was deeply disturbing on a simple tactical level: white supremacy was vulnerable both to the south and north of Belize City. Before the Caste War, in 1845, the 399 whites in the total recorded population of 9,809 constituted 4 percent. After the Caste War, in 1881, the 375 whites in the recorded population of 27,452 would represent 1 percent.

The president of Guatemala was predicting that if Indians took over Belize, they might revolt en masse against Europeans throughout Central America. Belize was identified as the most likely target in Central America for a rebellion. Some West India Regiment soldiers arrived as reinforcements in 1858, but these provided only temporary consolation. The need for Belize to attain some boundary accord with Guatemala became pressing. With a boundary, Britain could consider granting colonial status to the Settlement. Meetings were arranged by the Colonial Office in London and representatives of both sides agreed on boundary lines for a territorial treaty in 1859, thus smoothing the way for the birth of British Honduras.

But there was one major wrinkle. The president of Guatemala required his negotiator to obtain some compensation for Guatemala's generosity. An "Article 7" was notoriously added, vaguely worded, to suggest both "High Contracting Parties" would endeavour to build a road from Guatemala City to the Caribbean coast. Article 7 would prove to be a divider more invincible than the Berlin Wall.

The Guatemalan negotiator returned to the congress with good but misleading news: Britain was now obliged to build a road. Accordingly, the Anglo-Guatemalan Treaty was ratified in Guatemala in 1859. Guatemala would henceforth be able to maintain it had only recognized British sovereignty on the grounds that Britain had agreed to build a road. Without this road, they could claim the treaty was null and void. Britain was displeased with its negotiator Charles Lennox Wyke for opening a loophole. Nonetheless, Captain Henry Wray of the Royal Engineers was sent to make a survey for the most feasible route.

With this seemingly minor impasse arising from the southern end of Belize came news of heightened tensions with the Santa Cruz Maya in the north. Martial law was declared in northern Belize, around Corozal, after two designated emissaries of Superintendent Seymour, Lieutenants Twigge and Plumridge, were captured and humiliated by the Santa Cruz Maya. An invasion from the Maya was anticipated but they eventually apologized for misunderstandings.

Article 7

In 1861 the British cabinet agreed to ask parliament for the funds to implement the road-building scheme, but by this time diplomatic relations with Guatemala had soured to such an extent that the Colonial Office suggested delaying the move. The boundaries with Guatemala had been verified, agreed upon: there shouldn't be any need to build a road. The United States had plunged into a bloody Civil War—an imagined track through a mountainous jungle in an unnamed protectorate was a nuisance.

The great stumbling block of Article 7 led to complicated diplomatic exchanges. By 1863, Britain and Guatemala agreed to substitute a clause concerning the road: Britain could pay 50,000 pounds in lieu of the road. But Guatemala delayed ratification of this codicil and thereafter sought further advantages that Britain refused to grant. When the time elapsed for codifying the codicil, Britain argued that the preceding 1859 treaty held sway.

Guatemalans are keen to trace their dispute to 1670 when Sir William Godolphin went to Spain with instructions "to cultivate and improve the present alliance to a further increase and strictness of friendship and love." That year, England promised it would try to discourage its privateers from attacking Spanish towns and ships, in return gaining recognition of its rightful jurisdiction over New World territories such as Barbados, an English colony since 1605, and newly acquired Jamaica.

Godolphin neglected to specifically include, or exclude, Belizean territory in the treaty. Two years later Spain complained to England about foreign loggers in Belize. England made efforts to prohibit these loggers. From the Guatemalan viewpoint, if England believed it rightfully controlled Belize, why would it agree to suppress Englishmen engaged in the logwood trade at Spain's request?

It wasn't until 1717 that London resolved that British subjects should be able to conduct their logging enterprises any place that Spaniards had not settled. Spain hotly resisted this attempt by England to get some wiggle room out of the 1670 treaty. It expelled the British from Campeche in Mexico and began a series of policing attacks on Belize. English ships were scuttled or captured.

A Colony is Born

In the early 1860s, the Icaiche were again threatening the mahogany camps. The entire police force of the Settlement consisted of 25 officers in total, 19 in Belize City. The oligarchy in the Settlement had their legislative assembly in place. It was time, at last, to approach the Queen, and ask Britain to lay formal claim on Belize as a colony. From the British perspective, there was no telling how the Civil War in the United States would disrupt Central America and, by association, adversely affect Britain's widespread holdings in the Caribbean.

That's how and why British Honduras was born as a colony in 1862.

In 1870 elected members of the legislative assembly abrogated their own constitution and substituted a legislative council instead. This backward step was a prelude to British Honduras being upgraded to a Crown Colony under governorship from Jamaica in 1871. The elected body had become factionalized; taxation policies were topsy-turvy, depending on whichever sector of the business elite had dominance. With the mahogany business thriving, there were too many people gaining the right to vote: the troublesome democratic system ran the risk of allowing the hoi polloi some say in public affairs.

It was agreed that reversion to a system that essentially allowed the lieutenant governor to appoint legislators was more likely to protect the status quo.

The last of the prominent Indian resistance leaders, Marcos Canul, was killed in Orange Walk by British West India forces in 1872. The British Honduras Company, which owned half of all privately owned lands, changed its name to the Belize Estate and Produce Company (BEC) in 1875. The job of Lieutenant Governor was upgraded to a full-fledged Governor position when British Honduras became a separate colony, without Jamaica's administration, in 1884.

A northern boundary was formalized with Mexico in 1893, allowing Ambergris Caye to become part of British Honduras. Creole workers and some policemen rioted in 1894 when the currency was devalued. After the death of Queen Victoria in 1901, the British Empire began to unravel, eventually to be replaced by the Commonwealth of Nations.

In British Honduras, the mahogany industry was in decline and no longer viable on any large scale. For British overseers, the dog was dead, the party was over. Britain was saddled with the nuisance of maintaining a colony that could not feed itself. American foreign policy would increasingly call the shots in the Caribbean.

Chapter 12: Garveyism to Unionism

"There is absolutely no way that you will understand the 20th century history of British Honduras/Belize if you know nothing of Marcus Garvey/UNIA.... It is impossible for me to give you an adequate sense of how big Marcus Garvey was in British Honduras.... If you do not know what was happening in British Honduras in the 1920s, then you will not understand what is happening in the streets of Belize City with young, black males today."—Evan X Hyde, 2001.

Long ago, long before Belize became a British colony, all governmental and economic affairs were conducted through Kingston. The influence of Jamaica on the white managerial class is easily appreciated—there is a paper trail. But the proximity of Jamaica as an influence on the blacks of Belize is less easily understood. For the slaves of Belize, Jamaica represented the route backward to Africa in their dreams. That trail is in spirit, not paper. It connects Belize with a remarkable man named Marcus Garvey, a controversial businessman and prophet who was once revered and scorned and feared as the most powerful black man on the planet.

The yearning of slaves in the Caribbean to return home, literally or spiritually—to reverse their fates, to bid Jamaica farewell—was given a name in the late 1700s. It was a religious movement called Ethiopianism. The formalized concept of Ethiopianism can be traced to George Liele, a slave born in Virginia in 1752. Converted and baptized, Liele felt the call to preach in 1773. Despite prejudice against him, Liele erected a church on his own land in Kingston and became the founding father of the Baptist Church in Jamaica. To emphasize black pride and salvation, and to reconnect his parishioners to the richness of their black cultures, George Liele called his followers Ethiopian Baptists in deference to Ethiopia's considerable presence in the Bible. After Liele died, the concept and precepts of Ethiopianism continued to excite the hopes and dreams of Jamaican Baptists and would-be emancipationists. One such dreamer was Marcus Garvey.

Jamaica Farewell

Born in 1887, Marcus Mosiah Garvey grew up in the village of St. Ann's Bay on the northern coast of Jamaica, the youngest of 11 children. His father was a formerly prosperous printer and a well-read man who died in the poorhouse. As a master printer and foreman at age 20, Garvey led an unsuccessful printer's strike and was blacklisted. He inevitably became aware of the writings of Dr. Robert Love, a physician and social reformer who wrote for the *Jamaica Advocate* from 1894 to 1905. The *Advocate* would provide a model for Garvey's own publication, *The Negro World*, the largest "Negro" weekly in the United States, when it was published continuously from 1919 to 1933.

Around 1910 Garvey went to Costa Rica to work as a timekeeper at a banana plantation. There he was deeply distressed

The reputation of Marcus Garvey, the most powerful black man on the planet, was successfully undermined by J. Edgar Hoover before he became head of the FBI.

by the working conditions for black labourers. He was troubled further when he visited Panama. Garvey passed through British Honduras twice, in 1911 and 1912.

In Jamaica, Garvey founded his Universal Negro Improvement and Conservation Association and African Communities League on August 1, 1914. Its slogan was "One God! One Aim! One Destiny!" Popularly known as UNIA, this fledgling organization would soon spearhead a "back to Africa" movement for millions of blacks around the world. Garvey arrived in Harlem in 1916, where he stayed with a Jamaican family and found work as a printer. He earned enough money to quickly travel through 38 states and started a chapter of UNIA in New York in 1917. UNIA's festive parades were considered gauche by intellectuals, but during the war years Garvey's version of Ethiopianism evolved into a proud, quasi-religious response to racism in the Americas.

By 1920, UNIA claimed to have 1,100 branches in 40 countries and boasted a membership of six million (modern evaluations have placed that figure closer to one million). In addition to his newspaper *The Negro World*, Garvey ran a monthly magazine called *The Black Man*. At a month-long Harlem convention in 1920, UNIA ratified its Declaration of

The 'back to Africa' rallying cry of Marcus Garvey, depicted in this Harlem poster, circa 1925, brought hope to millions and laid some of the groundwork for Rastafarianism.

Rights of the Negro Peoples of the World. An estimated 25,000 blacks from around the world elected Garvey as provisional president of Africa.

Garveyism in Belize

Belize would have four UNIA chapters. These chapters arose in a climate that was ripe for protest. Two contingents of Creole volunteers went overseas for World War I in 1915 and 1916. Assigned to the Tigris-Euphrates area, they were prohibited from singing "Rule Britannia" with other troops and humiliated as second-class reservists throughout the war. Transported in cattle trucks, prohibited from white lodgings, disdained by white officers, they were also discriminated against in terms of their wages and pensions. British authorities deemed it counter to tradition to use "aboriginal troops" against a European enemy.

When the Creole troops returned to Belize on July 8, 1919, the overt racism of Governor Wilfred Collett (1913–1918) and rising food prices led to the Ex-Servicemen's Riot on July 22. The soldiers broke windows and assaulted officials, with three thousand citizens joining them in the streets. The rioters taunted whites, cursing the few members of the constabulary who opposed them.

Angered by alleged profiteering by merchants, the crowd gathered outside Brodie's, the main department store of Belize. Looting ensued. The Mother Superior of the Sisters of Mercy Convent recorded in her diary, "Carillo's Store, Lind's, Brodie's and many more are empty. Nothing to be seen but broken glass." Whites feared for their lives. The British warship HMS *Constance* soon arrived to disarm the protestors and reassert colonial control. Rioters were heard to exclaim, "This is our country and we want the white man out." Martial law was declared on July 26. Forty rioters were charged; 31 were convicted.

Further investigation by the Colonial Office into what caused the Ex-Servicemen's Riot concluded one factor was the admitted failure of wages to keep pace with the cost of living. Another cause was the Acting Governor Walter's ban of *The Negro World* in January 1919. Copies could be smuggled into Belize, but Herbert Hill Cain led a deputation to the Governor asking for its availability to be reinstated because *The Negro World* was not banned elsewhere in the West Indies.

Cain's delegation was not successful, and the ban was upheld, which led to smouldering resentment that became inflamed with the soldiers' protests. Acting Governor Walter consequently suggested the riot had been instigated by "the discontented negro element in the US." Colonial authorities agreed the "heightened racial consciousness among the colony's black labouring class" was the result of Garveyism and the "noxious" influence of his newspaper, as well as a feisty local newspaper called the *Belize Independent*, which was edited by Herbert Hill Cain and included a column called "The Garvey Eye" by L.D. Kemp.

Its location (shown in the postcard) has changed, but venerable Brodie's Department Store remains one of the few places in Belize that sells books beyond tourism titles.

The seeds of malcontent gave rise to the formation of the first of four UNIA chapters in Belize in April 1920. The new governor,

Sir Eyre Hutson, was invited to attend the unveiling of a UNIA charter for a membership of 800 blacks—a remarkable proportion in a society of 16,000. The governor declined to attend the ceremonies led by General Secretary Samuel Haynes, Benjamin Adderley, Calvert Staine and Herbert Hill Cain, but he rescinded the ban on *The Negro World*.

That year, the Black Cross Nurses Association of British Honduras was formed under the auspices of UNIA. In the United States, the need for Black Cross Nurses had arisen after black women were denied admission to the Red Cross Nurses voluntary sector. The nurses primarily supplied medical care to wounded black soldiers from World War I.

In Belize, it first became apparent that Black Cross Nurses were needed after a deadly three-month flu epidemic in 1918. The Belize Hospital was deluged, and medicines ran out. The public holiday to celebrate the November 11 armistice was cancelled. A soup kitchen was established outside the hospital to feed all the sick people who couldn't be admitted. The colonial government's preparedness and its concern for blacks were found to be lacking. "Life came to a standstill," according to nursing historian Eleanor Krohn Herrmann. "The flu actually brought to British Honduras a new kind of social awareness, cohesiveness and a heightened sense of national health needs."

In 1920, the would-be nurses went house-to-house to determine the number of occupants in each and the needs of each family. "Although untrained," writes Herrmann in *Origins of Tomorrow*, "the original Black Cross Nurses were eager and imbued with devotion to help the UNIA's general plan of welding the Negro people into a united group for effective mass action."

In the United States, Black Cross Nurses wore white uniforms with a black cross on their caps. In Belize the founders of Black Cross Nursing wore uniforms that clearly expressed their affiliation with UNIA, rather than with colonial authorities: their uniforms were green, cuffed in white at the neck, and their caps had a black cross in the centre. They also wore green enamel and brass shield-like pins. The labour leader Antonio Soberanis once referred to a Black Cross nurse as a Red and Green Cross Nurse, so adherence to the UNIA's colours was retained for several years. "Their work was admired and appreciated," Herrmann writes. "They were models for young girls to emulate and represented a state of womanly achievement toward which to strive."

Garvey came to Belize in July 1921. At the time he was easily the most popular black leader in America, and a brilliant orator, trying to establish a Black Orthodox Church with a black God. In Belize, he preached at four well-attended meetings. While taking care not to aggravate colonial authorities, he discussed racial pride, economic independence and the need to reconnect with Africa. "Since the white people have seen their God through white spectacles, we have only started out, late though it be, to see our God through our own spectacles. The God of Isaac and the God of Jacob, let him exist for the race that believe in the God of Isaac and the God of Jacob. We Negroes believe in the God of Ethiopia...we shall worship him through the spectacles of Ethiopia."

Garvey's idealism appealed to a successful Creole landowner in Belize, Isaiah Emmanuel Morter. The wealthy Morter was easily persuaded to accept "knighthood" within the Distinguished Service Order of Ethiopia at the 1922 UNIA convention. It didn't hurt that "Sir" Morter owned a 210-square-mile banana and coconut plantation, an island, plus 21 pieces of "improved" real estate lots. In 1922, Garvey also took care to provide Morter with a Trinidadian nurse who looked after him until his death in April 1924. The estimated value of his fortune was $300,000.

In his will Morter bequeathed $25 to his wife; the rest of his extensive holdings were allocated to the parent body of UNIA for Garvey's African Redemption Fund. The widow contested, alleging insanity, but it didn't wash. The Morter estate got messier when the chief justice in Belize ruled in 1926 that UNIA existed for illegal purposes, thereby rendering the estate invalid. Garvey's UNIA movement wilted in 1927 after its president, Benjamin Pitts was accused of misusing funds. Garvey visited Belize for a fourth and final time in 1929, but with difficulty: he held only one public meeting prior to his departure for Jamaica on February 28, 1929. Marcus Garvey died in relative obscurity in London in 1940, at age 53. He never set foot in Africa.

Hurricanes and Fire

After the Ex-Servicemen's Riot came the Depression and unemployment was rife. The *Colonial Report for 1931* noted "contracts for the purchase of mahogany and chicle, which form the mainstay of the Colony, practically ceased altogether."

Then came the hurricane.

Ramshackle Belize City was shattered by a hurricane and tidal wave on September 10, 1931, killing more than 1,000 people. Winds reached 132 miles per hour. Rooftops were torn away. Flooding was five feet deep. The greatest loss of life occurred in the Mesopotamia area "which was reduced to a few heaps of tangled wood,"

Before & After: Loyola Park, Belize City, in 1917; Loyola Park after the unnamed 1931 hurricane that killed one thousand people. *Belize Archives.*

according to journalist Ernest Cain. "The hurricane desecrated the East Indian community at Queen Charlotte Town" and the Women's Poor House disappeared into the sea "with all its inmates and duty staff." The streets were strewn with wreckage and "evil smelling mud." Legend has it Governor Burdon's manuscript for his three-volume history of British Honduras was miraculously spared because he had fortuitously placed it inside a secure tin box just the day before. Burdon has been portrayed as something of a hero for doing so, in British annals, but it has since been revealed that government wireless stations received warnings about the impending hurricane as early as the morning of September 8. The general populace was not sufficiently warned of its approach—but clearly Burdon knew enough to find a tin box.

In the wake of the hurricane, the proliferation of dysentery, malaria and yellow fever had to be managed by volunteer nurses. The population of Belize City, bloated by the recent return of hundreds of Belizeans who had been deported from Honduras, was largely dependent on soup kitchens. With a full-scale disaster at hand, relief was tentative, slow and inadequate. Governor Burdon had steadfastly rejected appeals for legalization of trade unions, minimum wage proposals and sick benefits. Now, in re-

During the Depression, British colonial authorities failed to adequately respond in the aftermath of the disastrous hurricane of 1931—giving rise to the unionist activism of Antonio Soberanis. *Belize Archives.*

turn for what little aid was forthcoming, Britain imposed treasury control with veto power for the governor in 1932.

While the general citizenry was mostly left to recover by its own devices, London acknowledged "the most awful calamity in the Colony's history" by bailing out the Belize Estate and Produce Company and Hoare family interests, loaning $200,000 for a sawmill in conjunction with a large grant of mahogany forest.

In 1932 a fire swept through Belize City, destroying three business blocks and eliminating 52 houses that had withstood the hurricane.

Desperate for work, a loose contingent known as the Unemployed Brigade took over the streets in 1934. Upon marching to the office of the new governor, they were encouraged to register for relief work breaking rocks. Approximately 1,800 registered; only 80 received work at 25 cents per day. As leaders of the Unemployed Brigade resigned in anger and disgust, Antonio Soberanis Gómez emerged as a spokesperson for the disadvantaged. As the first People's Hero of Belize, Soberanis would become famous for proclaiming, "I prefer to be a dead hero than a living coward."

"British Honduras for British Hondurans."

Born in 1897, Antonio Soberanis Gómez was the first-born child of Canuto Soberanis, originally from Izitas in Yucatán, and Domingo Gomez de Soberanis of Corozal. After only a few years of primary school, he left Orange Walk District to work in Panama. He also visited New York, Chicago and Boston, then joined the Volunteer Guard during World War II. A barber by trade, he helped lay the foundation for trade unionism in Belize after he participated in the Ex-Servicemen's Riot of 1919.

In his 1934 public letter to the governor, Soberanis requested a minimum wage, an eight-hour workday and 90 percent of jobs going to British Hondurans. "We are a new people, and we are aware to the facts," he challenged. "We are not going to be Railroaded into Slavery or Starvation." Soberanis held meetings at the Battlefield, the central square of Belize City, and formed the Labour and Unemployed Association (LUA). Boycotts of merchants were organized. The police commissioner noted Soberanis was called the Moses of British Honduras, "sent by God to lead the people to better things."

Soberanis gained a pay raise, from eight cents per hour to 25 cents per hour, for stevedores loading grapefruit in Dangriga. He led a 500-man brigade armed with sticks to shut down a Belize Estate Company sawmill. (The unemployed were pressuring sawmill workers to strike for higher wages.) In 1934 one demonstrator was shot in the neck during a labour protest. The merchants panicked. After 17 protesters were arrested, Soberanis brought bail and was arrested with them. In order to free Soberanis, one of the dissidents known as the Town Snakeman, Christopher Velasquez, tried releasing snakes in the police station. He went to jail for six months.

When Soberanis was eventually released, he caused a great stir at a rally in Corozal by calling the merchants of Belize bloodsuckers. He called the governor and the King crooks. His motto, "British Honduras for British Hondurans" was considered far too immoderate. He was arrested again but a sympathetic judge only gave him a fine.

In 1939, Soberanis and R.T. Meighan began the British Honduran Workers and Tradesmen Union, the first time the word "Union" was applied in Belize. After serving as its president in 1941, Soberanis went to Panama for nine years. He died in 1975. The shift from Garveyism in the 1920s, to unionism in the '30s, on to elected representation in the '40s, was a largely unheralded grind. Soberanis was later included in Belize's first set of commemorative stamps.

Natives First

Soberanis' Labour and Unemployed Association (LUA) activism encouraged the formation of Calvert Staine's Natives First movement in the 1930s and the General Workers Union in the '40s. The other pioneering political force was the rejuvenated United Negro Improvement Association. Of the few UNIA members who remained politically potent, Herbert Hill Cain published and L.D. Kemp wrote for the *Belize Independent*.

UNIA re-emerged after a 1935 court decision awarded the bulk of Isaiah Morter's estate to UNIA New York's Fund for African Redemption. The president of UNIA Inc., Lionel Francis, first visited Belize in 1935 and took up residence in 1941. Born in Trinidad, Francis had trained in Edinburgh as a physician and joined Marcus Garvey in 1920. He had served as the president of a Philadelphia UNIA chapter until 1929. In Belize, Francis dispensed with Garvey's "Back to Africa" visionary zeal and founded a much more conservative "Economic Society."

Professional and well spoken, Francis became the respectable face of labour within the colony. He quickly gained a seat on the 1941 Belize Town Board (city council), replacing Calvert Staines and his Progressive Party. Elevated to the position of president of the British Honduras Trades and Labour Union, Francis attended the Caribbean Labour Congress in Jamaica in 1947 and endorsed the proposed West Indian federation—in keeping with the designs of the colonial authorities. When financial irregularities arose from town board operations, Francis's star quickly fell. His UNIA-People's Group lost its power on the Belize Town Board in 1947, giving way to the Christian-based Natives First candidates.

In the 1930s, open-air forums at Battlefield Park called for unrestricted adult suffrage. In 1936, only the wealthiest 1.8 percent of the population could vote. From this foment, Calvert Staines generated the Natives First movement that attracted Creole industrialist Robert Turton and Creole lawyer Arthur Balderamos. Endorsed by Soberanis's LUA and the Citizens' Political Party, Turton ran on the Natives First platform and defeated C.H. Brown, the expatriate manager of the Belize Estate and Produce Company, in 1936. It was a major turning point in Belize history.

In 1941, trade unions were finally legalized, but employers were not obliged to recognize them. Joseph Blisset founded the Belize Independent Party, called for the expulsion of whites and also suggested joining the United States. With World War II underway, a new Employers and Workers Bill in 1943 finally eliminated the punitive terms of the 1883 Masters and Servants Act. That year the General Workers Union (GWU) was formed as a national organization and Father Marion Ganey, a Jesuit, kindled the credit union movement in Belize, advising a group of fishermen in Punta Gorda to organize themselves for joint economic power.

GWU president Clifford E. Betson, a shipbuilder, successfully negotiated GWU contracts, including a 60 percent wage hike for Belize City sawmill workers in 1947. The GWU also won all positions on the Stann Creek Town Board. Unionism, more than any other force, including racial solidarity, had given rise to political parties in Belize.

The Belize Town Board was the main forum for debating industrial issues; and although he won representation as a Natives First candidate in 1936, Robert Turton was too busy making money to pursue a sidelong career in politics. In 1944, eager to maintain an anti-Imperialist viewpoint on the Belize Town Board, he told one of his employees to stand for election with only three days' before the voting. Not surprisingly this employee, named George Cadle Price, did not win.

In 1947, the once all-powerful Belize Estate and Produce Company—the firm that exported nine-tenths of Belizean timber—was sold to J. Gliksten and Sons of London. The resultant transfer of 872,412 acres of forest to new controllers further destabilized the shaky economy. That year, Turton gave his secretary George Price sufficient notice to once more seek election.

George Price, Robert Turton's young secretary, gradually emerged as a priestly Messiah for a peaceful and constructive revolution. "There was no such thing as a blueprint," he said. "I just went along and made the plan as we went."
Permission of George Price.

Chapter 13: Liberator of Belize

"To think of George Price is to think of Belize."
— PRIME MINISTER SAID MUSA

If asked to name the greatest liberator of the Americas, most people might suggest George Washington of the United States. Or Simón Bolívar of Venezuela. Or Abraham Lincoln. Or Fidel Castro. Or Martin Luther King. One or two votes might go to lesser known leaders such as José de San Martin (Argentina), Bernardo O'Higgins or Salvador Allende (Chile), Augusto Sandino (Nicaragua) or Juan Perón (Argentina), plus Emiliano Zapata, Pancho Villa or Benito Juárez (Mexico).

Pierre François Dominique Toussaint l'Ouverture, commander of a slave army, gave rise to Haiti. Jacobo Arbenz of Guatemala led an enlightened but doomed effort to free his country from the clutches of the United Fruit Company and the CIA. The "Cincinnatus" of Latin America, José "Pepe" Figueres of Costa Rica, was once the only president of a democracy in Central America.

Nobody would pick George Price.

And yet George Price achieved what all those other liberators could not—a Peaceful Constructive Revolution—nationhood without bloodshed. "That does not mean that there was no isolated violent act," he once said, "but on the whole it was peaceful. I think that in itself is a revolution.

"We did more than decolonize. We created a nationality, we created an attitude of mind in the people wanting to be Belizeans, and to work to improve Belize, the society and its economy, its polity, that in itself is revolutionary."

George Price fought for most of his adult life to make Belizeans free, leading by example, not rhetoric. Having introduced "WAKE UP AND WORK" radio programs in the early 1960s, Price once arrived by skiff at the village of San Pedro. Wearing khaki pants, he walked down Front Street with his local party chairman, Enrique Staines Jr., and remarked, "Mr. Chairman, the streets are dirty—let's call on the soldiers of the Belize revolution to keep the place clean." Price proceeded to pick up litter as he walked; everybody followed suit.

From afar, it is possible to view George Price as a simple man born aloft by circumstances, elevated by the hopes of others. It wasn't even Price's idea to enter politics. His benign and decidedly priestly appeal was more enduring than endearing. He was diligent, conscientious; he kept to the straight and narrow. As such, the life of George Price provides a convenient national plot line, a tidy tale, when conjuring forth the 20th century history of Belize. The myth of George Price as a national saint, as a living Incorruptible, has been

DEMOCRACY INDEX

20th-Century Leaders	Elected
Cheddi Jagan (Guyana)	8 years
Michael Manley (Jamaica)	11 years
Margaret Thatcher (Great Britain)	11 years
Indira Gandhi (India)	15 years
Vigdis Finnbogadottir (Iceland)	16 years
Helmut Kohl (Germany)	16 years
Sir Robert Menzies (Australia)	19 years
W.L. Mackenzie King (Canada)	23 years
George Cadle Price	39 years

rigorously perpetrated by his long-dominant People's United Party (PUP). His elevation into the official position of Leader Emeritus is ironic when one considers he once said, "I am the servant of the people, their number one servant. It's all I wish to be."

In terms of longevity of elected leadership, George Price is unparalleled in the history of democracy—the most successful democrat ever to walk the earth. First elected in 1947, he served in public office during seven decades, compiling 52 years as an elected politician. After he became leader of the People's United Party (PUP), a party he co-founded, he was the leading domestic politician in his homeland for 39 years (including the colonial era).

In the Beginning, God Created

George Cadle Price was born on January 15, 1919. He was the eldest son, and the third-eldest of 11 children, in the home of his conservative, well-read father, Captain William Cadle Price. The family was respectable but not well-off. When George Price was an infant, the family kept a milk cow during a Spanish flu epi-

Price family, 1928. George Price, at far left, grew up with eight sisters: "I think living with mostly girls taught me not to be too macho. To be mild and modest."
Permission of George Price.

demic. At home, he and his sisters were taught to kneel and say prayers. There was no radio, and little knowledge of the outside world. Price was first educated outside the home by the Sisters of Mercy at the nearby Holy Redeemer Boys School, just down the street from his home.

"We saw the world through our educators," he once said. In 1927, at age eight, he was much impressed by the news received at the church that a Jesuit named Father Miguel Augustine Pro had been assassinated in Mexico by a firing squad, during the Mexican War of Cristeros. Apparently Jesuits could be heroes, too, just like Jesus.

At age 12 he was enrolled at St. John's College, near the seaside, where he was deeply influenced by one of his Jesuit mentors, Father Harkins, S.J., a dynamic contrast to his upright father. Father Harkins took George Price, age 15, to visit the "TB Hutments" on an isolated compound of the Poor House. After the teenager took the socks off a patient who was to receive the last sacraments,

George Price escaped injury at St. John's College after a 1931 hurricane caused the main school building to collapse. *Belize Archives.*

he wondered if he, too, would catch tuberculosis. The world could be base, unclean. Evil lurked.

Further evidence that hell on earth could exist arrived during his first year as a boarder at St. John's College. On the morning of September 10, 1931, Price had a terrifying, life-altering experience when an (unnamed) hurricane's tidal wave demolished the college. He had to wade and swim home, taking temporary refuge in a bakery. "I stood near Mrs. Lena Ynestroza and her two children in the bakery. It was not long after I got there when I felt the building shaking. Again I remembered my father's advice and ran out of the building into the yard over some ruins. The Wesleyan Church and the bakery had just crashed."

More than 1,000 people were killed. His father told his son he must have been saved for a reason. George Price would emerge like a Biblical figure who parted the waves between Guatemalan hostility on one side and British colonialism on the other.

Turton's Secretary

After the hurricane, the Price family could not afford to pay both home repairs and taxes on land Price Sr. had inherited in Burrell Boom and Haulover. In order to repair the house, he had to turn over some land to the government and sell some to Robert Turton, one of the richest men in Belize.

Most of the Jesuits who taught George Price were American; numerous were of Irish origin, antipathetic to the British, which partially explains why Price was able to develop such strong anti-imperial views, contrary to the traditionalist views of his father. At St. John's College, Price became a member of the St. Stanislaus Sodality and performed in dramas at Cathedral Hall. He wrote radio plays and produced pageants. Several programs were tributes honouring his Jesuit mentors; others reflected the importance of Mayan beliefs and stories, honouring the Maya-enriched spiritual world of his mother.

On August 28, 1936, Price left Belize in the company of Monsignor Facundo Castillo to study for the priesthood at the St. Augustine Seminary in Bay St. Louis, Mississippi, a Jesuit facility operated by the Fathers of the Society of the Divine Word. Here the young acolyte was introduced to Greek and Latin and furthered his training in music. He once dreamed of becoming a concert pianist.

Price hoped to go to Rome to continue his religious studies, but travel during World War II was difficult and dangerous: Mussolini held Italy; Nazi submarines lurked offshore. Instead, his teachers arranged for him to go to Guatemala City for one year to study ethics and logic at a Diocesan Seminary. "It opened my eyes and got me acquainted with the Spanish language," he recalled. Two decades later, when most other politicians in Belize were routinely condemning Guatemala, Price rose above their common level of bellicose rhetoric, saying, "While we shall not surrender one square centimetre of our national territory, we do not propose to spew recrimination or insults against our neighbours."

George Price returned to Belize in 1942, partly because his fa-

George Price graduated from St. Augustine Seminary in 1940. *Belize Archives.*

ther was ill. He had few, if any, practical skills but found work as a translator for Robert Sydney Turton.

It has been suggested that Turton was the bastard son of Major General Robert Straker Turton, who briefly served as acting colonial secretary and administrator in 1883. More importantly, he was the leading agent for chicle exports, trading with the Wrigley Chewing Gum Co., and a leading timber agent. "He used to ship out sometimes [US]$2 million worth of mahogany logs," Price once said.

Turton took Price with him on his business trips to Chicago, New York and Washington. While learning how to rub shoulders with rich men, Price was also able to visit the United Nations. But immersion in business and politics didn't sway his values. He remained a devotee of Papal encyclicals all his life, typically rising to attend Mass at Holy Redeemer Church every morning at 5:30 a.m. When Price once tried to explain Papal encyclicals to Turton, an earthly man with moral standards different from his own, his boss replied, "The Pope knew nothing about business."

For Turton, it was obvious the Belize Estate and Produce Company had enjoyed a stranglehold on the local economy ever since it was first registered as the British Honduras Company in 1859—just before the Settlement adopted the name British Honduras. This BHC/BEC dominance was akin to the enduring prominence of the Hudson's Bay Company in Canada.

Turton was elected to the Belize Town Board under the banner of the Natives First movement in 1936. He was a member of the governor's executive council. Along with Henry I. Melhado, whose family had become wealthy from liquor trading during Prohibition, he was one of the few Belizeans who had both the temperament and wherewithal to confront the status quo. His office hosted informal political gabfests with men such as Sir W. Harrison Courtenay, Reverend Gilbert Rodwell Hulse, Simeon Hassock and Fred Westby. One afternoon in 1944, after an intense discussion with Westby, Turton called Price into his office and instructed him to run as a candidate for the Belize Town Board. There were only three days to go before the vote. Price ran unsuccessfully, receiving 30 votes. So few people were eligible to vote in 1944 that this was not a bad showing.

Price's father died in 1945, bringing the 26-year-old, bespectacled secretary increasingly within the guidance of his employer. With Turton's support, Price joined a coalition associated with the St. John's College Alumni Association and the Christian Social Action Group. Along with John Smith and two other Christian candidates, Price ran under the banner of the Natives First movement in 1947. On November 19, he topped the polls with 156 votes.

In those days, when the Natives First foursome took control of the Belize Town Board, pressing issues of the day were deciding when the Swing Bridge should be opened and when households could dump their honey buckets into the canal. In this context, Price and his associates were radicals. They wanted a minimum wage, an all-elected council and creation of affordable rental housing on city-owned land. Price was opposed to Britain's proposed Federation of the West Indies, lumping all British dependents together into one state and he pledged to break local monopolies—no doubt to please his chief backer.

Price's concerns were always cultural as much as economic. Fond of playing the church organ, he increasingly used his modest talents to compose religious pageants. "There was no widespread radio or television," he once said, "and we tried to bring the doctrine of the Bible, the teachings, to the people." He had puritanical leanings in culture as well as religion. "We didn't want to import something from the United States," he said.

The Party That George Built
The trigger for the independence movement in Belize was money—devaluation of it—in 1949. As the top vote-getter on the Belize

Town Board, George Price was automatically thrust into the spotlight of a controversy that swept through Belize like a forest fire.

Britain devalued its pound in September. After much head scratching and apprehension—and promises from Governor Sir Ronald Garvey that devaluation would *not* occur in Belize—the governor, invoking his reserve powers to do so, devalued the colony's dollar on December 31, 1949, when most Belizeans would be distracted by their New Year's Eve preparations. The elected members of the legislative assembly walked out in protest as the edict was delivered. Being hewers of wood and drawers of water was one thing; having the value of their hard-earned money seemingly cut in half by the Brits was another.

Soapbox dissenters in Battlefield Park fuelled a sense of betrayal. It was obvious that devaluation had occurred largely to protect the interests of the Belize Estate and Produce Company: the balance of its trade with Britain had to be maintained.

Just as devaluation of currency had caused mahogany workers to riot in 1894, callous disregard for democracy on a monetary issue unleashed pent-up, anti-colonial feelings at the dawn of 1950. These feelings gave rise to the People's United Party (PUP) and the personal ascendancy of its secretary, George Price. "In Belize," Emory King would say at century's end, "the second half of the 20th century belongs to George Price. When the history of the period 1951–2000 is written,

George Price's old wooden house on Pickstock Street gets dressed with a PUP banner at election time. *Twigg photo.*

trained historians will be astonished by his achievements and foresight."

George Price and the PUP

Speakers at the Battlefield demonstrations against devaluation included John Smith and George Price. Protests against devaluation occurred immediately in the first days of January; some of the leaders of the protest reconvened at Price's residence at 3 Pickstock Street to form the People's Committee, forerunner of the PUP.

The People's Committee printed handbills from Goodrich Printing on Church Street, with only the names of John Smith and George Price attached, addressing "PATRIOTIC BRITISH HONDURANS!" in block capitals. "EVERYMAN'S PROTEST WILL COUNT. WE ARE ON THE VERGE OF STARVATION AND SLAVERY THAT WAS OUTLAWED BY WILLIAM IV IN 1833. WILL SLAVERY BE BROUGHT BACK TO US UNDER THE REIGN OF GEORGE VI? COME TO THE BATTLEFIELD DEMONSTRATIONS AND PARADE ON FRIDAY 8:00 P.M., JANUARY 6, 1950 AND REGISTER YOUR STRONGEST OPPOSITION TO DEVALUATION."

One of the originators of the People's Committee was Clifford Betson, president of the General Workers Union. He provided crucial melding with the GWU's organizational network around the country. Transportation and communication were enormous hurdles in 1950. As the middle-class intellectuals in the People's Committee gained support, Betson was honorifically shifted to the side as "patriarch of the union" and the GWU framework remained.

The People's Committee dissolved itself to create the People's United Party on September 29, 1950. John Smith, a teacher, was the leader; Leigh Richardson, chairman; George Price, secretary; Philip Goldson, assistant secretary. Price also became vice-president of the GWU soon afterward. Seemingly lacking in prestige, it was perhaps the key position in retrospect: as secretary and GWU affiliate, Price gained useful contacts throughout the country.

In July of 1951, the Belize Town Board was dissolved, by order of the governor, on the dubious grounds that the PUP-dominated council was refusing to keep a portrait of the King in its chamber. It was part of a larger clampdown. More famously, Philip Goldson and Leigh Richardson, as editors and owners of the *Belize Billboard*, were found guilty of sedition in October for an article that had appeared during the rising turbulence. The offending passage was a simple one: "There are two roads to self-government: Evolution or Revolution. We are now trying Evolution." Richardson and Goldson were sent to Her Majesty's Prison on Gaol Lane for one year's hard labour. It was obvious everyone had to take sides—there would be no comfortable middle ground. John Smith chose to resign when other PUP members refused to fly the British flag at public meetings.

With three-quarters of the original executive out of the picture, the coast was cleared for the seemingly unambitious George Price. Leigh Richardson served as PUP leader from 1952–56, but Price again topped the polls in the 1952 Belize Town Board elections. On April 28, 1954—the first election held with universal literate adult suffrage—the PUP won eight of the nine seats in the new legislative assembly, taking 66.3 percent of the vote. A dynasty was born. George Price would lead the PUP from 1956 until 1996—40 consecutive years.

Toilet Paper and Sedition

They say if a man is prepared for death, he can handle most earthly travails with relative equanimity. George Price escaped God's wrath a second time when an earthquake struck Mexico City in 1957. "I think, subconsciously, it must have had some effect," he has said, "that death can happen at any moment, that one should be prepared. *In the midst of life we are in death.*"

Price's steadiness under fire elevated his status tremendously—on at least four occasions—when his character was severely maligned by opponents.

He, too, was arrested for sedition. In 1958, fearing Price and his supporters could disrupt the impending visit of Her Royal Highness Princess Margaret, colonial authorities charged Price for "inciting disaffection" against Her Majesty the Queen and "defaming Her Majesty." These charges were laid in connection with remarks Price allegedly made about a parade held in New York to honour Queen Elizabeth and the Duke of Edinburgh. He happened to be in New York with Albert Cattouse at the time. He reported: "They rained down papers of all kinds from windows of high buildings. It was beautiful to see the papers floating down to the streets. When Mr. Cattouse and I picked up some of the paper off the streets, we saw some of it was toilet paper. This is the way the American people welcome distinguished visitors and I think they meant well in doing it." The prosecution claimed the reference to toilet paper was intended to be degrading.

Fearing Price's popularity, Attorney General Charles Henville successfully argued before Chief Justice Sir Clifford deLisle Innis that a common jury could not be used in this particular case because many persons would be summoned "whose opinion would be tainted with a very strong prejudice in favour of the said George Cadle Price." A "Special Jury" was duly empanelled. It was a bizarre twist, but Price kept his cool.

The Special Jury was selected based on an affidavit provided by Inspector of Police Arthur E. Bruhier who had claimed members of the People's United Party and the Christian Democratic Union were likely to be strongly prejudiced in favour of the defendant, that they necessarily would comprise at least one-third of any jury and that Price's followers were dangerously excited and posed a social threat.

The Crown's case against Price collapsed when Bruhier admitted under oath, when examined by defence lawyer Woolrich Harrison Courtenay, that he knew of no "state of excitement." He couldn't name a single PUP or CDU member whose name appeared on the list of common jurors and there was no joint National Council for the organizations as he had claimed. Other police testimony was revealed as a sham. It became clear the trial was an inept conspiracy. "I have nothing to say. I plead not guilty," Price said, refusing to call witnesses or allow the prosecution to cross-examine him.

He was found not guilty on both charges.

Lock, Stock 'n' Barrel Polkas

It is likely that the Toilet Paper Farce was an attempt at revenge by Governor Colin Hardwick Thornley. In 1957, Governor Thornley essentially accused Price of being a traitor over the government-controlled airwaves, only to have his attempt at character assassination enhance Price's reputation.

During their visit with Thornley to meet for the first time with the British secretary of state in London in November, a PUP delegation—consisting of George Price, Albert Cattouse, Denbigh Jeffery and Henry Bowman—also met informally for a meal with Guatemala's Ambassador Jorge Garcia Granados. The Guatemalan obligingly confided some details of the bargaining process with Britain to settle long-standing sovereignty issues with Guatemala.

When he learned of this unscheduled dinner from Jeffery and Bowman (according to PUP history), Governor Thornley squealed immediately to Secretary of State Alan Lennox Boyd who threw up his hands in alarm, appalled that the lowly Price delegation would take any independent action. The Anglo-Guatemalan dispute resolution process was clearly too delicate and important for Belizeans to have direct input. Having only recently graduated from mere observer status, Price and his colleagues were sent home in disgrace, accused by their betters of deceit and lack of good faith.

Upon his return, Thornley took the opportunity to bash Price's credibility, attacking him on a front where Price was strongest—his patriotism. "He [Price] was prepared in certain eventualities to see, you, the people of this country, handed over to the Guatemalan Republic 'lock, stock and barrel.'" It was a monstrous lie. But Price was not allowed any radio time on the British Honduras Broadcasting Service to refute the charges.

The PUP launched a counterattack. Their adherents literally rallied in support of Price, their "Popular Leader." The *Belize Times* provided a series of stinging editorials, alleging that Britain—not George Price—was intending to sell out Belizeans: "The alleged failure on the part of the Popular Leader was blown up out of all proportions. All this was done in what now appears to be an attempt to conceal the failure on the part of the United Kingdom, to inform the people of British Honduras that their future destiny was being 'settled' without their knowledge."

The editorials made it clear Britain had already renounced claims on the Bay Islands and the Mosquito Coast. It was alleged that the Foreign Office might be considering the advantages of increased trade between Britain and Guatemala, and the rest of Central America, as more important than holding on to Belize. A more sophisticated analysis was that Britain had received entreaties from oil companies interested in the petroleum potential of Belize; needing a way out of their ongoing talks with Guatemala, the Brits had scapegoated Price's delegation for engaging in secretive discussions that nullified the "above-board" process. Instead of sending Price home with his tail between his legs, Thornley and the Brits had conferred a halo. For all his troubles in Belize, orchestrating the sedition trial and the smear campaign, Thornley was later knighted.

"It has been my dedicated task," Price would tell the House of Representatives in 1965, "to lead the movement of Belizean independence from the chains of British colonialism; and I have no intention to exchange these chains for the colonialism of Guatemala or of any country."

Price was first accused of excessive collaboration with Guatemalan officials in the early 1950s. In the autumn of 1951, the Guatemalan consul in Belize gave Price BZ$500, purportedly as a contribution to the defence fund for Leigh Richardson's sedition trial. Price was also taken to task for, among other things, allegedly sending copies of his speeches to this Consul. For various PUP liaisons with Guatemala from 1950 to 1953, Commissioner Reginald T. Sharpe, appointed to conduct an inquiry by the colonial secretary in London, formally investigated Price and his PUP consorts. In March of 1954, Sharpe announced he was unable to substantiate most of the allegations. The Sharpe Inquiry served to fan the flames of independence. It was unveiled that the government's public relations officer, J.C.R. Proud, had been tampering with documents and intercepting PUP correspondence.

Guatemala was dangerous turf in the volatile 1960s, too. Politicians hoping to make some progress on finding a lasting accord with Guatemala were faced with an abiding dilemma: should sincere overtures be made in public, or must they be conducted privately? George Price fell afoul of that bind in 1967. A headline in the *Belize Billboard* declared, "Price's frequent visits to Guatemalan Border Area viewed with suspicion."

Price appointed an independent inquiry into whether he had been making clandestine contacts with Guatemalans in the Gallon Jug area since 1966. The editor of the *Belize Times*, George Frazier, couldn't substantiate the claims. Inquiry Commissioner Sir Colin MacGregor found Frazier "untruthful on all occasions," and was satisfied that Price had only visited the Gallon Jug area on April 20, 26 and May 3 to examine conditions for new roads. Whether or not that was entirely true became secondary in the minds of most

Belizeans; obviously the smear campaign was based on falsified claims.

Hurricane Hattie and Belmopan

In 1961, in the wake of Hurricane Hattie, George Price decided two deadly hurricanes in one lifetime was one too many to take. It was as if God were sending him a message. He made the controversial decision to erect a new inland capital, Belmopan, leading his people inland, "to build in time the new Belize of Maya splendour."

Whether Price's decision to build Belmopan from scratch was commonsensical for public safety reasons—or motivated by some innate desire to get closer to his mother's Mayan roots, or an age-old reflection of the urge of rulers to build lasting memorials to themselves—it alienated established Creole families in Belize City where most of them had lived for generations.

Blacks had literally "slaved away" to become the most well-placed racial group in the country. Creoles openly viewed Price's decision to reallocate reconstruction funds for Belize City to his pet project as prejudicial, even racist, because many of them held government jobs. Nobody actually *lived* in Belmopan. They much preferred to take their chances with hurricanes than pack their bags for Dullsville. Consequently, resentment against Belmopan and its location became an abiding cross for George Price to bear. As the Creole share of the country's population concurrently began to decrease, Belmopan became something of a dirty word in Creole.

In fact, the plan to build Belmopan had been included in an election manifesto entitled "PUP FOR PROGRESS" that was published months prior to the hurricane. It read "We shall encourage and promote the building of a new city, on better-sited terrain, which will entail no costly reclamation of land and which will provide for an industrial area." The PUP won all 18 seats in the new ministerial system of government in March 1961, so it had a mandate, arguably a unanimous one, to build Belmopan eight months prior to Hurricane Hattie, in October 1961. At issue was the designation of Belmopan as the capital of Belize—an important distinction that was *not* spelled out in the 1961 campaign literature. A committee selected the site for Belmopan in 1962 after the hurricane had damaged or obliterated 75 percent of the homes in Belize City. Its 15-foot tidal wave and 160 mph winds had also pummelled Dangriga, Mullins River Village, Hopkins, Sittee River Village, Gales Point, San Pedro and the cayes. It was prudent to choose a location 250 feet above sea level, at the juncture of the Western and Hummingbird Highways, near Roaring Creek Village.

Price went to London to discuss Belmopan, his proposed "jeweled City of Mopan radiating life and love and hope and joy" after his PUP regime achieved partial self-government in 1964. With a delegation also consisting of PUP cabinet members Rafael Fonseca, Lindy Rogers and Alexander Hunter, Price discovered the United Kingdom was not confident Belize could successfully undertake such a daring and large project.

Just as the Baymen had once solicited English cooperation by using the name of Admiral Burnaby on their humble constitution, Price invited Secretary of State for the Commonwealth and the Colonies Anthony Greenwood to visit Belize and travel 49 miles inland to see the proposed area for building. On October 9, 1965, at an elaborate—by Belizean standards—ceremony Price read his poem for the occasion, "Limestone Pillars of Belikin," alongside a newly erected "Maya Stela" that indicated in Mayan characters the year of Lord Greenwood's momentous arrival. To further propagate the connection of Lord Greenwood to the plan, whether Greenwood liked it not, Belize issued a postage stamp showing his name and the stela.

A contest was held to choose a name. The two citizens who submitted Belmopan as a conjunction of Belize and Mopan were each awarded a free lot in the proposed city. The first phase of construction, between 1967 and 1970, was undertaken by Pauling and Company construction, under the direction of the London architecture firm Norman and Dawbarn. The new legislative assembly atop Independence Hill was supposedly reminiscent of a Mayan temple.

On moving day for the government—August 1, 1970—there was only one store in Belmopan. For years afterward, government employees who moved to the subsidized housing made available in Belmopan received bus transport allowance to go shopping in Belize City.

The National Assembly held its first meeting in Belmopan on February 1, 1971. Until the Plaza Theatre opened in May 1973, free movies were shown twice a month at the market. By 2000, Belmopan had attracted approximately 7,000 residents and was the site of the main campus for the University of Belize. The George Price Centre for Peace and Development opened on September 21, 2002.

Prime Minister Rice, I Presume

Gaining independence was an incremental process. As of 1960, in accordance with a new constitution, the majority of the executive council was to be elected. In 1961, Belize obtained associate-member status in the United Nations Economic Commission for Latin America. In 1964, Belize gained internal, elected self-government. The governor's reserve powers were greatly reduced. The executive council that had advised the governor became a cabinet of ministers. The governor general appointed PUP leader George Price as prime minister. Britain retained control of defence, foreign affairs, internal security and terms and conditions of public service. The name Belize was formally adopted in 1973. The independence ceremony was in 1981.

A new capital. A new constitution. A new flag. A new name. A new university. A new deep sea port. A new social security system. A new water and sewerage system. A national anthem. An expanded economy. Universal adult suffrage. There aren't many improvements in Belize that George Price didn't oversee or help generate. He led his party to seven straight electoral victories until its first election loss in 1984.

The preceding year, in May, he had paid a working visit to the White House, discussing marijuana with Ronald Reagan and the struggles of the Belizean economy. Following their meeting in the Oval Office, the President of the United States mistakenly referred to his visitor as Prime Minister Rice, then corrected himself.

George Price, the good shepherd, was seldom disparaged in his waning political years. As modesty overtook him, it became increasingly difficult to countenance the United Democratic Party view of the "Leader Emeritus" as an authoritarian. "Having gained limited power," according to UDP literature, "Price was meticulous in trying to suppress opposition. He threatened civil servants, controlled the only radio station, reserved scholarships for the children of party activists and put close family members in positions of control."

Price became his country's first recipient of the Order of National Hero on September 19, 2000. He says he accepted membership on the Privy Council because he thought it might be helpful to his country. He has also received the Order of CARICOM (Caribbean Community and Common Market) in Barbados in 2001, the highest order conferred by the Caribbean's regional economic body. "Price conceived a nationalism that was more hemispheric than simply post-imperial," said CARICOM's Tony Cave at the ceremony. "He understood, perhaps better than any other Caribbean leaders of his time, the potential which resided in strong hemispheric relationships. In a sense, he was ahead of his time."

Five stamps have been issued in Price's honour and the government opened the George Price Boulevard on August 1, 2003, officially declaring Belmopan Day to mark the inauguration of a new route into the capital that Price had envisioned and built.

As an ascetic pragmatist—partly heroic, partly dull—George Price relied mainly on "providence" and papal encyclicals during his seven decades of democratically elected service to God and the little country he liberated with almost no bloodshed.

Chapter 14: Growing Pains

In 1956 there was a power struggle within the PUP. Britain wanted to place all its Caribbean holdings into one convenient political unit and the party was divided on whether or not Belize should become part of the proposed West Indian Federation. George Price and Nicholas Pollard vigorously opposed integration with the West Indian Federation; Philip Goldson and Leigh Richardson were more open-minded about it.

Overt discussion of ethnicity is avoided in Belizean politics, but issues of immigration are not. As a black man, Goldson felt he could not comfortably argue on behalf of excluding, or limiting, black immigration from the Caribbean. Goldson and Richardson were expelled from the party—according to PUP sources—but others have maintained Goldson resigned to assert his right to independent views. Either way, Goldson and Richardson had their *Belize Billboard* to get their points across. It was necessary for the PUP to have a rival publication: the *Belize Times* was founded under editor Nicholas Pollard in 1956.

In 1956, the rebels Goldson and Richardson formed the Honduras Independence Party (HIP) to combat the PUP. It merged with the National Party to create the National Independence Party (NIP) in 1958. Under Goldson, the second-most enduring politician in Belizean history, the NIP became the first serious opposition to the PUP.

Philip S.W. Goldson

Philip Stanley Wilberforce Goldson was born in Belize City in 1923. Unable to attend secondary school, he studied on his own to receive his junior and senior school accreditations. He started working as a journalist in 1941. After a six-year stint in the civil service, he became co-editor of the *Belize Billboard* with Leigh Richardson. As a trade unionist and general secretary of the General Workers Union, Goldson became a co-founder of PUP.

After Richardson and Goldson served one year of hard labour for their 1951 sedition conviction, Goldson returned to society hardened in his resolve to change it. As a member of the PUP, he won a seat in the British Honduras Legislative Council on the day he married Hadie Jones—April 28, 1954.

In the 1960s Goldson became one of the foremost black dissidents in Belize, but racism was not Goldson's primary concern. He vehemently opposed any possible British concessions to be made to Guatemala in the ongoing border dispute. Goldson's finest hour came in 1962 when he was excluded from membership in a Belize delegation that attended a British and Guatemalan summit on the border dispute held in Puerto Rico. Goldson went to Puerto Rico and demanded admittance. Refused entry, he staged a one-man picket protest. "His Puerto Rico vigil," according to United Democratic Party (UDP) Opposition Leader Barrow, "was the defining moment of an epic crusade that would continue well into independence and beyond."

Back in Belize, Goldson was charged with breach of the peace for using militant language in a speech. He led the first protest against the PUP government's exclusive use of the publicly owned radio station, later speaking for 8½ hours non-stop when the

Philip Goldson at left (with briefcase) was a member of the House of Representatives in 1965 with George Price (centre, front). *Belize Archives*

National Assembly finally introduced live broadcasts. In 1963 Goldson went on a hunger strike to protest exclusive PUP representation at a London Constitutional Conference. In 1966, he led large public protests against proposed mediation that might condescend to Guatemalan claims. For the same issue he blocked the Belize City Swing Bridge and went to New York to demonstrate at the United Nations. After addressing the Decolonization Committee of the UN, he returned in 1968 to become the first Belizean to address the UN General Assembly.

He finally gained a foothold in government as a cabinet minister in the UDP administration of 1984. Having run independently under his own National Alliance for Belizean Rights (NABR) banner, Goldson joined the UDP government as a one-man coalition member. He generated programs such as the Family Court, the Department of Women's Affairs and the Disabilities Services Division but according to some observers he was marginalized within the administration. He resigned from the UDP in 1991 when he refused to condone the Maritime Areas Bill. He retired from politics in 1998. Goldson was elected seven straight times from the Albert Division in Belize City. He owned and edited the *Belize Billboard* newspaper until 1971. The international airport bears his name.

Goldson was afflicted with glaucoma in 1978. A father of six, he died at 78, in 2001, while undergoing medical treatment in Florida. At Goldson's memorial service, UDP's Dean Barrow praised him as "Our North Star, our cynosure. There was never any doubt that at any moment he was prepared literally to die for Belize."

John Wayne vs. Frantz Fanon

If there's one moment when politics in Belize ceased to be a one-man show, it was New Year's Eve 1968. The '60s was a volatile era around the world, only slightly less so in conservative Belize. With visions of Martin Luther King, the Beatles and Vietnam War protests dancing in their heads, two idealistic young lawyers named Assad Shoman and Said Musa helped organize a protest outside the Eden Cinema in Belize City on New Year's Eve.

The theatre was showing a war movie called *The Green Berets*, starring John Wayne. The film was identified by the "Ad Hoc Committee for the Truth about Viet Nam" as Hollywood propaganda supporting the American military complex in Southeast Asia.

"This was the first political-cultural offensive against racism, US imperialism, cultural penetration and capitalism to occur in Belize," Shoman has claimed. Both Belizean-born, with Palestinian heritage, Musa and Shoman weren't just concerned about the downtrodden and disadvantaged in Belize, they were part of a new breed of agitators who were keen to identify the larger, capitalist forces that dictated inequality and poverty, both at home and abroad. Musa and Shoman would go on to become prime minister and foreign minister of Belize, respectively, at the turn of the century.

The Green Berets protest was a pivotal night in Belizean history if for no other reason than Robert "Rasta" Livingston, secretary of the United Negro Improvement Association (UNIA) noticed Evan X Hyde amid the demonstrators. Hyde had been giving talks for a few "bourgeois intellectuals," as he later put it, about "The Black Man in American Literature" down at the Bliss Institute in Belize City. Livingston invited the disaffected, college-educated Hyde to begin lectures on black consciousness at the Liberty Hall on Barracks Road. These talks, according to Hyde, became "the womb of the movement for black nationalism" in Belize.

As the young president of the newly formed United Black Association of Development (UBAD), Hyde openly referred to Belize as Afro-Honduras. "It was wild," he recalls, "but the message was winning the hearts and minds of many people, especially young black people. Be black and proud. Learn your history. Know about the deeds of your ancestors. Stand together for your rights. Be willing to die for what you believe in. Every white person until proven otherwise must be considered an enemy to freedom, justice, and equality, really."

Musa and Shoman joined UBAD to express their solidarity until they split in May 1969 to form their own activist association, with economist Lionel del Valle, called the People's Action Committee (PAC). Not yet a political party, it was meant to serve as the chief critic of Price's PUP. PAC literature pointed out "a vast amount of our fertile land is in the hands of foreigners who gained these lands by expropriating them." Hardly a revelation, but it was a way of taunting powers-that-be. PAC's rhetoric espoused a socialist vision: they were for free education and land reforms, against capitalism and racism. Clearly the nearby Cuban revolution of Fidel Castro was providing a model for change.

The 1960s' foment in Belize City also spawned a think-tank called the Society for the Promotion of Education and Research (SPEAR) in May 1969. The nine founders of SPEAR back in the Summer of Love were Assad Shoman, Evan X Hyde, Said Musa, Mac Alamilla, Everal Waight, Charles X Eagan, Abdullah (Justice) Ibrahim, Lionel del Valle and Ray Fuller. They sought "to encourage free thought and discussion and research into our social, economic, judicial and national life."

Free love in Belize was not nearly as threatening as free thought. In Trinidad, Dave Darbeau and Geddes Granger supported the National Joint Action Committee. In Grenada, Maurice Bishop spearheaded the New Jewel Movement. Emboldened, Evan X Hyde began working on his uninhibited black-run newspaper, *Amandala*, on August 13, 1969. Much of its "black-is-beautiful" rhetoric was contrary to Price's melting-pot view of Belize but Price didn't overtly present himself as a foe of the newspaper.

Momentum was afoot. In October, two upstart organizations briefly merged into the Revolitical Action Movement (RAM) with

Hyde as president. At the same time *Amandala* merged with PAC's publication *Fire* to become *Amandala with Fire*. Black intellectuals throughout the Caribbean were forming associations like UBAD and SPEAR. It was one thing for a colonial government to deal with a black upstart or two; it was quite another to suppress the resentment of an organization.

Many black intellectuals in the Caribbean were stirred by the works of a brilliant black psychiatrist from Martinique named Frantz Fanon, writer of *The Wretched of the Earth* and *Black Skin, White Masks*. The wisdom of Fanon continues to percolate in Belize. When the Old Prison on Gabourel Lane was converted into the Museum of Belize—a transition with an obvious symbolic significance—the Minister of Culture, Mark Espat, quoted Fanon in the catalogue for the first exhibition: "Culture never has the translucidity of custom; it abhors all simplification. In essence, it is opposed to custom, for custom is always the deterioration of culture." The brain trust of the PUP was steeped in Fanon.

Frantz Fanon, Emperor Haile Selassie, Malcolm X (El Hajj El Shabazz), Eldridge Cleaver and Martin Luther King were all providing contemporary avenues for the march of black liberation in the late 1960s. In Belize, as elsewhere in the Caribbean, black pride became as important as economics. Some counter-culturalists wanted to slay the dragon of capitalism; others argued the larger dragon of slavery had yet to be slain. Frantz Fanon once said, "The point is not to interpret the world, but to change it." So which dragon to slay?

The RAM attacked the "customary" Christian Democracy concept of the PUP, attracting the venerable Mayan activist Jesus Ken to its meetings. Ken's grandfather had been a leader of the Santa Cruz Maya during the Caste War; his pedigree was truly revolutionary. He had organized the Northern Cane Workers Union in 1961. He was a man of both talk and action. But the fraternal UBAD and PAC factions couldn't agree on how to change the world, they only agreed on how to interpret it. "Every time a black or brown man in the Western Hemisphere begins any kind of grassroots agitation amongst his people, the chances are the first people who will rush to his side and be his allies are people who are not considered black in the African sense, who are Marxist-Leninists, socialists or communists," recollected Evan X Hyde.

The RAM was split in January 1970. In February Hyde rekindled the UBAD, becoming its president in March. With RAM splintered, it was easier for the powers that be in Belize to retaliate.

On March 20 *Amandala* published a satirical review, more juvenile than vicious, of prominent PUP personalities. Hyde and his publisher Ismail Shabazz, a Muslim, were charged with seditious conspiracy due to the lampoon. In June 1970, Shoman and Musa served as defence lawyers, at no charge. In July, they won the case in Belize Supreme Court. There were celebrations in the streets. In the heady aftermath, Hyde generated a new, short-lived, black political party called the UBAD Party for Freedom, Justice and Equality. In a pamphlet called *The Crowd Called UBAD* he expressed his disdain for, and alienation from, the national vision of George Price.

"I say George Price is a Maya racist," Hyde charged. "There is no sincere black man in his government, only punks who have sold out their people and birthright for a fistful of dollars, a mess of pottage. Mayan racism must be neutralized. How are you going to speak of Belize united, sovereign and independent when you take money intended for the reconstruction of Belize City and Stann Creek, the towns almost destroyed by Hurricane Hattie, and build a segregated modern Maya ruins capital fifty miles closer to the guns of the Guats?"

But the PUP was unshakeable. The party would win 80 percent of the federal elections held from 1957 until century's end and 70 percent of municipal elections since self-government began in 1963.

The X Factor

"There is nowhere in Central America where black people are as powerful as they are in Belize." —Evan X Hyde, 2002

Evan X Hyde's life is a counterpoint to that of George Price. Both men attended St. John's College (SJC), but Hyde's Creole view of the Jesuit orthodoxy has been at odds with the habitual faithfulness of Price. Both men have felt deeply about their "Land of the free, by the Carib sea," but they were loyal to separate realms. One man emerged as the most influential politician of Belize; the other emerged as the most influential writer.

As the publisher and owner of *Amandala*, the country's leading independent newspaper, Hyde had more of his words digested by more Belizeans than anyone, including the novelist Zee Edgell or the historian Emory King. The disarming quality of his writing has a great deal to do with *Amandala's* continued popularity. His personalized riffs in print are antithetical to government press releases.

At age 12, Hyde began attending St. John's College. It was the only route upward to higher education. By 1962, when the Jesuits were pressuring Hyde to become a priest, he had concluded their leadership was cynical. He discovered they were not above manipulating the results of exams, playing favourites, but he still managed to win a new four-year scholarship program to an American university from the US Consolate.

Two of Hyde's friends, Ernest Moody and Wallace Campbell, were already in New York so he was eager to see beyond Belize. While attending Dartmouth College, Hyde was loaned a copy of *The Autobiography of Malcolm X*. It changed his life forever.

Members of the Brooklyn-based British Honduras Freedom Committee began updating Hyde on the unrest in Belize, as well as the text for "17 Proposals for Change."

After graduating in 1968, Hyde returned to Belize. "I could

have gone to just about any school I desired. I wished, however, to make revolutionary changes where the condition of my people was concerned, and so I sacrificed myself in the streets."

In Belize he taught English at the Belize Technical College. In the evenings he also taught an extramural department class at the Bliss Institute for the University of the West Indies. It was called "The Black Man in American Literature"—but it was too radical for the program's director, Vernon Leslie. "In 1968," Hyde has recalled, "there was almost no real black consciousness in British Honduras. The Opposition NIP was really 'Afro-Saxon' at its core, whereas all the ruling PUP kept referring to was the Mayan past."

At age 21, Hyde became president of the new United Black Association for Development (UBAD). Although UBAD was incorporated on February 9, 1969, it had coalesced from earlier gatherings. With no training in business or journalism, Hyde took $250 from UBAD members and laid the foundation for *Amandala*, along with Ismail Shabazz.

In early 1969, Hyde was invited to go with Said Musa, Assad Shoman, Silky Stuart and Lionel del Valle to meet George Price at his office. According to Hyde, Price was curious to know if any of the rising stars in the political ferment might be suitable and willing to serve as PUP candidates in the upcoming Belize Town Board elections.

The meeting with Price did not immediately bear fruit. Hyde ended up doing most of his fighting in court, not in the streets or at the ballot box.

He needed to have a perch somewhere. Unemployed for a year and a half, acquitted of sedition, Hyde took a teaching job at Wesley College in September of 1971. At 24, still politically naïve and desperate, Hyde didn't fully anticipate why he was being welcomed into Wesley College, an institution associated with the National Independence Party. He agreed to an alliance between his nascent organization, the UBAD, and the NIP, only to get caught in a power struggle between NIP's Philip Goldson and Dean Lindo, who had challenged Goldson for party leadership in 1969 and lost.

Lindo's People's Democratic Movement (PDM) boycotted the UBAD/NIP alliance for the 1971 Belize Town Board election. The PUP was elected yet again. UBAD/NIP received 38 percent of the vote.

When Goldson left Belize to study law in London, his NIP melded with the PDM and the Liberal Party to form the United Democratic Party. The new UDP leader Lindo decided that prideful Hyde, a potential rival, would be more dangerous inside the UDP tent than out of it. Having supported Goldson, Hyde was left out in the cold, even though he had received more votes in the 1971 Town Board election than any other UBAD/NIP candidate.

Hyde also felt like an outsider in the PUP camp. "The problem I had with the PUP was their over-emphasis in the Maya past, and ignorance of our African heritage. The PUP was so backward in 1970 that they banned Nina Simone's 'Young, Gifted and Black' from Radio Belize, the government-controlled monopoly radio station. So this was the type of disrespect for blackness that UBAD had to confront in 1970."

UBAD was a cultural movement at its outset, but veered into politics in 1970 when it ran a political party for four years, running a single candidate—Hyde—who gained only 89 votes in the Collet Division in the 1974 election, much to the delight of his UDP rivals. But those votes were enough to help the PUP candidate defeat the UDP candidate by one vote.

Hyde is still getting the last laugh. His son Cordel became a cabinet minister in the PUP's turn-of-the-century administration and, above all else, Evan X Hyde endures. Since 1974, Hyde's UBAD "Kremandala" movement has essentially functioned as a business consortium. Hyde became the first board chairman of KREM Radio, the first privately owned, commercial radio station in Belize.

In 2002, Evan X Hyde, after 40 years as an agitator, was elected as the chairman of the University of Belize, whereupon the UDP questioned his qualifications. Typically, Hyde challenged his critics head-on in *Amandala*. "I did not seek the notoriety which descended upon me beginning in late 1968," he wrote. "It is not that I am taken up with myself. This is how I make my living—telling stories."

Chapter 15: Free at Last

The birth of Belize occurred on June 1, 1973. On that day Belizeans formally shed the Spanish noun *Honduras* and the adjective *British*. On that day they were able to rise in the morning and call one another Belizeans. They had taken control of their own self-definition.

Belmopan became the new inland capital—an unimpressive development, easy to deride. But for George Price, it represented a new start, the challenge of making a destiny unencumbered by colonialism. And that was enough.

Politically, Belize became fully independent on September 21, 1981. In accordance with protocol, the Duke of Kent showed up to represent the Queen. Everyone had anticipated the event would be slated for September 10, in keeping with the annual celebration for the Battle of St. George's Caye, but Price chose the twenty-first. "I like magic numbers," he has said. "Three. Two and one make three. The Trinity."

George Price spoke for only seven minutes: three-and-a-half minutes in English, three-and-a-half minutes in Spanish. Belize joined the United Nations and became a fully independent member of the Commonwealth of Nations, with the Queen as its ceremonial head. Of 54 nations to gain Commonwealth membership in the 20th century, Belize was admitted fourth-to-last, followed only by St. Christopher (St. Kitts) and Nevis in 1983; Brunei Darussalam in 1984; and Namibia in 1990.

Belize introduced a social security system, but the future of its economy was largely still in foreign hands. Approximately 80 percent of the privately owned land in Belize—about 40 percent of the country—was owned by US nationals and US corporations. Americans had purchased the Belize Estate and Produce Company (BEC) just prior to independence.

In addition to United Brands, formerly the United Fruit Company, other major American investors in Belize after independence included Coca-Cola/Minute Maid (land ownership), Chase Manhattan (interest in Atlantic Bank), Hershey Foods (cacao), Texaco and Esso (petroleum), Yalbac (ranching), Prosser Fertilizer, Ramada Inns and Williamson Industries (assembling Dickie's Jeans). In 1981, roughly 60 percent of exports went to the United States; 35 percent of imports came from the US.

United Democratic Party

The UDP melded with the first major opposition to the PUP, the National Independence Party (NIP), in 1973. Since then the UDP and the PUP have been as inseparable as the rival characters in *Spy vs. Spy* comics.

The simple notion that the UDP is right of centre and pro-business, and the PUP is left of centre and pro-labour, is useful but not reliable. For instance, it was the UDP that extended diplomatic recognition to the People's Republic of China and the left-wing Sandinistas in Nicaragua; they didn't support the US ouster of General Manuel Noriega in Panama. It has been the PUP that has welcomed Taiwan into Belize.

Like the Democrats and Republicans in the United States, the PUP and UDP have monopolized the political marketplace, leaving little room for any new party. It's a formula for stability or stagnation, whichever way you want to look at it. Each party tries to undo, as much as outdo, the other. In 1997, for instance, having gained power a second time, the UDP managed to transfer valuable land at the Bel-China Bridge for its new party headquarters. In 2002, PUP's attorney general successfully argued that the land on which the UDP's offices stand belongs to the government of Belize, not the UDP. A compromise was worked out. At its outset, the UDP had affiliations with the United Black Association for Development (UBAD) to confront the "undefeated national juggernaut," but UBAD's Evan X Hyde later converted to the PUP.

The rise of power for the UDP was arduous. In 1979, confident of their first victory, the UDP had victory headlines printed in advance only to fall prey to the wily Price yet again. Theodore Aranda replaced UDP leader Lindo. Manuel Esquivel, a science teacher, took over from Aranda in 1982. He would serve two terms as prime minister, heading the party until 1998. Dean Oliver Barrow, a lawyer and a nephew of the first UDP leader, Dean Lindo, brought the UDP into the new millennium.

It took 11 years for the UDP to rise to the top. The first democratic transition of power occurred in 1984 when it swept 21 of 28 seats in an expanded house of assembly. Price had run in his traditional Freetown Division and lost. Derek Aikman, an energetic orator who had attended college in the United States and served as a page in the US Senate, achieved the greatest political upset in Belizean political history. He turned the tide against Price partly by winning a legal case that claimed approximately 60 names on the voters list were bogus. The UDP was able to infer Price's long-time supremacy was not entirely earned. The UDP would make similar claims that the PUP was rigging the voters' lists in 2003.

Aikman's detractors later suggested he had some help from the United States. In '84, when American television became widely accessible, Belizeans were able to receive Chicago-based WGN.

Belizeans became ardent followers of the Chicago Cubs. After his election victory, Aikman was able to arrange a visit by popular Cubs outfielder Gary Matthews, on leave from the Cubs' training camp in Arizona. If the UDP has had some supportive linkage with the American embassy, it would not be surprising: George Price's refusal to support Ronald Reagan's invasion of Grenada could have cost him the 1984 election.

It was Price's first election loss since 1944. Indefatigable, at age 65 he pledged to rebuild his party. Although he would no longer have access to his battered government Land Rover with the Belizean flag fluttering on the hood, he could always borrow a car from his brother-in-law. He would continue to type policy papers on the reverse side of old campaign flyers. It was all for the best. "The election showed the world what we know about democracy," said Price. "We are gracious losers but in five years time we know the people will make us winners once again. I feel like a great burden has been removed from my shoulders. I'll be much freer now to tend to the job of rebuilding the party."

Having lost in the Fort George division to his perennial rival Dean Lindo, PUP's Education and Economic Development Minister Said Musa made clear his designs on the PUP leadership. "We came over as old and tired," Musa said. "Corruption was creeping into the government and the leader was not dealing effectively with it."

Manuel Esquivel, the second-ever prime minister of Belize, had ties with the defunct Liberal Party, but he was a relative neophyte in politics. The UDP quickly fell under the sway of the American embassy. A Voice of America transmitter was installed in Punta Gorda soon after his victory. The number of Americans at the embassy in Belize City greatly increased during his first tenure, as did the presence of Peace Corps volunteers.

In 1987, the UDP created the Security and Intelligence Service (SIS), a secret service agency. Help from the American International Development (AID), whose headquarters in Belize were located next to the American embassy, peaked in 1985 and 1986. Between 1983 and 1989, mainly when the UDP was in power, Belize received more than $94 million in US economic assistance—with strings attached. As much as possible, American funds had to be used to purchase American goods and services.

Counter-narcotics operations were boosted by $2.5 million in Foreign Military Sales and the training of some special officers in the US under the auspices of the International Military Education and Training program.

The UDP came under heavy criticism when it shut down the country's post-secondary educational institution, Belize College of Arts, Sciences and Technology (BELCAST), created in 1978, and replaced it with an affiliation with the University College of Belize, a two-year, American-based college program administered by Ferris State University of Grand Rapids, Michigan. The UDP even waived its "sovereign privileges and immunities" so that any disputes arising from the unusual arrangement would be settled within the Michigan Court of Claims.

The impression that Belize was only making itself ripe for American pickings was complicated by complaints that Peace Corps workers were taking away local jobs. It didn't help when the former head of the American AID Mission, Neboysha Brashish, was convicted for unduly using his influence to secure jobs and contracts for close family members. US Ambassador to Belize Malcolm R. Barneby also caused a stir in 1988 when he stepped down in order to become a "consultant" for the purchase of 700,000 acres in northeast Belize.

Some of the major business players at the time included Santiago Castillo, Nestor Vasquez and the seventh-generation Belizean Barry Bowen, owner of the Chan Chich Lodge, Coca-Cola franchise distributor and Belikin Beer magnate. Bowen's father had started Crystal Bottling Works. Barry Bowen began brewing Belikin beer in 1971. His business interests expanded to include the Belize Aquaculture Project (shrimp farm) and the Gallon Jug

Experimental Farm that supports his "green" rainforest coffee project. He also supported the publication of a superb collection of Belize photos by Thor "Bushman Ollie" Janson called *Belize, Land of the Free by the Carib Sea*.

Some of Esquivel's supporters had trading rivalries among themselves. After rising star Derek Aikman helped to oust Dean Lindo as UDP party chairperson in 1988, party solidarity sagged. Lindo was aligned with Housing Minister Hubert Elrington and Minister of Foreign Affairs Dean Barrow, who would ultimately succeed Esquivel as party leader. In Belize, politics is always complicated by the influence by oligarchic and monied families that include the Youngs, Urbinas, Bowmans, Espats, Estephans, Perdomos, Roes, Menas, Bedrans, Castillos, Feinsteins, Godreys and Zabanehs, plus the banker Lord Michael Ashcroft.

PUP Again

In September 1989, Prime Minister Esquivel was 44 years old; George Price was 70. Price won the national election by a very slim 15-13 margin. The PUP quickly dismantled SIS, the semi-clandestine security system that had repressed dissidents and harassed community activists and PUP members. The UDP had muzzled freedom of the press. Price, the leader once accused of

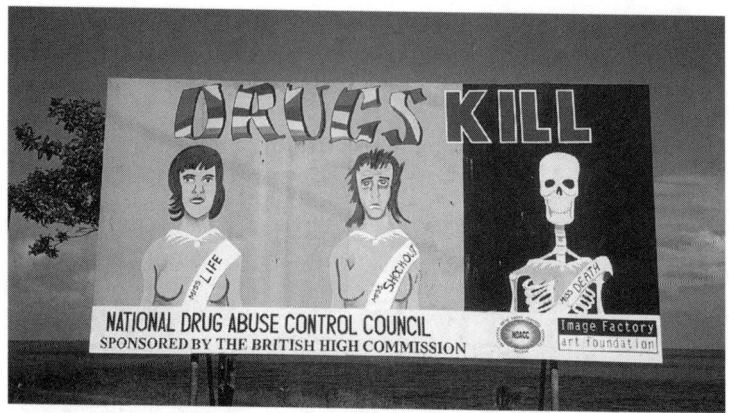

As a transshipment point for cocaine from Colombia to the United States, Belize is a haven for a new breed of offshore pirates with cell phones. *Twigg photo*.

hogging the government airwaves for the PUP, now legislated reduced government control of media and loosened libel laws. He vowed to stop the hugely unpopular practice of selling Belizean passports, began to dismantle ties with Ferris College in Michigan and tightened restrictions on property sales to foreigners (including the eventual termination of the lease facilitating the Voice of America relay station at Orange Point).

Predictably, as soon as the PUP nudged its way back into Belmopan, the American AID assistance dropped to $7 million in 1990. The PUP nonetheless maintained education as a high priority, raising its budget allocation to roughly 17 percent in the 1990s—compared to 3.3 percent in 1930 or 8 percent in 1951. Also in 1990, in keeping with its Belize First mandate, the PUP decreed that the leader of the Belize Defence Forces must be a Belizean.

Based at the Price Barracks near the Goldson Airport, the BDF was formed in anticipation of independence in 1981 as a paramilitary merger of the Belize Volunteer Guard and Police Special Forces. It co-ordinated anti-drug smuggling and border surveillance. It had always been commanded by British officers and trained by British, American and Canadian advisors. The extent to which the BDF became a puppet of American foreign policy during the first Esquivel terms has yet to be fully disclosed.

Allegations have been made that the CIA was running a cocaine operation out of the Belize airport to help finance their Contra campaign against the Sandinista government of Nicaragua—back in the days of Oliver North. The newspaper *Amandala* has suggested crack cocaine via Belize was the basis for the outbreak of a cocaine epidemic among blacks in South Central Los Angeles.

In 1990, the new PUP government replaced the Dangerous Drugs Act of 1980 with the Misuse of Drugs Act to stiffen penalties and create its National Drug Abuse Control Council. Minor trafficking offences called for fines of up to $12,500 and jail terms of five to ten years. More serious drug trafficking brought fines of

$50,000 or else three times the street value of illegal drugs that were seized, plus seven to 14 years in jail. This legislation also allowed the PUP government to seize vehicles and profits.

No matter which party reached Belmopan, policing in Belize was a perennial election issue. The high murder rate, low wages, gang warfare, corruption and poor training had combined to make the reputation of the civic Belize Police Force (BPF) more than a little shaky.

Topsy-Turvy

Sensing tough times ahead, George Price called an election 18 months earlier than was necessary in 1993. On June 30, 1993, the UDP squeaked to victory with a slim 16-13 margin.

House of Representatives

	1979	1984	1989	1993	1998
PUP	12	7	15	13	26
UDP	6	21	13	16	*3

with Philip Goldson's National Alliance for Belizean Rights party

Needing money in 1993, the government auctioned 450 parcels of land to Americans to gain an infusion of $4 million and opened traditional Maya territories in Toledo District to Malaysian logging companies.

The second UDP tenure ran its full five-year limit. The party was running scared and was crushed on October 27, 1998, losing all but three of 29 seats in the House of Representatives after Said Musa had replaced George Price as PUP leader in November 1996.

Chapter 16: The New Millennium

A new millennium required a new man. On August 28, 1998, the third-ever prime minister of Belize, Said Wilbert Musa, regained power for the PUP when his party won 26 seats compared to only 3 for the UDP. Percentages of the vote were 59.2 percent for the PUP and 40.8 percent for the UDP. Musa asked Price to serve in cabinet as senior minister but Musa no longer walked in the shadow of the nation's founder. More intellectual than Price, Musa was just as likely to take advice from his long-time ally Assad Shoman.

Campaign poster for Prime Minister Said Musa, a liberal-minded lawyer elected for a second term in 2003.

Born in San Ignacio, Cayo District on March 19, 1944, Musa was the son of Hamid Musa, of Palestinian origin. From a colonial backwater and a family of modest means, Said Musa was able to graduate from St. John's College and study at Manchester

University where he attained an Honours degree in Law in 1966. The following year he brought his family to Belize where he served as a circuit magistrate and a Crown Counsel in the Public Prosecutor's Office.

Musa entered private practice with Shoman, then with Lawrence Balderamos. With Shoman he helped create the People's Action Committee (PAC) and the Society for the Promotion of Education and Research (SPEAR). He joined the PUP in 1974. As an unsuccessful PUP candidate that year, he was appointed as a senator for the 1974–79 term. In 1979 he was elected to the legislature from the Fort George division of Belize City. Prior to his ascension to PUP leadership and the job of prime minister in 1998, Musa served as Attorney General and Minister for Education, Foreign Affairs, Economic Development, plus Sports and Culture.

Manchester native Joan Millicent married Said Musa in England. As a registered nurse specializing in ophthalmic nursing, she taught at the Belize School of Nursing and has strongly supported the Belize Council for the Visually Impaired. As well as being a strong advocate of literacy, she served as president of the Belize National Women's Commission.

Status of Women

The status of women in Belize ranked 58th out of 174 countries in 2000 according to the UN Human Development Index. Ongoing efforts to improve health and the status of women have had a long way to go.

Women were 98 percent disenfranchised in the 1930s. In 1950, the minimum age for women voters was lowered from 30 to 21. Women could not sit as jurors until 1972. In its 1975 constitution, the PUP created the United Women's Group and Women's Marshals, but the subordination of women was deeply ingrained. Kathy Esquivel, wife of the former UDP prime minister and first president of the National Women's Commission, claimed women were under-represented politically because "women are never the people to whom political favours are owed."

In 2000, women headed 24 percent of Belize's 52,000 households, about one-half of which were two-bedroom homes occupied by five or more people. At the same time the proportion of women in the workforce had increased by 32 percent since 1991.

Novelist Zee Edgell is the first Belizean writer to be widely read outside Belize and Governor General Dame Minita Gordon served from independence in 1981 until 1993, but for the most part women's roles have been restricted to the domestic realm. The most noteworthy exception is lawyer Lisa Shoman, who has served as an ambassador to the United States, permanent representative to the Organization of American States and high commissioner to Canada—among other responsibilities. Born in Belize in 1964, she was educated at Florida University, the University of the West Indies and Norman Manley Law School. Other important and respected women of Belize include Gwendolyn Lizarraga, Jane Usher and Dolores Balderamos Garcia. In 2003, Sylvia Flores replaced George Price as minister of defence.

Zee Edgell became the first Belizean writer to reach an international audience with the publication of her first novel, *Beka Lamb*.

One of the most famous cases in British Honduran legal history concerns the plight of Nora Parham, the first and only woman to be hanged to death. She was hung on June 5, 1963, for the murder of her common-law husband, Ketchell Trapp, a policeman who had abused her and other women. Nora Parham had eight children, all boys, and she was pregnant at the time of her conviction. The hanging was delayed until she could give birth. Citizens circulated a petition with 2,000 signatures, calling for clemency, but the British legal system was impervious to public opinion.

In 1979, activists including Cynthia and Zoila Ellis founded the Belize Organization for Women and Development (BOWAND) to broaden awareness of women's issues. In 1985, Cynthia Ellis and Regina Martínez subsequently created the Belize Rural Women's Association with its quarterly newspaper, *The Belize Woman*. Dorla Bowman founded Belize Women Against Violence (WAV). "Domestic violence," according to the Ministry of Human Development, Women and Children and Civil Society during Musa's first term, "continues to plague our society today more than ever before." Jewel Patton-Quallo spearheaded the Family Life Association. Dr. Marla Holder spearheaded the opening of an emergency facility for victims of abuse in 1998, since renamed SAVES-Marla's House of Hope. SAVES stands for Sexual Abuse Victims Education and Support Program.

The majority of women, until recently, had their first child while in their teens. In Belize, a nation brought to independence by a devout Catholic, the illegality of abortion has had severe consequences. It's not entirely surprising to discover terse news bulletins from Love FM about criminalized young women: "A woman previously charged with concealment of birth is now charged with murder. Police upgraded the charge against 24-year-old Juliana Choc of Santa Elena Village, Toledo, following the discovery of a newborn in a pit latrine in Punta Gorda Town in April of this year."

A study conducted in the 1990s by the non-profit Alan Guttmacher Institute of New York has claimed 80 percent of the estimated five million abortions annually conducted in Latin America were illegal and therefore life-threatening to the mother. Tom Barry of the Inter-Hemispheric Education Resource Center claimed more than 15 percent of women admitted to hospital in Belize City during the 1980s suffered from injuries sustained by illegal abortions.

With an election in the works in 2003, Prime Minister Musa promised to provide at least 8,100 Belizean women over 65 with social security pensions, vowing it was time to recognize the work of "women in the home who take care of the children, who clean that house, who cook that food, who really make sure that their things run from Sunday to Sunday, that make sure the children get to school on time, that they have clothes, that they have shoes, that they have food."

Health

In 2001 the World Heath Organization ranked Belize 69th out of 190 countries for health standards. (France ranked first; Myanmar/Burma ranked last.) But among the Caribbean and Central American states only Guyana had a worse AIDS infection rate in 1991, according to the UN Program on HIV/AIDS. In 2005, National AIDS Commission chairperson Dolores Balderamos Garcia estimated at least 2 percent of the population had HIV/AIDS, twice the rate of Honduras and Guatemala. According to the Pan American Health Organization, more than 1.7 million people in Latin America are living with HIV/AIDS, with Brazil accounting for more than one-third of that total.

Schooling has been mandatory until age 14 and has remained mainly in the hands of religious groups. Catholic and Christian fundamentalist schools have not forcefully encouraged condom use or sex education. "I go begging for condoms," said a community health nurse in Seine Bight. The government cited 2,000 documented HIV cases in 2002 but the stigma attached to the disease makes such estimates questionable. Cabinet responded by reducing sales taxes for HIV/AIDS medications and enhanced the National AIDS Program in its recurrent budget. Treatment procedures in Belize have sometimes been complicated by interventions of "herb specialists" who attempt folk remedies.

Turn-of-the-century life expectancy in Belize was 69 years for men and 73.5 for women. The infant mortality rate was 25 per 1,000 births; the birth rate was 32 per 1,000; the death rate was only five per 1,000. Children were born out of wedlock as often as not, especially in Belize City.

According to the Labour Act, Chapter 297, nobody was obliged to work more than 45 hours per week, but some doctors were working as much as 250 extra hours per month, more than twice the legally required hours.

Infusion of contracted Cuban doctors within the Cuban Medical Brigade has greatly enhanced the health care system, but there are always *problemas*. In 2001, at least 10 Cuban doctors married in Belize. "These doctors come to Belize pretending to do charity work," one Belizean doctor complained in 2002, "then they marry the Belizean men or women. These people use our Belizean men and women as a convenience to get their legal documents. Most of them are already married in Cuba, so they commit bigamy here in Belize."

With a Belizean passport, it's possible to reach the United States, where some 70,000 Belizeans choose to reside. Of Belizean emigrants near the turn of the century, 84 percent went to the United States and just 4.6 percent went to the rest of Central America. Only 2.7 percent went to Mexico. Of people emigrating from Belize, 40 percent were from the Belize (City) District. Early in the new millennium Senior Police Superintendent Bernard Lino was investigated for irregularities in the issuance of Belize Immigration documents but was later exonerated on the grounds that his signature had been forged.

Crimes and Punishments

Increasingly Belizeans have demanded harsher measures to combat crime. Led by the Belize Chamber of Commerce and

Industry, 1,000 Belizeans attended a rally in 2002 "to express solidarity and to protest the crippling effect of rampant crime holding our society hostage." More than 100 businesses closed for a one-day protest against the escalation of violent crime, much of which was tied to the cocaine trade. Heroin was also a problem. A tip-off led to the country's biggest-ever heroin bust in April 2001. Four men in a white taxi near the bus depot were nabbed with 2.8 kilograms of heroin taped around their waists. It was a typical situation: Hondurans had been hired by a Colombian to transport the heroin into Belize.

"The truth of the matter," said Prime Minister Musa, "is that in our country we are faced with particular problems over senseless cold-blooded murders and the people are calling for action." The penalty for murder in Belize was death by hanging, but nobody had been hung since the 1980s. Hattieville Prison was overflowing with killers. In November of 2001, Andrew Kelly, 25, was convicted for killing Yan Li Chan, a shopkeeper, making him the fourth Belizean to be convicted of murder in one month. In February 2003, there were four separate violent deaths over one weekend.

Police Station, Belize City. *Twigg photo.*

Belize shocked the European Union by drafting a constitutional amendment, in July 2002, to restrict appeals to the (British) Privy Council for Class A murder cases, thereby clearing the way for executions again. At the same time the Pentagon was scaling back its $19 billion anti-narcotics budget to concentrate on terrorism, leaving Belize on the frontlines against the Colombian drug cartels.

"My response to the European Union," said Musa, "[is to] assist us in fighting crime, perhaps then the attitude of the Belizean people might change when they see the world is helping us." Jamaica's Prime Minister P.J. Patterson had just won re-election by vowing to tackle the crime wave that was threatening to ruin his island's tourism industry. Barbados was making much the same move. Some criminals were being sent back to the Caribbean from the United States. Few families were unaffected by crime and violence. The PUP tightened liquor laws in 2001, leading to controversial 2:00 a.m. closures for bars in San Pedro after a teenager from a prominent family was killed by Gurkha special forces soldiers at the infamous Rose Garden brothel outside Belize City, originally built to serve British troops.

This well-known brothel, located on the main highway near the Price Barracks, was originally built to serve British soldiers. They're gone—but not the sex trade. *Twigg photo.*

In the 1980s, British military authorities had dealt with the problem of wandering, rum-riddled Brits by condoning Raul's Rose Garden, conveniently located near the main Price Barracks. The establishment provided dimly lit alcoves for entertaining the soldiers in the back of the building—mere hovels. Most of the young women were Latinas from surrounding countries. British Army medical officers had inspected the sex trade workers for communicable diseases on a regular basis. The nightclub closed when most of the British soldiers left Belize, but reopened again to serve local clientele. Belize has been criticized for its inability to police its growing sex trade.

We Hungry, but Dem Belly Full!

Some Belizeans were disgruntled after the government appeared to fast-track a controversial development project, the Chalillo Dam, against the recommendations of environmentalists inside and outside the country; other Toledo District citizens claimed relief resources were not evenly distributed after Hurricane Iris, but social unrest only became violent on July 30, 2001, during a 12-hour riot at the Orange Walk Tower Hill Toll Bridge.

Angry bus passengers threw stones at Belize Defence Force (BDF) soldiers, injuring two of them, after the commissioner of transport refused to renew permits for the Tillett and Castillo buses to transfer their northern passengers to Belize City. The Tillett family had associations with the UDP.

BDF soldiers in riot gear, armed with M-16 rifles, retaliated with tear gas. One soldier reportedly shot into the crowd. One person took a bullet in the arm, another in the leg. Protesters had armed themselves with sticks, stones and bottles after Commissioner Arthurs ordered buses stopped and emptied around 5:15 a.m. on a Monday, when many commuters were on their way to work.

Bus passengers were venting their frustration because many felt bus fares charged by the country's major bus company,

Novelo's Bus Lines, were too high. Novelo's had acquired control of 60-year-old Batty Brothers Bus Services Ltd. and controlled roughly 75 percent of the bus transportation market, operating most of the major runs.

Prime Minister Musa ordered a commission of inquiry. The transport commissioner was judged impervious to suggestions for improvement and ill-suited for his position. As well, the BDF needed to learn modern techniques for control and dispersal of "riot assemblies." Finally, the inquiry process rebuked Amelio Tillett Jr. for defying the non-renewal of his permit by using a charter permit to maintain his run. In April 2002 cabinet directed the Ministry of Transport to establish legal published transit rates by Statutory Instrument. The government admitted the Novelo's bus consortium had, in some cases, charged fares above their maximum permitted rates.

Lord of Belize

Another problem for Musa's government was how to curtail the influence of British peer Lord Michael Ashcroft, executive chairman of Belize Telecommunication Limited (BTL). Dubbed the "Tories' Troublesome Tycoon," Ashcroft once donated £3 million to the Conservative Party in England.

To show its clear support for an incoming alternative to BTL's unpopular telecommunications monopoly, the International Telecommunications Company (INTELCO), Musa's government issued press releases on an almost weekly basis touting the generosity of INTELCO for donating 5,000 computers as part of the Internet for Schools Project.

Lord Aschroft had the means and the motive to fund the rival UDP against the PUP. UDP leader Dean Barrow's former wife was a BTL lawyer and Ashcroft's Belize Bank interests were represented by Barrow's law firm, Barrow and Williams. But Barrow had to be careful because neither BTL nor Ashcroft was popular. Lord Ashcroft, when he was Conservative Party treasurer in Britain, had incited ridicule for requesting the formal title Lord of Belize. "Belize runs through my bones," Ashcroft said, "from my schooldays onwards and all through my life."

Economic Woes

In 2000, the trade deficit grew due to dropping export prices for sugar and bananas. "Unhappily, Belize is too small," said Musa. "We cannot attract competitive privatization. We are dictated to by the World Bank and IMF. At times it pays us to borrow on the commercial market and pay 10 percent or 11 percent."

The prime minister needed to inject dollars, change and optimism. It was akin to pushing a boulder uphill. But his resolution and his footing held. In a country with only three paved roadways in 2001, he travelled extensively nevertheless—on 2,500 km of roads, only 25 percent paved—to fly the flags of patriotism and hope.

The despised monopoly of the BTL telecommunications network led to expensive and poorly maintained service. *Twigg photo.*

The government claimed it had attracted BZ$800 million in private sector investments between 1988 and 2003. The chief development was the creation of 1,000 more hotel rooms. Belize also developed a BZ$8 million tilapia fish farm project in association with Fresh Catch Belize Ltd. This was the first private sector project jointly funded by the Inter-American Development Bank and the Latin American Agribusiness Development Corporation. It was optimistically expected to yield 4,000 tons of fish per year in the wake of the Cherax Belize Ltd. closure in 1999.

New aquaculture businesses would operate in areas called

Export Processing Zones. Projections made by the Ministry of Agriculture and Fisheries trumpeted the "possibility" of Belize increasing its shrimp yield from three million pounds in 1998 to as much as 42.3 million pounds for export by 2005, creating more than 1,000 jobs and almost BZ$300 million in foreign exchange earnings. Belize was also developing new papaya, pepper, honey and soybean industries. Acreage for aquaculture doubled. A Korean company was exporting tiles. A Taiwanese company was assembling electronics. Small steps, but progress.

The relationship between Taiwan and Belize was multifaceted and controversial. The contributions of the Taiwanese government enabled Belize to undertake major projects such as the renovation of its former penitentiary to create a National Museum and the development of a Regional Language Centre at the University of Belize. Minister of Works Vildo Marin unveiled a plaque to declare the opening of the 17.4-mile Section 4 of the Southern Highway Upgrading Project—yet another project partly funded by a loan from the International Co-operation Development Fund of Taiwan. But Belizeans were suspicious of Taiwanese generosity. The arrival of Taiwanese Premier Yu Shyi-kun with a 35-member entourage in August 2002 was not greeted as good news by the man on the street.

Taiwan's influence has resulted in some niche speciality exports including mushroom powder from the Corozal area and the establishment of a hybrid-rice-seed-making farm in Blue Creek. In addition, the Taiwanese encouraged Belize to produce Sea Island cotton for export.

Pushing That Boulder

Nobody could accuse Said Musa of not trying.

Musa undertook a tour of the country to explain a proposed accord with Guatemala. With quiet poise, he continued to deal with international alarm about the Chalillo Dam project, public insecurity about crime, Guatemala border negotiations and the after-effects of four major storms in three years. He personally investigated the violence that emerged from the Tower Hill bus riot, visiting the wounded in the hospital and taking measures "to ensure there is no monopoly situation" in the transportation business. He also dealt with international flak when his government sought to rescind the ability of convicted murderers to seek repeal of the death penalty at the Privy Council level.

In his 2003–2004 budget speech, Musa noted the United States' economy grew a meagre 2.4 percent in 2002; Europe's growth was expected at around 1 percent; Japan's economy would shrink half a percent; and Canada's projected 3.4 percent increase was ranked as stellar. "In this ocean of lacklustre economic performance and despair, Belize makes its mark by posting a formidable 4.4 percent growth in GDP for 2002. Belizeans will be proud to know that we are beneficiaries of a growing BZ$1.7 billion economy, up by over BZ$100 million from 2001."

Musa claimed unemployment had dropped to 9.1 percent from 11 percent in 2001. "For the first time in modern Belize, the domestic overdraft of Central Government was not used, showing a positive $2.1 million, with additional deposits of BZ$22 million at the end of 2002." He claimed the PUP had lowered the average lending rate from 16.3 percent to 14.5 percent.

Musa's national tour ended at the new University of Belize, established in Belmopan along with the Regional Language Centre and the George Price Centre for Peace and Development. "My government came into office on a firm commitment of zero tolerance for impropriety, corruption and abuse of power and during the last four years, we have worked tirelessly to deliver on this solemn commitment," Musa said.

Musa Rewarded

The people of Belize went to the polls on March 5, 2003. For the first time since Belize gained independence in 1981, the incumbent party was re-elected. The PUP won handily, taking 22 seats; the UDP won seven. It wasn't the landslide victory of 1998 when the PUP won all but three seats, but for Musa it was a vote of confidence that no other leader of Belize had had since George Price in the 1970s. The turnout of 99,560 voters out of a possible 126,261 registered electors showed the extent to which elections are taken seriously in Belize. But civil discord and economic problems plagued Musa's second term, leading to a severe decline in his popularity by 2006. Belizeans were able to buy shares in their country's telephone system, the talks for possibly resolving territorial disputes with Guatemala resumed and cruise ships injected some tourist dollars, but levels of violence and poverty persisted.

A new political party called VIP (Vision Inspired by the People) ran a full slate of candidates for Belmopan City Council elections in 2005.

Seeds of Distrust

In 1937, the new President of Guatemala, Jorge Ubico, offered to drop Guatemala's claim if Britain paid 400,000 pounds. In effect, he was offering to sell British Honduras, or asking for a bribe. Ubico suggested President Roosevelt of the United States should be asked to arbitrate when Britain decided not to sell territory it already possessed. Britain declined the arbitration proposal, too.

In 1939, when Britain was diverted by Hitler, Guatemala announced it was nullifying the treaty of 1859. In 1945, to further assert its territorial claims, Guatemala defined "Belice" as its 23rd Department in its new constitution. This led to grandstanding by two Guatemalan politicians.

In 1958, President Miguel Ydígoras Fuentes carried a copy of the Guatemalan constitution across the border at the remote Benque Viejo police station and asked for permission to proceed into Belize. Not to be outdone, one of his political opponents, Francisco Sagastume, led 19 followers across the border at Pueblo Viejo in 1962, claiming he was liberating the territory. Half of the Segastume invasion party proceeded to San Antonio where Sagastume burned a Union Jack and photos of Queen Elizabeth and the Duke of Edinburgh. The local Maya, many of whom had fled Guatemalan oppression, were less than hospitable. Sagastume drove toward Punta Gorda but ran out of fuel. He and a Belizean associate were arrested and sentenced to 10 years' hard labour. They served only nine months before their sentences were commuted.

Talks resumed in 1961 between Guatemala and Britain only—and George Price protested. Guatemala repeatedly broke off border talks in 1962 after Belizeans were accorded observer status at negotiations.

When the Belizean weightlifting team was invited to San Salvador for the 1962 Central American championships, the Guatemalan team refused to accept Belize as a country. Costa Rica and Honduras voted for acceptance of Belize; Guatemala and Nicaragua voted to oust them. El Salvador, as the host nation, didn't vote. The Belizeans refused an offer to compete as individuals, so the Belizean weightlifters didn't compete.

George Price rejected an irritating proposal from Guatemala to make Belize into an "associated state." Guatemala broke off diplomatic relations with Britain and threatened war with Belize in 1963. Price went to London to plead the Belizean case. Diplomatic relations between Guatemala and the United Kingdom were truncated when Belize gained more internal self-government. Britain agreed to allow President Lyndon Johnson to appoint an American lawyer, Bethuel M. Webster, to mediate the dispute in 1965. His draft treaty in 1968, now known as the Webster Proposal, was so completely in favour of Guatemala, making Belize City into a duty-free port, that it had to be completely rejected by Belizeans.

After Guatemala again broke off its negotiations with Great Britain in 1972, Britain sent 8,000 troops and an aircraft carrier to undertake amphibious exercises. In response, Guatemala assembled troops at the border.

The name of British Honduras was changed to Belize in 1973, prior to independence. It was one way of testing the sovereignty waters without declaring fully-fledged nationhood. Premier Price took Belize's case to the United Nations in 1975. During a December vote, the General Assembly recognized the right of the Belizean people to self-determination by a vote of 110 in favour, 9 against and 16 abstentions. During this vote, Cuba became the first Latin American country to support Belize.

In 1976 Price went to Panama and befriended Jamaican Foreign Minister Dudley Thompson. This led to a little-appreciated meeting with Tanzanian Foreign Minister Salim Ahmed Salim. It was the Tanzanian who encouraged Price to seek an international stage for his independence movement, to form a coalition among the anti-colonialists. The Caribbean and Commonwealth leaders who became allies included Guyana's President Forbes Burnham, Jamaica's future Prime Minister P.J. Patterson, Barbadian Prime Minister Errol Barrow, President Julius Nyerere of Tanzania, Fidel Castro of Cuba and Kenneth Kaunda of Zambia.

Most importantly, General Omar Torrijos of Panama became a Belize supporter at the Summit Meeting of the Non-Aligned Countries held in Colombo, Sri Lanka, in August 1976. Torrijos understood Price's situation full well: he was trying to regain sovereignty of the Panama Canal Zone. Torrijos provided crucial support at the next UN General Assembly session that discussed Belize. Panama became the first Central American country to vote against Guatemala's claim.

In 1977, when President Jimmy Carter condemned the human rights record of Guatemala, suspending military aid to the butchers in control, Israel responded by sending military advisors and weapons to Guatemala. The CIA was clearly at odds with the President. When the Sandinistas overthrew the Nicaraguan dictatorship of Anastasio Debayle Somoza in 1979, the leftist Sandinistas expressed unequivocal support for Belize. President José

López Portillo of Mexico also became a staunch ally. In 1980 the Organization of American States (OAS) overwhelmingly supported Belize. This prompted the United States to finally jump onto the independence bandwagon for Belize.

Just prior to Belize achieving independence, a last-ditch proposal to resolve the border dispute was initialled on March 11, 1981. Ultra-right forces in Guatemala and anti-PUP forces in Belize labelled it a sell-out. Violent demonstrations resulted in four deaths in Belize, plus property damages to PUP leaders and their families. A state of emergency was declared.

After independence was attained on September 21, 1981, Prime Minister Price addressed the UN General Assembly on September 25. "Let the people of Belize remain a nation in waiting no longer. In this, the year of the 15th anniversary of the Declaration on the Granting of Independence to Colonial Countries and Peoples, let not a people who have struggled for national independence for 25 years, and who have been self-governing for twelve years, be condemned to further unnecessary delay in achieving their just goal."

Unfortunately, the most vicious of the Guatemalan military dictators, General Efraín Montt, seized power on March 23, 1982. It has been estimated that Britain spent $18 million annually in the 1980s to maintain its military presence in Belize, roughly double the defence budget of Belize. When Marco Vinicio Cerezo Arévalo gained power in Guatemala as a civilian in 1985, a new Guatemalan constitution was created, but seeds of distrust and fear had spread widely. Communal Mayas on both sides of the hoped-for border were branded as communists by the regimes supported by Ronald Reagan's White House.

The border dispute continued, exacerbated by countless accusations of trespassing, for the next 15 years or so.

A glimmer of sanity prevailed in 2000 when both sides agreed to accept a "line of adjacency," based on the de facto border, in order to deter cross-border squatting. In May 2001, there was a major breakthrough when a delegation from the Belize Chamber of Commerce went to Guatemala and signed a memorandum of agreement to promote trade between the two countries. The following month Guatemala sponsored Belize to become a member of the Central America Federation of Chambers of Commerce.

But on November 22, 2001, in the San Vicente area of remote Toledo, a patrol of Belizean police and BDF soldiers shot and killed three Guatemalan men armed with machetes. All were named Ramirez; all were allegedly 150 yards within Belizean territory. According to a swiftly issued press release from Belmopan, Belizean security officers "acted in self-defence in preservation of their lives." Where exactly was the Guatemala/Belize border? For months there had been an ongoing dispute between farmers in the area about alleged encroachments. An inquiry commission spoke with nine Belize Defence Forces soldiers and visited the Ramirez farm to collect testimony from five female witnesses close to the deceased.

Five months later, Chief Magistrate Herbert Lord reiterated that Belizean soldiers had acted "extremely well under the given circumstances." No circumstances were cited but an autopsy report from the Office of the General Prosecutor of Guatemala, "indicated that none of the fatal shots came from behind. None of the deceased were shot in the back."

In May, the government of Belize announced $48,000 in compensation was to be paid to the children of the three dead Guatemalans. This was to be done strictly as a "humanitarian gesture." It was a small price to pay for not stalling delicate talks underway between Belmopan and Guatemala City to possibly resolve the long-standing border dispute.

Guatemalan President Alfonso Portillo visited Belize in February 2002, the first Guatemalan head of state to do so in half a century. "It's a situation which we urgently need to resolve," he said, "and that we will resolve this year...we have the best intentions and the best relations between both governments to resolve the differendum [sic] we have...There are so many things that Belize and Guatemala can do together. Why not form a free trade zone together?"

Neither Portillo or Said Musa wanted to have such a volatile issue decided during an election year. Guatemala and Belizean negotiators agreed on terms for a binational referendum to finally resolve the impasse. OAS facilitators recommended referenda be held in both countries simultaneously on November 30, 2002.

When Pope John Paul II visited Guatemala in 2002, he made a point of providing an audience for Belizean Foreign Affairs Minister Assad Shoman. Prime Minister Musa of Belize traipsed into every corner of Belize to sell the agreement, only to have Guatemala renege on the date planned. OAS Secretary General Gaviria and his facilitators failed to establish an alternate date for the vote.

The Belize/Guatemala border rivalry has few contemporary parallels in both length and complexity. Guatemala has always argued Britain has repeatedly respected Spanish claims to sovereignty in international treaties and Belizeans have always argued Spain has never administered Belize or established permanent settlements. Just as Belizeans prefer to ignore the myriad legalistic points that have fueled Guatemala's aggressive claims, Guatemalans refuse to register the irrefutable evidence that Belizeans unanimously reject affiliation with Guatemala.

But on September 7, 2005, Ambassador Assad Shoman, Chief Negotiator with Guatemala, and Guatemala's Foreign Minister Jorge Briz signed "An Agreement on the Framework of Negotiation and Confidence Building Measures between Belize and Guatemala."

"It is really not good for Guatemala, for Belize, and for the countries of the Americas to have such a dispute continue into the 21st century," said Shoman.

The on-again, off-again political tango between Guatemala

and Belize is of little interest to most tourists—other than the fact that it has complicated travel to and from nearby Tikal—but ongoing hostilities with Guatemala have prevailed in the minds of Belizeans as *the* greatest threat in their lives for more than a century.

Chapter 17: Tourism

The island getaway of San Pedro is mentioned three times in pop singer Madonna's song "La Isla Bonita," with its jingle-like refrain, "All of nature, wild and free." But until she came along, the most famous comment about Belize had been made by Aldous Huxley.

In a dashed-off travel memoir called *Beyond the Mexique Bay*, published just prior to his immigration to the United States in 1937, the English author of *Brave New World* wrote, "If the world had any ends, British Honduras would certainly be one of them."

Of course it's easy to claim that Belize is *still* one of the ends of the earth. The Huxley quotation is seldom supplied in its entirety. "British Honduras is not on the way from anywhere to anywhere else," Huxley continued. "It has no strategic value. It is all but uninhabited and when Prohibition is abolished, the last of its profitable enterprises—the re-export of alcohol by rumrunners who use Belize as a base of operations—will have gone the way of its commerce in logwood, mahogany and chicle.

"Why do we bother to keep this strange little fragment of the Empire? Certainly not from motives of self-interest. Hardly one Englishman in fifty thousand derives any profit from the

Britishness of British Honduras. But *le coeur a ses raisons*. Of these the mere force of habit is the strongest."

Huxley's assessment remained apropos throughout the 1940s and '50s when UFCO vessels sailed to New Orleans on a monthly basis. The Toledo District was only reachable by sea. In the early 1950s, an all-weather road to Dangriga had yet to be completed. British West Indian Airways had weekly flights to Jamaica. Biweekly services could connect travellers to Mexico City via

How tourism was promoted in a 1953 government publication, *British Honduras: Portrait of a Colony*. Author's collection.

Guatemala City, Tegucigalpa and Chetumal. There was a monthly boat to Liverpool and London. The first and only major hotel in Belize for many years was the Fort George Hotel, built by the Colonial Development Corporation. When it opened in 1953, the room rate was $10 per night. In the 1960s, only 11,000 visitors came to Belize annually. Few were tourists. The presiding PUP administration "virtually frowned" on tourism according to a UN report. A representative of the new administration said it was reluctant "to turn Belize into a nation of waiters."

It was the hoteliers on Ambergris Caye who put Belize on the vacation map. In the mid-'60s, Celi McCorkle opened a one-bathroom Holiday Hotel in San Pedro. By century's end there were more than 50 registered hotels in San Pedro and McCorkle was recognized as the first recipient of a new Tourist Minister's Award. The number of foreign visitors to Belize rose to 30,000 in the 1970s, increasing to 64,000 in the 1980s and tripling to 190,000 in the 1990s.

The new UDP administration in 1985 made tourism its second-highest priority; it had ranked seventh under the PUP. When the PUP was re-elected, the big-game hunting associations in the US who had petitioned Belize to open up the country to jaguar hunting were out of luck: the PUP tried to place greater emphasis on ecotourism. The identification with nature, as being integral to the character of Belize, came with independence in 1981. That year a national parks system was envisioned. The remarkable spate of new reserves that were created over a 10-year period, both governmentally and privately, serves as the marketing basis for ecotourism in the new millennium:

1982: Half Moon Caye
1983: Ix Chel Farm and Tropical Education Center (private)
1984: Crooked Tree Wildlife Sanctuary
1985: Community Baboon Sanctuary (private)
1986: Cockscomb Basin Wildlife Sanctuary

1986: Blue Hole National Park
1986: Society Hall Nature Reserve (private)
1987: Hole Chan Marine Park
1987: Rio Bravo Conservation Area (private)
1988: Shipstern Native Reserve (private)
1990: Guanacaste National Park
1990: Bladen Nature Reserve
1990: Monkey Bay Wildlife Sanctuary (private)
1991: Five Blue Lakes National Park
1991: Laughing Bird Caye
1991: Chiquibul National Park
1991: Monkey River Development Area
1991: Manatee Development Area
1991: Corozal District East Development Area
1991: Burrell Boom Development Area

By 2000 Belize was calling itself one of the world's top 10 adventure travel destinations. By 2002, cruise lines such as Carnival, Norwegian and Royal Caribbean were arriving on a year-round basis, making Belize the fastest-growing cruise ship destination in the Caribbean. In his 2003–2004 budget address, Prime Minister Musa reported there were newly scheduled flights by US Air from Charlotte, Air Jamaica from Montego Bay, by Continental from Newark and by American from Miami. Austrian Airlines planned a regular service via Havana. Overnight arrivals had risen by 1.8 percent, resulting in about 200,000 tourists per year.

More than half of the visitors to Belize head to the cayes for snorkelling, fishing, sun and sex, attracted primarily to the Hispanic town of San Pedro on Ambergris Caye, secondarily to Caye Caulker. Madonna, Harrison Ford and Cyndi Lauper were among the celebrities who bunked in at the Victoria House Hotel on Ambergris Caye.

Other famous visitors include Charles Lindbergh (1927, 1929), Princess Margaret (1958), Muhammad Ali (1966), Jacques

Cousteau (1967) and Prince Andrew, Duke of York (2002). Pope John Paul II made a ceremonial visit in 1983, but he never left the airport. Vacationing Canadian Prime Minister Pierre Elliott Trudeau stayed at remote Glover's Reef when he was still married to Margaret Trudeau. Queen Elizabeth was fed stewed gibnut, a large rodent tasting like rabbit, dubbed "the Royal rat" by the London press. Jerry Jeff Walker ("Mr. Bojangles") has hosted an annual music festival. And Tiger Woods has stayed at Cayo Espanto.

Considering the extent of the tourist invasion in the 1990s and the modest amount of facilities, the atmosphere for tourism remained remarkably unspoiled on the islands. Each has its own history. **Tobacco Caye** reputedly attracted Puritan tobacco growers in the 1600s, overseen by Captain Samuel Axe. **Queen's Caye** was named for the daughter of James I, Queen of Bohemia. Smithsonian scientists operate a marine lab on **Carrie Bow Caye**. East of Dangriga, **Man-O-War Caye** is renowned for its colony of frigate birds. The pirate Blackbeard (Edward Teach) found sanctuary on **Water Caye** in 1717, sailing onward to **Sapodilla Caye** to prey on Spanish shipping.

Ambergris Caye, the largest island of Belize, was once a thriving Mayan trading centre. There are several archaeological sites. It was also the focus for sperm whaling, leading to the logical assumption that the name Ambergris Caye must be derived from the secretions of ambergris—"grey amber"—that washed ashore prior to overwhaling. Pirates collected the excrement because oil from it was highly valued for making perfumes. In fact, it is just as likely that Ambergris Caye derives its name from Spanish maps that called the area *Costa de Ambar*—the Amber Coast—because the fossilized resin from trees known as *ambar* was prized for jewellery and medicinal purposes. The island was part of a peninsula, connected to the Yucatán peninsula, until a narrow canal was made by the Maya to facilitate easier trading. Dozens of ships have sunk off Ambergris Caye, including the salvaged HMS *Yeldham* from 1800 and the still-missing *Water Witch*, a British frigate that foundered in 1793, supposedly carrying $2 million worth of gold and silver bars. Formerly claimed by Mexico, the 25-mile-long caye has its hub at San Pedro, where transportation by golf cart is preferred. Some residents claim pirate ancestry. The Belize Agriculture Company first held title to the land. It was sold to a Mr. Welsh and a Mr. Golf in 1842. Mayans fleeing the Caste War took up residence in the 1850s. After a series of owners in the 1860s, Corozal Magistrate James Humes Blake purchased Ambergris Caye at auction for $625 in 1869. Fishing families claimed one of Blake's descendents, Anita Alamilla, was charging exorbitant rents in the mid-1900s. The PUP government eventually surveyed and issued lots to some of the original settlers after Belize became self-governing in 1964.

Caye Caulker was known on early English maps as Cay Corker and as *Cayo Hicaco* by the Spanish, possibly because it was a favoured place for sailors to replenish their cork water bottles, but more likely because boats were often caulked in its protective bay. After Luciano Reyes purchased the island in 1870, he sold lots to a few families whose descendents developed a lobster-fishing industry in the 1920s. Legend has it Captain James Cook introduced lobster traps to Caye Caulker in the late 18th century—which is undoubtedly hokum. Founded in 1960, the island-based Northern Fishermen's Co-operative Society Ltd. became a model for other co-operatives in Belize. Shipbuilding remained integral, as evidenced by displays at the Belize Marine Terminal and Museum. By the turn of the millennium, manatee and rainbow parrot fish were still common; lobster and conch fishing continued. The season for catching the spiny Caribbean lobster (*Panulirus argus*) is limited—from July 15 to March 15.

Caye Chapel, formerly a coconut plantation, was a favoured R & R spot for British soldiers who stayed at the since-demolished Pyramid Hotel. Kentucky-based Larry Addington bought Caye Chapel and completed a deluxe par 72, 6,843-yard golf course that he designed for himself and for guests in his 12, $1,000-per-night villas built at the turn of the millennium. Environmentalists protested the construction due to dredging and maintenance procedures; the expansion project countered by importing a special hybrid grass called Paspalum that is supposed to require 50 percent less pesticide, irrigation and fertilizer. During the construction phase Addington made himself essential in Belize by providing two $100,000 donations for a small but modern hospital in nearby San Pedro. The golf course accepted day visitors when it was not accommodating its clientele, primarily American conventioneers. It was the first golf course built in Belize since British colonial days.

Cayo Espanto, just off Ambergris Caye, is also for the rich. Just as Europeans once routinely retreated to the baths to "take the cure," visitors to this tiny island's resort, which was created as a restorative retreat, can luxuriate in a slower, first-name-basis atmosphere for $1,500 per night, excluding a 17 percent service charge. **Goff's Caye,** about the size of a football field, is just 12 miles east of Belize City. It attracts snorkellers for short visits. **Spanish Lookout Caye** is a 234-acre mangrove island, 10 miles southeast of the city. Also nearby for day-trips are **Sergeant's Caye**, **English Caye** and **Rendezvous Caye**. **Glover's Reef** is 70 miles southeast of Belize City and named for the pirate John Glover. Glover's Reef National Park is a circular stretch of coral. Pottery remains indicate the Maya visited the reef in pre-Conquest times.

The **Turneffe Reef** is a chain of 32 islands that form an oval approximately 50 miles long and 10 miles across, creating a lagoon for trophy fish such as king mackerel and marlin. Pirates brought female captives to **Maugre Caye** ("meagre" in Creole) after sacking the Spanish fort of Bacalar. Turquoise water and schools of iridescent fish attract tourists to a 166-acre resort on **Blackbird Caye** on the eastern side of the reef. **Calabash Caye** is the focus for 28-day marine survey expeditions managed by Coral

Cay Conservation Ltd. in London. **Hontin Caye**, as the name suggests, was supposed to be haunted.

Ranguana Caye and **Laughing Bird Caye**, a protected area for birds, are about 25 miles southeast of Placencia. **Lighthouse Reef** is the farthest offshore atoll. It attracts treasure-seekers in search of the Spanish galleon *Juan Baptista* that sank on June 21, 1822. It's named for a solar-powered lighthouse on **Half Moon Caye**, a 45-acre natural monument to protect red-footed boobies, overseen by the Audubon Society. Camping is permitted. German submarines were able to use Half Moon Caye as a refuelling base in World War II. It has some of the clearest waters in Belize, visibility 200 feet.

Maya Sites

The world's appreciation of Mayan civilization has increasingly focused on Belize, where Mayan ruins are relatively unexposed.

Anthropologists and archaeologists have divided Mesoamerican history into seven periods:

Early Preclassic – 2500 to 800 BC
Middle Preclassic – 800 to 400 BC
Late Preclassic – 400 BC to 250 AD
Early Classic – 250 to 600 AD
Late Classic – 600 to 900 AD
Early Postclassic – 900 to 1200 AD
Late Postclassic – 1200 to 1500 AD

Some include a Colonial period, from 1521 to 1821, and a Modern period, from 1821 to the present, to affirm Maya habitation in Belize has been continuous. The Department of Archaeology in Belmopan oversees ruins in accordance with the Ancient Monuments and Antiquities Ordinance of 1971. Seven sites have been open daily to the public: Altun Ha, Xunantunich, Santa Rita, Lamanai, Cerros, Lubaantun and Nim Li Punit.

With the noteworthy exception of Altun Ha, within easy

driving distance of Belize City, most of the Mayan sites are relatively undeveloped for tourism. If you don't head immediately to the idyllic islands, as most travellers do, you'll find roads are potholed, gas stations scarce, service unpredictable. It's unwise to drive at night. From north to south, here is a brief introduction to the principal Mayan sites that have been unearthed, disentangled or spotted from overhead.

Santa Rita. Within walking distance of Corozal, near a Coca-Cola plant, it was formerly the site of the Mayan city of Chetumal, distinct from the current Mexican city of Chetumal across the border. Santa Rita was a thriving trade centre on Corozal Bay until Spanish contact in the 1500s. It was abandoned after military incursions led by Alonso Dávila in 1531. The Maya went to Chequitaquil, a few leagues up the coast, but were attacked there, too. Eventually Mayan warlord Nachancan drove away the Spanish, but Dávila established the fort of Bacalar that blocked traditional trade routes. Late Postclassic. There is only one extant structure: a series of connected doorways. Burial sites and some pottery from 2000 BC have also been unearthed.

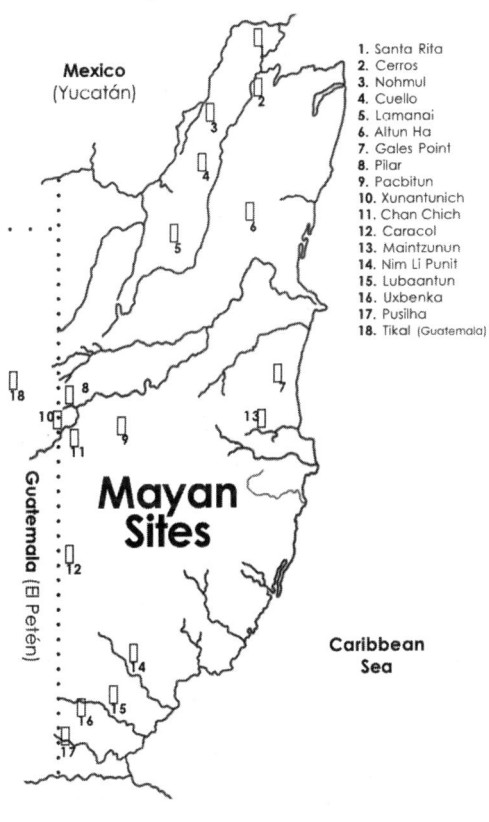

1. Santa Rita
2. Cerros
3. Nohmul
4. Cuello
5. Lamanai
6. Altun Ha
7. Gales Point
8. Pilar
9. Pacbitun
10. Xunantunich
11. Chan Chich
12. Caracol
13. Maintzunun
14. Nim Li Punit
15. Lubaantun
16. Uxbenka
17. Pusilha
18. Tikal (Guatemala)

Mexico (Yucatán)

Guatemala (El Petén)

Mayan Sites

Caribbean Sea

Cerros. Near the mouth of New River, the name means "hill." It is accessible by boat from Corozal. It was registered with the Belize Department of Archaeology by Peter Schmidt and Joseph Palacio in 1969. Cerro Maya Foundation in Dallas made plans for a tourist site with Metroplex Properties, but the scheme went bankrupt. It was excavated by David Friedel of Southern Methodist University, 1973–79. Maya Hill Archaeological Reserve now covers 52 acres. Late Preclassic. Trading centre for salt, jade, obsidian. Emerged as a ceremonial centre with a 3,600-foot canal, 18 feet wide, 6 feet deep. There are two ball courts, tombs, three acropolises and plazas. The largest structure is 72 feet high.

Nohmul. About eight miles north of Orange Walk Town, on private land. The name means "great mound." Used by the Maya in both Late Preclassic and Late Classic Periods, the site was neglected and looted for many years. It was first recorded by Thomas Gann, British medical officer and amateur archaeologist, in 1897. He returned numerous times to uncover tombs and take artifacts back to the British Museum, lastly in 1936. Mapping and excavations were begun by Norman Hammond (1970s); major excavations followed (1980s).

Cuello. The oldest evidence of Mayan settlement within Belize—from 2500 BC. It's reachable by taxi from Orange Walk Town. Not much to see.

Lamanai. Located eight miles west of Crooked Tree Wildlife Sanctuary on a 950-acre reserve. Accessible via boat on New River Lagoon from Guinea Grass or Shipyard, near Orange Walk Town; also reachable via San Felipe Village in dry season. Resorts and guides provide tours. A major site with more than a dozen major structures. The Temple of the Mask features a stucco mask thought to be Kinich Ahau, the Sun God. The dominant Preclassic building is 56 feet high. Long inhabited, from 1500 BC until the 1800s, it flourished during the 6th and 7th centuries. The Maya resisted Christian missionaries around 1570. Relics include two

16th-century Spanish churches, plus a derelict 19th-century sugar mill. First uncovered by Thomas Gann in 1917. Also explored by J. Eric Thompson (1930s), William Bullard Jr. (1960s), Thomas Lee (1967). The main excavation work was supervised by Dr. David Pendergast, Royal Ontario Museum (ROM) in the 1970s. The name Lamanai means "submerged crocodile." It's one of the few sites that retained its original name.

Altun Ha. Of the estimated 600 archaeological Mayan sites in Belize, the main tourist attraction has been Altun Ha. Six miles inland, about 35 miles north of Belize City, this site flourished as a ceremonial centre for 10,000 people around 950 AD, falling into disrepair by 1400 AD. Altun Ha is famous as the source of the Jade Head representing the Sun God, Kinich Ahau, from 600 AD. Altun Ha was recognized as an historical site in 1957 by A.H. Anderson, Belize's first archaeological commissioner. Some preliminary work was done by W.R. Bullard in 1961. The story goes that Anderson invited Canadian archaeologist Pendergast to investigate the site after a villager from nearby Rockstone Pond Village tried to sell a large, carved jade pendant unearthed from the site in 1963. The ROM undertook large-scale excavations in 1964

Temple of the Masonry Altars, Altun Ha. *Vivien Lougheed*

under the direction of Dr. Pendergast and his wife, along with Creole and Maya workers.

According to Pendergast, unique sacrifices were staged on the altar atop Structure B4, the tallest building at 60 feet high. Pendergast allocated the name Altun Ha, meaning "rockstone pond," in reference to a large water reservoir that never ran dry. The "Temple of the Sun God" is depicted on Belikin Beer bottles, one of the two original brands made in Belize. The magnificent Jade Head of the Sun God Kinich Ahau was found in 1968 on the wrist of a ruler interred in the earliest of seven tombs within Structure B4, the Temple of the Masonry Altars. Weighing 9.75 pounds and at 14.9 centimetres high, it's the largest carved jade artifact in Belize. It is much valued as a national treasure: it's the national symbol of Belize and appears on the nation's currency, although it is seldom on public display. In cooperation with the Inter-American Development Bank, the government undertook a major enhancement and development program to restore major Maya sites, including Altun Ha, in the new millennium. The discovery of the Jade Head in the temple suggests Altun Ha was used as a centre of sun worship, not just sacrifice. The pedestal for sacrifices is atop the temple. The temple underwent eight phases of construction and contained as many as seven tombs for priests, so archaeologists have concluded there must have been continual occupation of Altun Ha until the Maya empire inexplicably collapsed around 900 AD. The Maya liked to rebuild their structures, partially destroying them to make them anew. This makes deciphering Mayan hieroglyphics even more problematic for scholars.

Dr. Pendergast estimates in his book *Altun Ha* (1969) that as many as 8,000 Maya lived at one time near the site. The settlement began as early as 200 BC; construction projects began as early as the second century AD. There's some evidence to suggest the Maya returned to the site in the 14th or 15th centuries.

According to Pendergast's contract, excavated artifacts were to be housed within a new Mayan gallery in the Royal Ontario Musuem. The Jade Head did reach Canada, travelling as far as the Glenbow Museum in Alberta. For decades it became Belize's version of the Elgin Marbles. "Basically the ROM never got its act together," said Dr. Dorie Reents-Budet, Director of the Museum of World Cultures at the University of North Carolina. "This is a priceless loss to the people of Canada."

El Pilar. Only 32 miles east of Tikal near Bullet Tree Falls, 12 miles north of San Ignacio, it's believed to be far larger and important than Xunantunich, and is mostly unexcavated. It was inhabited for 15 centuries. There are temples, 25 plazas, ball court, and water catchments; Classic Period. Its survey commenced by Anabel Ford of the University of California at Santa Barbara in 1982. Included in the World Monuments Fund's list of 100 Most Endangered Sites in the World in 1997, the area was designated a national park in 1998. Its mysteries are yet to unfold. The source of its Spanish name is obscure. Site for the annual Maya Culture Day.

Pacbitun. Situated at the entrance to Pine Ridge, in the Cayo District. Its name means "stones set in earth." One of the oldest sites, occupied from 1000 BC until Late Classic period. It contains at least 24 temples, the largest 50 feet tall, a ball court, stelae, a causeway, and evidence of Mayan musical instruments. Nearby, the traditional Mayan Mopan village of San Antonio, famous for its healer Don Elijio Panti, attracts patients from all over Belize. Pacbitun was not registered as a protected site until 1971. Ground surveys were conducted by Trent University (1984); excavations were overseen by Paul Healy of Trent (1980s).

Xunantunich. Eight miles west of San Ignacio, near the Guatemalan border, at San Jose Succotz Village, this small but major site contains El Castillo, 130 feet high. Easily reached via the Western Highway and approachable by a hand-operated pedestrian and car ferry across the Mopan River, it affords a panoramic

The El Castillo tower at Xunantunich can be visited after crossing the Mopan River on a hand-winched ferry. *Vivien Lougheed*

view. It was occupied until 900 AD. Excavations suggest a major earthquake occurred at that time, possibly explaining the sudden abandonment of ceremonial sites. It's the longest government-operated Maya tourist site in Belize. It was first investigated by Thomas Gann (1894-95), followed by Teobert Maler (1924) of the Peabody Museum of Harvard; Gann returned (1924) and removed carved hieroglyphs, location now unknown. Other archaeologists included J. Eric Thompson (1938), Linton Satterthwaite (1950), amateur Michael Stewart (1952-57), Euan Mackie of Cambridge (1959-60) and David Pendergast (1979). Belize's Archaeological Commissioners A.H. Anderson (1959), Peter Schmidt (1968-71), Joseph Palacio (1978-79), Elizabeth Graham and Harriot Topsey also explored Xunantunich. The name means "stone maiden" but it's of recent, local origin. Xunantunich was reopened in 2003 after a fibreglass reproduction of the original carved stone frieze was added high up on the east wall of El Castillo. The reproduction has been used to cover the original work, eroded by weather. Classic Period.

Caracol. The largest site in Belize, larger than Tikal, it's remote and difficult to access, near the Guatemala border, approximately 50 miles south of San Ignacio. It was settled around 300 BC and occupied into the Late Classic Period. Caracol was accidentally rediscovered by loggers in 1938. It contains the Canaa Pyramid, or Sky Palace, two metres higher than El Castillo, and tombs for group burials and non-rulers. Glyphs record a war with Tikal, in 562 AD, in which Lord Water of Caracol was victorious. This war possibly explains the collapse of Tikal, 60 miles to the northwest. Stelae trace royal lineage. Caracol's population reached as high as 150,000 in its prosperous Classic phase under Lord Makina-hokkawil. It was inexplicably abandoned in the middle of the 10th century. A.H. Anderson explored the Temple of the Wooden Lintel in 1938, the only building visible at the time. His field notes on future work were destroyed when Hurricane Hattie hit Belize City

As a thriving metropolis in the 6th century, Caracol once controlled the rainforest area of Guatemala that includes the Mayan city of Tikal. *Vivien Lougheed*

in 1961. Arlen and Diane Chase from the University of Central Florida oversaw explorations from 1985 onward. For many years a small sign— "The Rumours Are True" —greeted visitors at the site.

Maintzunun. The name means "Small Hummingbird." Situated off Hummingbird Highway, about 10 miles north of Cockscomb Wildlife Sanctuary, in foothills above coastal plane, this modest Late Classic site was discovered by a tree planter with the Forestry Department, Ernest Gongora. It was examined by Cambridge University students under direction of Allan Moore (1987).

Nim Li Punit. This site was rediscovered in 1976 by oil company employees and was looted soon afterward. The name means "big hat" in Kek'chi Maya; it refers to the headgear worn by the priests depicted on one of the 25 stelae. It's the tallest carved stela in Belize at 31 feet. This stela was not erected. The Late Classic site accommodated up to 5,000 Maya in the area, from 700 to 800 AD. The site was surveyed by Richard Leventhal in 1983; he discovered a royal tomb in 1986. There are two plazas and a ball court. It's accessible by trail from the Southern Highway and is about 25 miles northeast of Punta Gorda.

Lubaantun. From atop the highest temple, the Caribbean is visible 20 miles away. This Late Classic ceremonial site is approachable by car from San Pedro Columbia village off the Southern Highway, about 15 miles north of Punta Gorda. The name means "place of fallen stones." There are five plazas, three ball courts and unusual architecture: no mortar and rounded edges of buildings. Lubaantun was occupied only briefly from 700 to 890 AD. The governor sent Thomas Gann to investigate around 1903. He was followed by R.E. Merwin (1915), T.A. Joyce (1926) and J.E. Thompson (1927) and Norman Hammond (1970s). A "crystal skull" was found at Lubaantun during explorations by F.A. Mitchell-Hedges for the British Museum in 1926. Most archaeologists dismiss it as a fake, but scientists can't fully explain the method of carving used to make it. The daughter of F.A. Mitchell-Hedges, Anna Mitchell-Hedges, kept the crystal skull with her in Kitchener, Ontario. The Fallen Stones Butterfly Farm, which produces butterflies that are exported to Europe in the chrysalis stage, is near Lubaantun.

Uxbenka. This small ceremonial site, nine miles east of Guatemala, was only identified in 1984. Surveyed by Richard Leventhal. Located near Santa Cruz Village, three miles west of San Antonio, in Toledo District. Also called Uxbenton or *Uch Ben Cah*, the name means "ancient place."

Pusilha. Located just one mile east of Guatemala. It's unusual for its walled-in ball court and a long building that's 400 feet long, 130 feet wide, but only 16 feet high with no arches. Monuments include zoomorphs, carved to appear animal-like, in forms of jaguars and ocelots. Glyphs date from 500 to 700 AD. Pusilha River is a branch of the Moho River, south of Punta Gorda. Pusilha is accessible by boat.

Ambergris Caye

Significant Mayan sites have also been found offshore, first at the north end of Ambergris Caye in 1986. A local Maya named Francisco Cruz Reyes was digging a well behind his house when he found a Mayan grave. Texan archaeologists arrived and named the site Ek Luum, "black earth." They also identified another site on the same caye called Chac Balam.

When the Americans returned in 1987, the Belizean owner of the property cleared two acres to accommodate 15 tents for the excavation team and a film crew, as well as building a cooking tent. The Americans unearthed a three-coloured Mayan vase decorated with three monkeys, as well as 300 Mayan graves. In the final week of work, a fire was built to control the mosquitoes. It flared out of control, spreading to fruit trees and the vegetable garden, and ruined Francisco Cruz Reyes's main source of income and food. The scientists went home with evidence that as many as 10,000 Maya had once lived on Ambergris Caye, adjoining a valuable salt mine. Francisco Cruz Reyes was forced to evacuate his home.

There's also a Mayan site called Marco Gonzales on the southern tip of the peninsula.

Chalillo Be Damned

The Chalillo Dam construction project at the turn of the century galvanized attention on the inevitable industrialization-vs.-environment debate that must continually occur in Belize. Efforts to stop the highly questionable $30 million hydroelectric project were led by American-born "zoo lady" Sharon Matola of the Belize Zoo and Tropical Education Center. Located 29 miles west of Belize City, on the road to Belmopan, the zoo was opened in 1983 when Matola adopted 17 animals left behind by a film crew. As a coalition member of the Belize Alliance of Conservation Non-Government Organizations (BACONGO), Matola helped attract foreign media and conservationists, such as David Suzuki and

Harrison Ford, to examine the proposed Chalillo Dam project on the Macal River.

In November 2001, the government's National Environmental Appraisal Committee (NEAC) decided the benefits of the "Macal River Upstream Storage Facility project would outweigh the environmental costs." According to BACONGO, the 400 people who demonstrated against the government in Belmopan in November 2001 did so because they feared "the dam would flood habitat for the Scarlet Macaw, and the tapir, Belize's national animal. It would lead to higher electricity rates and undermine the country's growing nature-based tourism industry."

A Canadian-based company, Fortis Inc., had acquired ownership of approximately 95 percent of the Belize Electric Company. The developer promised to relocate crocodiles, construct artificial breeding sites for the macaw, transplant five protected plant species, undertake captive breeding programs for wildlife and leave a 20-metre buffer zone of vegetation along the edge of the Macal River. In return, Fortis reportedly gained long-term operational rights.

Suspicion of corruption within Belize arose from the Chalillo project but more damaging was the impression that Belize might be squandering some of its natural purity. Most of the ecotourism managers were opposed to the deal. Meanwhile the Belize government found itself in a bind because it had hoped to fulfill one of its election promises—to reduce electricity rates. "I sincerely believe that Chalillo will provide us with cheaper, cleaner power," Prime Minister Musa stated in February 2002. This led prying reporters such as the Canadian Broadcasting Corporation's Terry Milewski to traipse down to his office, unscheduled, and attempt to confront him with some potentially embarrassing mathematics.

"In all the arguments that Belize Electricity Limited and her parent company, Fortis, have put forward to advance the case for the proposed Chalillo Dam," the *Belize Reporter* editorialized in

2001, "we have seen nothing to show that Chalillo will in any way reduce the cost of electric power to the Belizean consumer."

Matola was one of four applicants who filed suit against the Government of Belize. UDP leader Dean Barrow successfully argued before Chief Justice Abdulai Conteh in February of 2002 that the alleged "illegality, procedural impropriety and irrationality" of the Department of Environment's decision to "green light" the project was sufficient to merit a judicial review.

The environmentalists were suggesting that the government had contravened its own Environmental Protection Act. Road building was allowed to commence prior to the completion of an environmental impact study. Barrow also argued that no public hearings were held. Section 23 (5) of the Environmental Protection Act stated, "When making an EIA [Environmental Impact Assessment] proposal, developer shall consult with the public and other interested bodies or organizations."

The Chalillo Dam project was stalled. Matola and two other applicants withdrew their applications in favour of the BACONGO intercession. In May 2002, Maya naturalist Eligorio Sho travelled to Canada to urge Fortis investors to put pressure on the power and real estate firm to abandon its plan to sell its output to Belize Electricity, also owned by Fortis. It was the second straight year environmentalists targeted the Fortis shareholders' meeting in St. John's, Newfoundland. In December the Supreme Court ruled a public hearing must be held on the 7.5 MW Chalillo project. On December 22, 2002, Sharon Matola and Tony Garel of the Belize Zoo hosted a "Fortis Forget It Day!"

But after the 2003 election, the government's commitment to Fortis was reconfirmed and the courts upheld the procedures that were taken for environmental protection. The environmentalists had been beaten in Belize. In the summer of 2003, Friends of the Earth, the Natural Resources Defence Council and Belizean environmental groups took their appeal to the Privy Council in

London, launching the first major environmental lawsuit in the history of Belize. But in 2004, the PUP administration of Said Musa held firm.

In September 2005, Belize Electric Company (BECOL) announced completion of its Chalillo Dam hydroelectric facility. The lake created by the dam is intended to store water that will enable generators at Chalillo, and downstream at the Mollejon Hydroelectric Plant, to produce electricity at a steady, year-round rate. Electric power generated by the Macal River system is anticipated to double output for the country. A third facility is planned downriver from Mollejon at Vaca Falls.

A Nation of Waiters

Tourism in Belize has the appearance of a healthy industry. According to the Tourism Board, tourists spent US $111.5 million in 1999, up from $108.3 million in 1998. In the 1990s about half of all tourists were Americans. The hype was contrary to a summary in *Belize First*, a well-written newsletter from the US, reporting that at least 16 of the country's hotels and resorts were changing hands, had been recently sold or were on the block at one time in 2000.

The government of Belize invested a huge amount in the Ramada Hotel, only to see the country's largest hotel go into bankruptcy. The people of Belize reportedly lost their investment when it was sold. The Ramada reopened as the Fiesta Inn. Then its 118 rooms and suites became the Princess Hotel. Without remodelling the overpriced rooms, the Princess underwent a refit for the first major casino in Belize, open from noon until 4 a.m. Ostensibly the Princess casino was to be run on a membership-only basis—allowing attendants to deny entry if they don't like the cut of your jib—but the jibs of Chinese Belizeans and tourists have been liked well enough to allow easy access. With its free grub and booze, the Las Vegas-styled casino opened with lots of slots, gaming tables, video poker and a bevy of imported Russian dancing girls.

Initially a tiny casino on Caribena Street in San Pedro provided the lone competition for the Princess operation, but the lure of gambling revenues proved irresistible to a government reduced to a BB credit rating, two notches below investment grade. In 2000 the government reportedly planned to sell a bond to help finance a $100 million four-star hotel on Ambergris Caye.

"We will need to go to the private capital markets in the US," said Keith Arnold, governor of the Central Bank of Belize. On a more pragmatic level, the government's small equity investment program allows the government to become a partner in businesses, leading some critics to reinterpret the meaning of the national motto, "Flourish Under the Shade." Most of the tourism entrepreneurs who benefit from these improvements are not obliged to spend their profits in Belize, meanwhile the government takes out loans to improve infrastructure.

As disparities between the entrepreneurial, white, mostly American tourism masters and the majority of Belizeans in the service industry continue to grow, social and political tensions are inevitable. Few incidents of tourist molestation are mentioned in travel books, but it happens. In May 2002, six armed men robbed 10 tourists of more than $6,000 when they were visiting a Mayan site in the Cayo District. Channel Five reported, "Police expect the robbers may be Guatemalans." In June 2000, Leroy Dunn made an unprovoked attack on a Swedish tourist, hitting her on the head with a board. He was convicted by the Quick Trial Court just hours later and by the end of the day he was in the Hattieville Prison serving a two-year term.

It was the American poet Gary Snyder who said the best way to save the world is to stay home.

Jungle locales increasingly attract a curious sub-species of tourist: the ecotourist, who likes to hike, paddle or dive reverentially into the pristine places that mankind has yet to spoil. Some of the natives are getting restless about this. "Everybody hides under the 'eco,'" observed Nazario Ku, a Maya curator of a museum at the Lamanai Archaeological Reserve, "but what ecotourism really means is destruction of the rainforest."

Unfortunately the government has lacked the expertise or manpower to diligently monitor adventure playground tourism ventures once they are approved. In the Garinagu village of Hopkins, located south of Dangriga, resort developers were accused of illegally including five acres of the Hopkins cemetery in their site plan. It was further alleged in 2002 that a bulldozer had levelled the shorelines, disregarding the 60-foot beach resort mark. The Department of Environment issued a stop order to the Hopkins Harbour Development project for the area under dispute, known to the locals as Hawaii, but the ancestors had already rolled over.

The Selling of Belize

Ex-pats, as they're called, dominate the hotel industry. The rising tide of tourism began in the 1970s. One of the first American eco-entrepreneurs was John Carr, "an honest-to-goodness cowman from Montana," who, with his wife Carolyn, arrived in 1977 and created their Banana Bank Lodge for birdwatching and horseback riding. It's amid 4,000 acres of jungle and ranchland near Mile 46 of the Western Highway. Promotion material states, "There is even a beautiful jaguar that they have raised since she was abandoned as a baby."

Two American wildlife biologists envisioned the ecotourism and conservation project at Gales Point in 1991. The idealistic experiment was designed to help preserve manatees and to benefit the local community, but it proved fractious and arguably detrimental. Since 1993, Francis Ford Coppola's five-star Blancaneaux Lodge has invited guests to "float to San Ignacio in a dugout canoe, or relax in a villa by the Macal River." He also purchased

Turtle Inn in Placencia, fixing it up after Hurricane Iris. Texans Bill and Allison Moore purchased their own offshore caye. New Yorker Robert Frackman owned the five-star Inn at Robert's Grove. In Cayo, Jay and Pamella Picon opened the Mopan River Resort in 1999, building a ferry service to their 10-acre compound with thatched cabanas, mahogany cabinets, VCRs and TVs. The Lamanai Outpost Lodge has had Australian ownership. And so on.

Not all entrepreneurs were high rollers. Unassuming Tom Benson, a retired general contractor from Pensacola, bought a school bus and pulled his 25-foot-boat all the way to Punta Gorda to operate a bed and breakfast called TC's By-The-Sea. The bed and breakfast concept has a much tonier approach at Villa Boscardi, in Belize City, operated by an Italian émigré family.

Rosita Arvigo gained prominence as the author of a book about herbal medicines, *Sastun*, written with Nadine Epstein, after an elderly *curandero* shared his knowledge with her. Arvigo and Epstein also collaborated on *Rainforest Home Remedies: The Maya Way to Heal Your Body & Replenish Your Soul*. Arvigo opened a spa and wellness centre, complete with facials, massages, pedicures and aromatherapy, to be followed by a bush-medicine camp for children.

The splendid commercial photographs of American Tony Rath, a resident of Dangriga, portray Belize as everyone would prefer it to be—they are art as much as reality. People are posed just right. His website is sophisticated. Women in bikinis stare out to sea, faceless. In contrast, the equally impressive images of ex-pat Thor "Bushman Ollie" Janson are spirited and natural, showing Belize in a more realistic, day-to-day light. The difference between the two styles makes clear how the image of Belize can be flexible and manipulated, from an idyllic eco-paradise getaway to a friendly, multi-racial, backward enclave.

"What is being sold is a Western, idealized image of tropical rurality and exotic culture devoid of the ugliness associated with real Third World poverty, inequities and globalization," claims the Third World Network. "In their consumption of natural Belize, international tourists bypass the reality of British colonialism, slavery, racism." This stance is based on researcher Jill M. Belsky's *An Examination of Community-based Ecotourism Discourse and Practice in Gales Point, Belize* (2000, available via Columbia University Press).

Ample literature is available on land acquisition and citizenship: basically—get a lawyer. Telephone calls and e-mails from afar don't always merit quick responses. "Property information is not that easy to find here," cautioned one tourism guide in Dangriga. "For example, to find a survey, you have to know the name of the surveyor, rather than the name of the property owner. I once found a great research title on birds in Stann Creek. The book was filed under 'T' because the title was *The Amazing Birds of Southern Belize*."

It has been possible to buy your way in. In 1996, under the heading of "Help Us Build A New Nation," the Finance Ministry placed a small ad in an international newspaper advertising citizenships at the price of $25,000, which rose to $50,000 in 1997. This buy-your-passport plan soon proved unpopular with Belizeans because the Economic Citizenship program obviously raised the cost of real estate. As well, some successful applicants such as an "American shyster" and a "Sikh terrorist" were generally assumed to be unworthy of citizenship. It was alleged that one drug baron from Mexico managed to buy his passport in a single day. Whereas the transfer tax on a sale of property for non-Belizeans was 10 percent of the purchase price, usually paid by the buyer, that 10 percent surcharge was waived for the high rollers. The Economic Citizenship program was tarnished by allegations of corruption. It was easy to imagine middlemen pocketing hidden surcharges from unsavoury applicants.

The Retired Persons Incentive Act was passed in early 1999 to encourage qualified retirees 45 and older to come to Belize—but only if they're from the US, Britain, Northern Ireland or Canada.

The income of these retirees from outside Belize was not taxed in Belize: importation of their household goods and a car or boat could be tax-free, but retirees couldn't work in Belize and they had to deposit their monthly pensions or investment incomes into a Belizean bank.

Provided you're not a proven axe-murderer and you meet the monthly income level, the Belize Tourism Board, the administrators of this program, could green-light the Immigration Department to grant Qualified Retired Persons Status.

Just two of numerous titles about the complexities of entry, obtaining citizenship, residency papers and property are *How to Become a Resident of Belize without Going Completely Crazy* by Bill and Claire Gray, and *How to Invest or Retire in Belize* by Belize Film Commissioner Emory King. One of the best writers about Belize on an ongoing basis, Lan Sluder of *Belize First* magazine, has also written an adapter kit.

Tourists can be confounded by competing media. The biased papers can be full of vitriol. Manners can be deceptive, too. While Belizeans appear laid-back and tolerant and the pace of business is unhurried, Creole humour is sharp-edged. A young Belizean woman can walk down the street in a T-shirt proclaiming "Once You've Tried Black, You'll Never Go Back" and merit nary a glance, but visitors must take care when they fraternize off the beaten track.

The Future

According to Minister of Home Affairs Ralph Fonseca, speaking in November of 2005, "The country's annual imported oil bill is now well over one hundred million dollars a year and growing." To assist cash-strapped Belize, Venezuela pledged to provide preferential petroleum prices to Belize in keeping with the new PetroCaribe Energy Cooperation Agreement.

Addressing the United Nations assembly on September 15, 2005, Prime Minister Said Musa noted 52 percent of the Belizean population was less than 19 years old, 51 percent of Belizeans were living in rural areas and the population density was 10.9 persons per square kilometre. The struggle for self-determination was as difficult as ever, but he remained optimistic.

"The poet/songwriter Woody Guthrie said it best," Musa told the UN on its 60th birthday. "'This land is your land, this land is my land,' and with a bit of poetic licence I would say, 'From the majestic Maya Mountains to the tropical coral islands, from the proud Rio Hondo to the old Sarstoon, this land was made for you and me.'"

In keeping with his rhetoric, Musa reversed the privatization of Belize Water Services Limited in 2001, when control had been purchased by Cascal, BV, a Netherlands registered company. In October 2005, the government bought back 33 million shares (82.68 percent of issued share capital) in BWSL at the original price of US$24.8 million, thereby returning majority control to the Belizean public. In the same month the government offered shares for sale, only to Belizeans and Belizean companies, in Belize Telecommunications Ltd. at a price of US$2.71 per share.

"Belize is on the rebound," Musa pronounced, just prior to the country's 24th birthday. "We are putting our national house in order. And the nation we proudly call Belize will endure, will revive and will prosper. This rebounding is not an accident. It is occurring because the Belizean people, despite an irresponsible call for sustained civil disobedience, chose the rule of law and democracy over anarchy and raw emotionalism.

"It is occurring because our government maintained calm and focus, continued to work with the social partners and made substantial reforms in the management of public finances and in the handling of the people's business. Most of all, Belize remains stable and continues to grow because Belizeans across the entire nation, in the midst of the countries difficulties, continued to produce, to farm, teach, nurse, work and build."

Timeline

1508—A former navigator for Christopher Columbus, Vicente Yáñez Pinzón, discovers the Belizean shoreline with his sailing partner Juan Díaz de Solís, but they don't go ashore.

1511—A shipwrecked Spanish soldier named Gonzalo Guerrero "goes Native" for 20 years, living in the Corozal area and undoubtedly setting foot in Belize.

1524—Hernán Cortés, founder of Mexico City, leads a fantastical expedition of soldiers through the Maya Mountains. He becomes the first European to enter Belize from the eastern interior.

1630—Puritans establish the colony of Providence south of the Mosquito Coast.

1630s—Buccaneers and privateers pillage the Spanish and use Belize as their safe haven.

1655—England conquers nearby Jamaica. The Caribbean becomes a war zone.

1670-1700—Hard-drinking Baymen begin exporting logwood from their base on a little island off the mouth of the mosquito-infested Belize River.

Edward Teach, aka Blackbeard, discovered the pleasures of Ambergris Caye a few centuries before Madonna.

1701—Fly-by-night buccaneers and their Mosquito Indian mercenaries capture the Maya and sell them as slaves.

1755—In response to the "Battle of Labouring Creek" the year before, the Spanish rout the English Baymen and burn their settlement to the ground.

1765—Based on unwritten rules derived from public meetings, Burnaby's Code is drafted and signed by 85 people. It will serve as a constitution until 1862.

1773—The first major slave revolt occurs when 40 slaves combine to slay particularly odious slave masters. This frontier justice is thwarted by Royal Marines from HMS *Diligence*.

1776—The Reverend Robert Shaw, an Anglican missionary, arrives from the Mosquito Shore. The Church of England is formally established in Belize in 1777.

1779—Spanish from the fort of Bacalar, just north of the Hondo River, successfully attack St. George's Caye, taking away 250 slaves and a few settlers.

1783—The Versailles Treaty proposes Baymen shall have logging rights between the Sibun and Belize Rivers.

1786—The Convention of London formally extends logging rights southward to the Sibun River for logwood and mahogany harvesting.

1787—The population of Belize is vastly altered by the arrival of 2,214 "British subjects" from the Mosquito Shore.

1788—The Maya attack mahogany works on the New River.

1790—A census records 2,656 inhabitants in the Belize City area.

1791—The practice of obeah, supernatural religious practices brought from Africa, is outlawed upon penalty of death.

1793—The British frigate *Water Witch* founders off Ambergris Caye, supposedly going down with $2 million worth of gold and silver. Countless sunken ships will attract divers for centuries.

1798—At the Battle of St. George's Caye, outnumbered Baymen and their slaves convincingly repel the Spanish with the assistance of HMS *Merlin*.

1800—Banana plantations allow American and British investors to generate a trade route to New Orleans.

1802—The first Garinagu (Garifuna) arrive. They're a black-skinned hybrid race of escaped slaves and Amerindians who were forcibly expelled from St. Vincent Island by the British in 1797. They will chiefly reside at Stann Creek, later renamed Dangriga.

1812—The government provides funds for St. John's Cathedral, the first Anglican Church in Central America, and the foundation stone laid.

1814—Government House is built.

1820—The fourth slave revolt since 1765 occurs. The Supreme Court is established without consultation or complaint from Spain.

1821—Spain dismantles its New World Empire. Mexico and Guatemala will begin to make territorial claims on Belize.

1832—Led by Alejo Beni, 40 more Garinagu land near the mouth of Stann Creek on November 19, giving rise to a national holiday in Belize called Settlement Day.

1847—Refugees flood into Belize from the north during the Caste War in the Yucatán (1847–53).

This was the perspective from Fort George, now part of Belize City, in 1842, from *British Honduras: Portrait of a Colony, 1953*.

1857—"Extortion" fees are paid to the Icaiche tribe at Blue Creek by Belizean mahogany merchants. Rum and sugar are exported to England for the first time.

1859—In exchange for peace and sovereignty, Britain agrees to build a road for Guatemala to the Caribbean coast. A British–Guatemalan treaty is signed. Guatemala never gets the road.

1862—The Colony of British Honduras is founded.

1865—The first imported Chinese labourers – 474 in all – arrive in the Corozal District, then are taken to the Toledo District where they'll become an integral minority.

1868—Approximately 150 ex-Confederate soldiers migrate after the American Civil War, chiefly north of Punta Gorda, at Cattle Landing.

1871—British Honduras becomes a crown colony of Britain administered from Jamaica.

1875—The British Honduras Company becomes the Belize Estate and Produce Company. The London-based company owns half of all privately owned lands.

1884—British Honduras finally becomes a separate crown colony, detached from Jamaica. Guatemala threatens to repudiate the treaty of 1859 because a once-agreed-upon road still does not exist.

1893—The northern boundary is clarified when Mexico agrees to a Treaty of Boundaries with the British. San Pedro on Ambergris Caye is officially within British jurisdiction.

1903—Dr. Thomas Gann visits Mayan ruins at Lubaantun and recommends the site ought to be protected and preserved. The first automobile arrives.

1905—The telephone exchange is established.

1906— The first electric streetlights are installed in Belize City.

1908—Canada offers free land in British Honduras to any Sikhs who will leave Canada. No one accepts.

1915—A radio telegraph is established.

1919—George Cadle Price is born on January 15. Creole soldiers of the British Honduras Contingent in World War I, angered by racism overseas, spark the Ex-Servicemen's Riot to protest white rule, racism and low wages.

1921—The Jamaican-born African redemptionist Marcus Mosiah Garvey, founder of the Universal Negro Improvement Association, visits British Honduras.

1923—Afro-Belizean patriot Philip Stanley Wilberforce Goldson is born on July 25.

1925—William Jex Bowman opens the first citrus-packing plant at Sarawee, having planted 300 budded grapefruit trees imported from Florida in 1913.

1927—Charles Lindbergh lands on the Newtown Barracks cricket grounds in the *Spirit of St. Louis*, scouting flight paths. He returns in 1929.

1929—The Great Depression ruins mahogany and chicle sales, commencing a decade that will serve as the crucible for Belizean politics.

1931—The worst hurricane in Belize's history levels much of Belize City, killing more than 1,000 people. Labour activist Antonio Soberanis is jailed for leading protests.

1934—The Unemployed Brigade takes over the streets of Belize City on February 14. The governor offers stone-breaking relief work to mollify them.

The hurricane of 1931 decimated much of the housing in Belize City. *Belize Archives.*

1935—Soberanis organizes a strike in Stann Creek and, under a new sedition law, is later jailed for a Corozal speech. A new constitution is passed to limit eligible voters due to literacy, property and income qualifications.

1936—Democracy dawns: Creole Robert Turton wins a seat on Belize's Legislative Council.

1937—A mahogany logger named Rosa Mai stumbles upon the lost metropolis of Caracol, the largest Mayan site in Belize.

1940—Joseph Blisset founds the Belize Independence Party and calls for the expulsion of whites.

1941—Trade unions are legalized, but laws don't require employers to recognize them. Mass meetings demand unrestricted adult suffrage. Blisset forms the Belizean Labour Party.

1943—The Employers and Workers Bill finally eliminates the punitive terms of the 1883 Masters and Servants Act. The British Honduras Workers and Tradesmen's Union (founded by Soberanis in 1939) becomes General Workers Union, and expands into a national organization.

1945—Guatemala's new constitution cites "Belice" as that country's twenty-third department (or state).

1946—A new weekly newspaper called the *Belize Billboard* presents pro-American, anticolonial views, harkening a new era for political debate. It will become a daily paper in 1950.

1947—Opposing immigration, George Price is elected for the first time.

1950—On January 2, protesters meet at 3 Pickstock Street, home of George Price, to form the People's Committee. It leads to the foundation of the People's United Party (PUP) on September 29.

1951—In July, the governor dissolves the PUP-dominated Belize Town Board on the grounds it has refused to hang a portrait of King George VI.

1952—Radio Belize, a government-run broadcasting system, goes on air. The General Workers Union attempts a national strike.

1954—Universal adult suffrage for literate Belizean adults is established. A new constitution provides for internal self-government. Price and the PUP take eight of nine seats in the new Legislative Assembly, the beginning of a 30-year PUP winning streak.

1956—The Honduran Independence Party (HIP) is formed. Price and Nicholas Pollard form a new trade union, the Christian Democratic Union. *The Belize Times* begins publication for the PUP. George Price is elected leader of the PUP, a position he'll retain for 40 years.

1958—Philip Goldson forms the National Independence Party.

1959—Some 3,000 Mennonites emigrate from Mexico and Canada (Manitoba), buying 100,000 acres along the Hondo River.

1960—Large-scale Mayan archaeology begins. The government signs an agreement with the Royal Ontario Museum (ROM) for excavation of Mayan ruins.

1961—Hurricane Hattie devastates Belize City, killing 275 and leaving 10 times as many homeless. Price announces a new capital called Belmopan will be built inland.

1964—PUP leader Price becomes premier. Britain retains control of defence, foreign affairs, internal security and the civil service. A two-chamber legislature is introduced.

1965—Muhammad Ali visits. The first hotel opens on Ambergris Caye.

1968—The Jade Head – the most spectacular relic in Belizean archaeology – is uncovered by ROM crews led by Pendergast. It becomes the national symbol of Belize.

1969—Writer and activist Evan X Hyde's black consciousness lectures lead to the creation of the United Black Association for Development (UBAD) in February. Hyde begins his long association with a new independent newspaper, *Amandala*, on August 13, 1969.

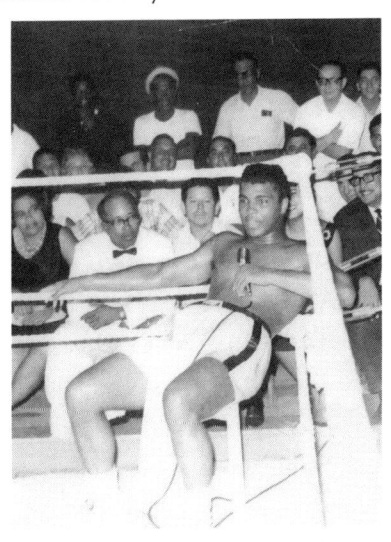

Muhammad Ali visited Belize shortly before he refused to comply with the American draft. *Belize Archives.*

1971—Belmopan – an amalgam of "BEL"-ize and "MOPAN," the main tribe of the Maya – becomes the capital.

1973—British Honduras changes its name to Belize. The United Democratic Party (UDP) is formed as a coalition of the National Independence Party (NIP), the People's Development Movement (PDM) and Liberal sectors.

1978—The Belize Defence Force (BDF) is created to counter Guatemalan threats.

1980—Rising oil prices and plummeting sugar prices drastically lowers the GDP. Belize approaches bankruptcy.

1981—On September 21, Belize becomes an independent nation under the PUP. A new constitution retains the Queen of England as the ceremonial head of state. Membership within the UN comes a few days later.

1983—Pope John Paul II visits but never leaves the airport.

1984—The UDP gains a landslide victory under Manuel Esquivel in December. A Voice of America transmitter is installed at Punta Gorda.

Sharon Matola of the Belize Zoo was one of the community leaders who protested against the Chalillo Dam project. *Belize Archives.*

1984—British-owned sugar giant Tate and Lyle lays off 600 employees at Libertad and divests a 90 percent share of its Tower Hill plant, marking the decline of the sugar business, the country's most vital and productive industry since 1959.

1986—American zoologist Alan Rabinowitz convinces Belize to set aside 3,600 acres in the Cockscomb Basin for the world's first jaguar reserve.

1989—Price and his PUP are narrowly elected. The PUP dismantles SIS and encourages freedom of the press. Hyde's *Amandala* newspaper leads to the birth of KREM radio on November 17, breaking the government's monopoly on the airwaves.

1991—Guatemala recognizes Belize's sovereignty. Diplomatic relations are re-established.

1993—The UDP is victorious for a second time under Esquivel.

1994—The UK withdraws 3,000 military personnel, leaving only a few troops as a symbolic deterrent to Guatemala.

1998—The PUP wins a sweeping victory under Said Musa.

2000—American sprinter Marion Jones dazzles the world by wrapping herself in the Belizean flag at the Sydney Olympics, winning five medals and putting her mother's homeland on the map.

2001—Hurricane Iris hits southern Belize.

2002—The George Price Centre for Peace and Development is opened in Belmopan. A ratification referendum on the Guatemala border agreement is postponed.

2004—Strikes and public demonstrations proliferate; saboteurs shut down telecommunications; civil unrest and increasing crime acerbates a faltering economy.

2005—An October poll released by the Society for the Promotion of Education and Research (SPEAR) pegs the approval rating for Prime Minister Said Musa at 19.8 percent. Cabinet deliberations in November lay the groundwork for implementing a Goods and Services Tax (GST), as well as the reintroduction of a semi-professional basketball league.

2006—Prime Minister Musa's administration is beset by more economic problems. January negotiations to resolve the border dispute between Guatemala and Belize are postponed yet again, rescheduled for Washington, DC.

Further Reading

O. Nigel Bolland, *The Formation of a Colonial Society: Belize from Conquest to Crown Colony* (Baltimore, 1977)

William David Setzekorn, *Formerly British Honduras: A Profile of the New Nation of Belize* (Athens, Ohio, 1981)

Robert Leslie, ed., *A History of Belize: Nation in the Making* (Benque del Viejo Carmen, Belize, 1983, revised 1995)

O. Nigel Bolland, *Belize: A New Nation in Central America* (Boulder, Colorado, 1986)

Byron Foster, *The Baymen's Legacy: A Portrait of Belize City* (Belize City, 1987)

Assad Shoman, *Party Politics in Belize, 1950-1986* (Benque Viejo del Carmen, Belize, 1987)

O. Nigel Bolland, ed., *Colonialism and Resistance in Belize: Essays in Historical Sociology* (Benque Viejo del Carmen, Belize, 1988)

Byron Foster, *Warlords and Maize Men* (Belize City, 1989)

Robert Horwich & Jon Lyon, *A Belizean Rain Forest: The Community Baboon Sanctuary* (Gay Mills, Wisconsin, 1990)

Tom Barry, *Inside Belize: The Essential Guide to its Society, Economy and Environment* (Albuquerque, New Mexico, 1992)

Rosita Arvigo & Michael Balick, *Rainforest Remedies: One Hundred Healing Herbs of Belize* (Tin Lakes, Wisconsin, 1993)

Peta Henderson & Ann Bryn Houghton, eds., *Rising Up: Life Stories of Belizean Women* (Toronto, 1993)

Rosita Arvigo, Nadine Epstein & Marilyn Yaquinto, *Sastun: My Apprenticeship with a Maya Healer* (San Francisco, 1994)

Irma McLaurin, *Women of Belize: Gender and Change in Central America* (New Brunswick, New Jersey, 1996)

Toleda Maya Cultural Council, *Maya Atlas: The Struggle To Preserve Maya Land In Southern Belize* (Berkeley, California, 1997)

Anne Sutherland, *The Making of Belize* (New York, New York, 1998)

Donald C. Simmons, Jr. *Confederate Settlements in British Honduras* (Jefferson, North Carolina, 2001)

Acknowledgements

I am grateful to George Price for his co-operation, and especially Gregorio Ch'oc and Augustine Flores for their insights, and I regret my interviews with these three individuals cannot be contained herein.

Permission to replicate archival photos was provided by George Price and Belize Archives. I wish to acknowledge the friendly staff of the Belize Archives, particularly Marvin Pook, for their assistance. Belize Cabinet secretary and historian Robert Leslie, Belize historian Lita Krohn and Prime Minister Said Musa have kindly read the manuscript and generously provided their constructive comments and corrections. I am indebted to them, but hasten to add any shortcomings or errors are my own.

Thank you, as well, to all other Belizeans who have helped me directly, or indirectly, along the way. As much as possible, I have refrained from injecting my own preferences and experiences, but feel obliged to mention the hospitality of the people of Placencia and Monkey River in particular, where much of this book was conceived and written over the years.

A.T. 2006
Vancouver, Canada
www.alantwigg.com

Index

A abolition, 96-100
abortion, 178-179
Active, HMS, 53
Addington, Larry, 200-201
African Communities League, 123
African Redemption Fund, 127
AIDS/HIV, 179
Aikman, Derek, 169, 172
Alamilla, Anita, 200
Ali, Muhammad, 198, **229**
Altun Ha, 202, **205**
Alvarado, Pedro de, 35
Amandala, 160-161, 162, 163, 166, 173, 229, 230
Ambergris Caye, 21, 24, 120, 197, 198, 199-200, 212, 216, 224, 226, 229
Anderson, A.H., 205
Anglo-Guatemalan Treaty, 117
aquaculture, 185
Aranda, Theodore, 169
Arawaks, 101
archaeological ruins, *see* Mayan sites
Arévalo, Marco Vinicio Cerezo, 191
Arthur, George, 69
Arvigo, Rosita, 27, 218
Ashcroft, Lord Michael, 172, 184
Atkins, John, 49
Austin, John Gardiner, 72
Axe, Samuel, 42, 199

B Bacalar, 24, 116, 203
"back to Africa" movement, 123
Banana Bank Lodge, 217
bananas, 74-75, 224
Barneby, Malcolm R., 171
Barrow, Dean, 169, 214
Barrow, Thomas, 64
Bassett (Superintendent), 105
Battle of Labouring Creek, 51, 223

Battle of St. George's Caye, 64-66, 86, 94, 224
Batty Brothers Bus Services Ltd., 184
Baymen, 48, 50, 51-58, 60-61, 62, 64-65, 67, 68, 94, 223, 224; "Articles", 55
Belikin Beer, 171, 206
Belize, origins of name, 9-10
Belize Agriculture Company, 200
Belize Alliance of Conservation Non-Government Organizations (BACONGO), 212, 213, 214
Belize Billboard, 155, 156, 158, 228
Belize City, 11, 15, 17, 18, 19, 20, 21, 39, 57, 69, 80, 90, 105, 106, 115, 128-129, 130, 131, 133, 149, 150, 159, 162, 180, 182, 189, 224, 225, 226, 227, 229
Belize College of Arts, Sciences and Technology (BELCAST), 171
Belize Defence Force (BDF), 173, 183, 192, 230
Belize Estate and Produce Company, 70, 71, 120, 133, 139, 140, 142, 168. *See also* British Honduras Company
Belize Independent, 108
Belize Independent Party, 133
Belize Marine Terminal and Museum, 200
Belize Telecommunication Limited (BTL), 184
Belize Times, 155
Belize Town Board, 133, 141, 144
Belize Water Services Limited, 221
Belize Zoo and Tropical Education Center, **21**, 212
Belmopan, 149-151, 167, 187, 229
Belmopan Day, 153
Benbow, "Admiral" John, 40

Beni, Alejo, 106, 225
Bennett, Marshall, 64, 99
Benson, Tom, 218
Betson, Clifford E., 133, 143
Bishop, Maurice, 159
Blackbeard (Edward Teach), 40, 199
Blackbird Caye, 201
Black Cross Nurses, 126-127
Black River, 57
Bladen Nature Reserve, 198
Blake, James Humes, 200
Blancaneaux Lodge, 217
Blisset, Joseph, 133, 227
bloodwood, *see* logwood
Blue Creek, 186
Blue Hole National Park, 198
Bochub, Amin, **29**
Bowen, Barry, 171
Bowen, Mansfield William, 87-88
Bowman, Dorla, 178
Bowman, Henry, 146
Bowman, William Jex, 76, 107, 227
Boyd, Alan Lennox, 146
Brashish, Neboysha, 171
Brig Badger, HMS, 57
Brigand's War of 1795-96, 104
British Honduras, colony of, 9, 93, 117, 119-120, 190, 226, 229
British Honduras Company (BHC), 70, 71, 120
Briz, Jorge, 193
Brodie's Department Store, 124, **125**
Bruhier, Arthur E., 145-146
brukdown music and dancing, **90**
buccaneers, 40-41
Burdon, Governor, 129
Burnaby, Sir William, 53
Burnaby's Code, 54-55, 62, 223
Burrell Boom Development Area, 198
bush medicine, 13, 26-27, 218

C Calabash Caye, 201
Camock, Sussex, 42
Campeche, 41, 45, 46, 48, 49, 80, 119
Canaa Pyramid, 209
Canada, 73, 136, 177, 207, 214, 226
cannibalism, 33, 34, 101-102
Canul, Marcos, 120

Caracol, 209-**210**, 227
Carib Development and Sick Aid Society (CDS), 107-108
Carib Town, 105
Caribs, 101-105
Carr, John, 217
Carrie Bow Caye, 199
Carter, Clarissa, 86
Carter, Jimmy, 190
Cascal, BV, 221
Caste War, 114-116
Castillo, Santiago, 171
Catholic Church, 103, 106-107, 114, 116, 178, 179
Cattouse, Albert, 145, 146
Caye Caulker, 200
Caye Chapel, 200
Cayo Espanto, 199, 201
Cerros, 202, 204
Chac Balam, 24
Chalillo Dam, 21, 183, 186, 212-215
Chatoyer, Joseph, 103, 104
Chequitaquil, 203
Chichanha Indians, 113, 115
chicle, 73-**74**, 227
Chinese Belizeans, 15, 72
Chiquibul National Park, 198
Chiquita Brands, 76
Cho, Julian, 25
Ch'oc, Gregorio, **23**, 28-29
citrus, 70, 76-77, 107
Claiborne, William, 41
cocaine, *see* drug trafficking
Cockscomb Basin Wildlife Sanctuary, 13, 197, 230
Collett, Wilfred, 124
Columbus, Christopher, 31
Commonwealth of Nations, 167
Community Baboon Sanctuary, 197
Constance, HMS, 124
Convention of London, 58, 224
Convention Town, 61
Cook, James, 53, 200
Coppola, Francis Ford, 20, 217
Corozal, 186, 203
Corozal District East Development Area, 198
Cortés, Hernán, 36-37, 223

Coxon, John, 48
Creoles, 15, 88-91, 100, 149
crime, 17-18, 173-174, 180-183, 216, 231. *See also* drug trafficking
Crooked Tree Wildlife Sanctuary, 197, 204
cruise ships, 188, 198
crystal skull, 211
Cuba, 116, 160, 180, 190
Cuello, 204
Cygnet, 62

D Dampier, William, **38**, 49
Dangriga, 105, 110-111, 150, 225
Darbeau, Dave, 160
Dávila, Alonso, 203
de Aguilar, Jeronimo, 35
de Cerezeda, Andrés, 35
Delgado, Fray José, 10
del Valle, Lionel, 160
Despard, Catherine, 60, 63
Despard, Edward Marcus, 57, 59-64
Despard, James, 63
devaluation of currency, 142-143
Dorsetshire Hill, 104
Douglas, John
drug trafficking, 17-18, 171, 173-174, 182

E East Indian Belizeans, 16
Eboe Town, 80
ecotourism, 197-198, 213, 216-217
Edgell, Zee, **177**
Ek Luum, 212
El Castillo, 207, **208**
Elfrith, Daniel, 42
Elizabeth, Queen, 199
Ellis, Cynthia, 178
Ellis, Zoila, 178
El Pilar, 207
Elrington, Hubert, 172
Employers and Workers Bill, 133, 228
English Caye, 201
Equiano, Olaudah, **78**, 79
Esquivel, Manuel, 169, 170, 172
Ethiopianism, 121-122
Ex-Confederates, 72
Export Processing Zones, 186
Ex-Servicemen's Riot, 124-125

F Fallen Stones Butterfly Farm, 211
Fancourt, Charles St. John, 114
Fanon, Frantz, 161
Farrell, James, 55
Ferris College, 171, 173
Fitzgibbon, David, 55
Five Blue Lakes National Park, 198
flag, national, 95, **97**
Flores, Augustine, 111-112
Flores, Sylvia, 177
Fort George, 176, 225
Fort George Hotel, 197
Fortis, 213-214
France, 64, 104
Frazier, George, 148
Free Coloureds, 88-89
Fuentes, Miguel Ydígoras, 188
Fuller, Ray, 160

G Gales Point, 150, 217
gambling, 215-216
Ganey, Father Marion, 133
Gann, Thomas, 204, 205, 226
Garcia, Dolores Balderamos, 177
Garcia, Marcia, 27
Garden of Gethsemane, 109
Garifuna Settlement Day, 108-109, 225
Garinagu people, 15-16, 76, 101-112, 116
Garland, HMS, 84
Garvey, Marcus, 121-**122**-**123**-124, 127-128, 226
Garvey, Ronald, 142
General Washington, 56
General Workers Union (GWU), 133, 143, 144
George Price Centre for Peace and Development, 151, 231
Glover's Reef, 201
Godolphin, William, 118-119
Goff's Caye, 201
Goldson, Philip, 143-144, 155-**158**, 165, 227, 228
Granger, Geddes, 160
Great Britain, 39, 46, 47, 51, 53, 56-58, 60-61, 64, 72, 94, 114-115, 117-120, 130, 136, 141, 142, 147, 151, 155, 188-189, 191, 225, 226, 229, 231

Great Depression, 128, 227
Guanacaste National Park, 198
Guatemala, 15, 29, 37, 51, 114, 117-118, 139, 146-148, 156-158, 186, 188-189, 190-194, 225, 226, 228, 230, 231
Guerrero, Gonzalo, 33-36

H Half Moon Caye, 197, 202
Hammond, Norman, 204
Harkins, Father S.J., 137
Hattieville, 90
Hattieville Correctional Institute, 17-18, 181, 216
Haulover Creek, **8**, 20, 52, 57, 59
Hawkins, John, 79
Haynes, Samuel, 126
Henville, Charles, 145
Hilton, Anthony, 43
Hinchingbrook, 57
Hodge, John, 71
Hole Chan Marine Park, 198
Hondo River, 24, 35, 48, 53-54, 84, 113, 116, 224, 229
Honduran civil war, 105
Honduras Almanack, 9, 43, 49, 100
Honduras Independence Party (HIP), 156, 228
Hontin Caye, 202
Hopkins, 21, 110, 150, 217
Hunter, Peter, 62
Hurricane Hattie, 18, 149-150, 162, 209, 229
hurricane of 1931, 128, 138, 227
Huxley, Aldous, 195
Hyde, Cordel, 164
Hyde, Evan X, 77, 160, 162, 163-166, 169, 229, 230

I Ibrahim, Abdullah, 160
Icaiche Maya, 115-116, 119, 225
Independence Hill, 151
independence movement, 91, 95, 96, 142, 148, 151, 190-191, 230
infant mortality, 180
INTELCO, 184
Ix Chel Farm and Tropical Education Center, 197

J Jackson, William, 43
Jade Head, 205-206, 229
Jamaica, 16, 41, 46, 47-48, 49, 50, 65, 80, 96, 97, 115, 119, 120, 121-123, 136, 182, 196, 223, 226
Janson, Thor "Bushman Ollie", 172, 218
Jeffery, Denbigh, 146
Jones, Basil, 55
Jones, Hadie, 156
Jones, Marion, 11-12
Juan Baptista, 202

K Ken, Jesus, 161
King Ferdinand II, 32
Kinich Ahau, 205
KREM radio, 165, 230

L Labouring Creek, 51, 223
Lamanai, 202, 204-205
Lamanai Outpost Lodge, 219
Lambey, Juan Pablo, 109
Las Cuevas Research Station, 12
Laughing Bird Caye, 202
Lawrie, James Pitt, 64
Lawrie, John, 55
Lea, Charles, 72
Liele, George, 122
life expectancy, 180
Lighthouse Reef, 202
Lindbergh, Charles, 198, 227
Lindner, Carl, 76
Lindo, Dean, 165, 172
Lino, Bernard, 180
Lizarraga, Gwendolyn, 177
logwood, 43, 45-50, **67**, 223, 224
Lomé Convention, 75
London Covention, 60, 61
Love, Robert, 122
Loyola Park, **128**
Lubaantun, 202, 211
Lucas, Adeline, **110**
Lynch, Sir Thomas, 48
Lyttleton, 53

M Macal River, 213
MacGregor, Colin, 148
mahogany, 45, 53, 57-58, 61, 62, 67-**68**-71, 73, 120, 128, 130, 224, 225, 227

Maintzunun, 210
Malcolm X, 161, 163
Manatee Development Area, 198
Man-O-War Caye, 199
Martínez, Regina, 178
Martinique, 102
Masters and Servants Act, 133, 228
Matola, Sharon, 212, 214, **230**
Matthews, Gary, 170
Maud, Joseph, 55
Maugre Caye, 201
Maya Culture Day, 207
Maya Hill Archaeological Reserve, 204
Maya Mapping Project, 25
Mayan sites, 29, 199, 201, 202-**203**-212, 229
Maya people, 15, 23-29, 33, 34-35, 68, 71, 76, 106, 114-115, 117, 118, 189, 199, 223, 224, 229
McCorkle, Celi, 197
Melhado, Henry I., 140
Mennonites, 16, 76, 229
Merlin, HMS, 65-66, 224
Mermaid, 65
Mestizos, 15, 71, 76, 90, 114, 116, 117
Mexico, 15, 24, 28, 36, 37, 69, 89, 114-116, 119, 120, 137, 144, 200, 225, 226
Millicent, Joan, 176
missionaries, 80, 106, 204, 224
Mitchell-Hedges, F.A., 211
Modyford, Governor, 47
Monkey Bay Wildlife Sanctuary, 198
Monkey River Development Area, 198
Montt, Efraín, 191
Mopan River, 86, 207
Mopan River Resort, 218
Morgan, Henry, 10, 41
Morter, Isaiah Emmanuel, 127
Mosquito Indians, 41, 42, 61, 90
Mosquito Shore, 51-52, 60, 64, 147, 223
Mullins River Village, 150
Musa, Hamid, 175
Musa, Said, 77, 109, 159-160, 162, 164, 170, 174, 175-176, 181, 182, 184, 185, 186, 187-188, 193, 213, 215, 221, 231

N Nachancan, 203
National Alliance for Belizean Rights (NABR), 158
National Independence Party (NIP), 155-156, 165, 168, 228, 229
National Joint Action Committee, 160
Natives First movement, 141
Negro World, The, 123, 125, 126
Nelson, Horatio, 57
New Jewel Movement, 160
New River, 24, 204
New River Lagoon, 204
New Spain, 36
Nim Li Punit, 202, 210
Nohmul, 204
Noj Kaax Meen Elijio Panti National Park, 26-28
Northern Cane Workers Union, 161
Northern Fishermen's Co-operative Society Ltd., 200
Novelo's Bus Lines, 184

O obeah, 106-107, 224
Olmecs, 24
Omoa, 57
Orange Point, 173
Orange Walk Town, 120, 204
Organization of American States (OAS), 191

P Pacbitun, 207
Panti, Don Elijio, 26-28, 207
Parham, Nora, 177-178
Paslow, Thomas, 64, 86-87
Patterson, P.J., 182
Patton-Quallo, Jewel, 178
Peggy (slave), 87-88
Pendergast, David, 205-206
People's Action Committee (PAC), 160, 176
People's Committee, 143
People's Democratic Movement (PDM), 165
People's United Party (PUP), 96, 137, 142-147, 149-150, 155, 156, 160, 161, 164, 168-170, 172-174, 175-176, 184, 187-188, 191, 197, 228, 230, 231

Pine Ridge, 207
Pinzón, Vicente Yáñez, **30**-32, 223
pirates, 39-41, 201. *See also* privateers
Pitt, William, 52
Placentia, 42
Pollard, Nicholas, 155
Pope John Paul II, 193, 199, 230
Portillo, Alfonso, 191
Portillo, José López, 191
Portugal, 39
Price family, **138**
Price, George Cadle, 20, 22, 96, 133, **134**, 135-153, 155, **157**, 160, 162, 163, 164, 167, 169, 170, 172, 174, 175, 189, 190, 191, 226, 228, 229, 230
Price, William Cadle, 137
Princess casino, 215
privateers, 17, 32, 39, 41, 44, 55, 57, 223
property sales to foreigners, 173
Providence Island, 42-43, 44
Providence Island Company, 43
Pueblo Viejo, 188
punta dance, 110
Punta Gorda, 105, 189, 226
Puritans, 41, 223
Pusilha, 211

Q Q'eqchí, 28
Qualifed Retired Persons Status, 220
Queen Charlotte Town, 129
Queen's Caye, 199

R Rabinowitz, Alan, 13, 230
Radio Belize, 165, 228
Raleigh, Walter, 71
Ramos, Thomas Vincent, 107-109
Ranguana Caye, 202
Rath, Tony, 218
Raul's Rose Garden, **182**
Reagan, Ronald, 17, 152, 191
Rendezvous Caye, 201
Revolitical Action Movement (RAM), 160-162
Reyes, Francisco Cruz, 212
Reyes, Luciano
Richardson, Leigh, 143, 155, 156
Rio Bravo Conservation Area, 198

rivers of Belize (map), **52**
Roatan, 42, 57, 60, 104
Roeg, Nicholas, 21
Rosado, José Maria, 116
Royal Ontario Museum (ROM), 205, 207, 229

S Sagastume, Francisco, 188-189
Salim, Ahmed Salim, 190
San Antonio, 26, 189, 207
Sandinistas, 190
San Felipe Village, 204
San Jose Succotz Village, 207
San Pedro, 150, 198, 200, 201, 226
San Pedro Columbia village, 211
Santa Rita, 202, 203
San Vicente, 192
Sapodilla Caye, 199
sapodilla tree, 73
Sarawee, 76, 108, 227
Scarlet Macaw, 213
Security and Intelligence Service (SIS), 176
Sergeant's Caye, 201
Settlement Day, 108-109, 225
Seven Years War, 52
sex trade, 182-183
Shabazz, Ismail, 162, 164
Shaw, Robert, 224
Shipstern Native Reserve, 198
Shoman, Assad, 115, 159-160, 162, 163, 175, 176, 193
Shoman, Lisa, 177
Sibun River, 105
Sinnott, Christopher, 55
Sittee River Village, 150
Sky Palace, 209
slavery, 15, 43, 51, 61, 66, 67, 79-88, 93-100, 102, 103, 105, 224, 225; census figures, 85
Smith, John, 143
Soberanis, Antonio, 127, 227
Society for the Promotion of Education and Research (SPEAR), 160, 176, 231
Society Hall Nature Reserve, 198
Spain, 28, 37, 39, 43-53, 56-58, 61, 62, 65, 67, 69, 76, 119, 193, 225
Spanish Lookout Caye, 201

St. George's Caye, 10, 50, 55, 56, 58
St. John's Anglican Cathedral, 113, 225
St. John's College, 137, 138, 139, 163, 175
St. Vincent Island, 101, 224
Stann Creek District, 42, 77, 90, 105, 106, 107, 108, 110, 116, 133, 162, 225, 227
Stochl, Father John, 112
sugar, 64, 70, 71-73, 230
Summit Meeting of the Non-Aligned Countries, 190
Swing Bridge, **8**, 20, 158

T Taiwan, 77, 168, 186
TC's By-The-Sea, 218
Teaser, 65
Temple of the Mask, 204
Temple of the Masonry Altars, **205**
Temple of the Wooden Lintel, 209
Terra Nova medicinal plant reserve, 13, 27
Thompson, Dudley, 190
Thornley, Colin Hardwick, 146-147
Tickler, 65
Tikal, 209
Tillett, Amelio Jr., 184
Tobacco Caye, 42, 199
Toilet Paper Farce, 145-146
Toledo District, 15, 25, 28, 29, 73, 90, 174, 183, 196, 226
Torrijos, Omar, 190
Tortuga, 9, 40, 42, 43, 45
tourism, 16, 22, 73, 182, 188, 195-221
Towser, 65
Toznenitzin, dona Elvira, 35
trade unions, 129, 130-133, 143, 160, 228
Traditional Healers Foundation, 27
Treaty of Godolphin, 47
Treaty of Paris, 53
Treaty of Versailles, 57-58, 224
Trinidad, 160
Trudeau, Pierre Elliot, 20, 199
Turneffe Islands, 39
Turneffe Reef, 201
Turtle Inn, 218
Turton, Robert, 133, 139, 140, 227

U Ubico, Jorge, 188

unions. *See* trade unions
United Black Association for Development (UBAD), 91, 159, 161, 164, 165, 169
United Brands, 168
United Democratic Party (UDP), 152, 158, 165, 168-172, 174, 175, 184, 188, 197, 229, 230, 231
United Fruit Company, 74, 168
United Nations, 151, 158, 167, 190, 220, 230
United States of America, 17, 77, 93, 114, 118, 119, 122, 126, 133, 152, 168, 169, 171, 173, 180, 188, 190, 191
Universal Negro Improvement and Conservation (UNIA), 123, 124, 126
University of Belize, 151, 171, 187
Uring, Nathaniel, 46-47
Usher, Jane, 177
Uxbenka, 211

V Valdivia, Pedro, 33
Vasquez, Nestor, 171
Vespucci, Amerigo, 32
Victoria House Hotel, 198
Villa Boscardi, 218
Vincyland, 101
VIP (Vision Inspired by the People), 188
Voudon ("Voodoo"), 107

W Wallace, Peter, 9, 42, 43, 44-45
Walter Raleigh, 102
Water Caye, 199
Water Witch, 199, 224
Wodehouse, Philip, 114
women, status of, 176-179
World Garifuna Organization, 111
World War I, 124
World War II, 139, 202
Wray, Henry, 118
Wyke, Charles Lennox, 118

X Xunantunich, 202, 207-**208**-209

Y *Yeldham*, HMS, 199
Young, Toledo & Company, 113, 115
Yucatán, 115-116